Three Weeks to
eBay
Profits

Three Weeks to
eBay
Profits

REVISED EDITION

Go from Beginner
to Successful Seller
in Less than a Month

Skip McGrath

STERLING

New York / London
www.sterlingpublishing.com

STERLING and the distinctive Sterling logo are registered trademarks of Sterling Publishing Co., Inc.

Library of Congress Cataloging-in-Publication Data Available

10 9 8 7 6 5 4 3 2 1

Published by Sterling Publishing Co., Inc.
387 Park Avenue South, New York, NY 10016

© 2009 by Skip McGrath

Distributed in Canada by Sterling Publishing
c/o Canadian Manda Group, 165 Dufferin Street
Toronto, Ontario, Canada M6K 3H6
Distributed in the United Kingdom by GMC Distribution Services
Castle Place, 166 High Street, Lewes, East Sussex, England BN7 1XU
Distributed in Australia by Capricorn Link (Australia) Pty. Ltd.
P.O. Box 704, Windsor, NSW 2756, Australia

Manufactured in United States of America
All rights reserved

Sterling ISBN 978-1-4027-6570-4

For information about custom editions, special sales, premium and corporate purchases, please contact Sterling Special Sales Department at 800-805-5489 or specialsales@sterlingpublishing.com.

THIS BOOK IS LOVINGLY DEDICATED to my mom, June Springer. Mom never failed to encourage me in my endeavors, she taught me the value of hard work, and, at eighty-six, she herself still works every day. From a very young age, I learned from my mom to reach for my dreams—no matter how impossible they seemed—and that it was all right to be afraid of something as long as you didn't let your fear stop you from doing what you wanted to do or going where you wanted to go. She is gentle, sweet, and generous—sometimes to a fault—and none of my success in life would have been possible without her love and support. My gratitude to this extraordinary woman knows no bounds.

✦ CONTENTS ✦

WEEK
3

BUILDING AND GROWING YOUR BUSINESS 185

ACKNOWLEDGMENTS

When you pick up a book, you see the title and the author's name. However, unlike with a movie, where the credits roll across the screen at the end, you never get to see the names of all the people working behind the scenes to help bring that book to fruition. An author spends countless hours writing a book, but a lot of work by other people actually figures in the final product.

My editor, Meredith Hale, got married in the middle of this project, and I had to get used to her new last name. Meredith was enthusiastic about the book from day one, and worked tirelessly with me from the initial outline right up to the final edits. She contributed solid ideas and pointed out flaws in my organization, always keeping you, the reader, in mind. Editorial assistant Lindsay Herman watched over both of us to make sure we didn't miss anything.

Copyeditor Diana Drew spent hours poring over every word of my prose—shortening run-on sentences; correcting grammar, spelling, and agreement problems; and coming up with simple ways to express complicated ideas. If you find this book easy to read, thank Diana. Getting all the little details right is always important. For this I thank my daughter-in-law, Lissa McGrath, an author and eBay seller in her own right, for checking all the links, fees, and little details that I missed. I'm also grateful for her help with updating images and references.

Before a book is printed, much thought goes into the layout and design. The cover of *Three Weeks to eBay Profits* was designed by Kevin Baier. The interior was designed by Christine Heun and by Oxygen Design. All details and issues, large and small, were overseen by Michael Fragnito.

Lastly, I would like to thank my agent, Marilyn Allen. Marilyn understands what publishers are looking for and helps me channel my ideas into successful proposals and projects.

✦ INTRODUCTION to the Revised Edition ✦

WELCOME TO EBAY, the world's greatest marketplace—electronic or otherwise. More than 86 million people have bought or sold items on eBay during the last twelve months. Over 7 million items are listed for sale on eBay every day, and 1.2 million sellers make a full- or part-time income on eBay.

In 2008 more than $48 billion worth of merchandise changed hands on eBay. Yet eBay itself sells nothing but access to its platform. eBay does not sell one antique or collectible, one razor blade, even one digital camera—although tens of thousands of digital cameras are sold on eBay each month. It is you and I who do the selling. If every eBay seller were an employee of eBay, it would be the largest private employer in the world—larger than Wal-Mart and Lowe's combined.

When you launch an eBay business, you are opening a store in a city of 86 million people. Except you have no rent, no employees, no costly advertising, and very little overhead. What could be better?

But eBay is not a static marketplace. Over the years I have seen many changes, including several major changes since the first edition of this book was released in 2006. There have been changes in fees, selling practices, feedback, payment methods and systems, and how eBay buyers find your items. These changes have required sellers to change how they list their auctions, how they ship their items, and how they relate to and communicate with their customers. Learning these updated techniques is what will put profits in your pocket on the new and improved eBay.

I have been selling on eBay for over nine years, and writing books and newsletters about selling on eBay for the past eight. During that time, I have spoken to and answered e-mails from hundreds of readers seeking advice. Although the questions always differ in their specifics, a basic theme recurs: "OK, I'm registered on eBay. What do I do next?" That question first prompted me to write this book.

At first glance, selling an item on eBay looks simple. But once people become immersed in the process, they are confronted with dozens of choices and decisions related to auction titles, item descriptions, payment, shipping, image placement, eBay promotional options, and more. As they start to list their first two or three items for auction, new sellers begin to wonder if they can really build an eBay business—or is this whole thing just too complicated?

It *is* somewhat complicated—but not overly so. Almost anyone can master selling on eBay: You just need to take the time to understand the process and the unique nature of the eBay selling platform. Over 10 million people have sold items on eBay and over 1.2 million sell on a regular basis. With some guidance and perseverance, you, too, can join the ranks of those 1.2 million professional sellers.

What makes this book different from all the others that teach the ins and outs of selling on eBay? Most books on this subject tend to focus on mechanical aspects of the process, answering questions like the following: How do I upload photos? How do I get paid? How do I create a listing? Understanding how all these elements work is certainly important, and we do cover these points clearly. But rather than getting bogged down in details soon to become second nature, this book offers answers to one simple, yet all-encompassing, question: How do I make money on eBay?

Three Weeks to eBay Profits is designed to take you through the process, step by step, in a logical manner so you understand and master each step. Why three weeks? It won't take you three weeks to sell your first few items—you can do that within a few days of starting. But we are talking about reaching PowerSeller status—not just making a few quick sales.

Setting up and organizing your business, researching and finding the right products, and putting in place the automated systems and services to save you time will take the average person about three weeks. If you are not currently working and are doing this full time, you may actually master all these steps even sooner. On the other hand, if you have a full-time job and can only devote a few hours to your eBay business every evening, it may take you four or five weeks before everything is humming along and you are making money consistently week after week.

How you define success on eBay depends on your personal goals and how eBay fits into your life. If you are a stay-at-home parent or a working person just looking to supplement your income, you might be looking to make an extra $100–$200 a week. However, if you are trying to replace your income from a job lost to downsizing, then your vision of success might be earning $500 or $1,000 a week—or more. Both scenarios are doable—it's just a matter of time, work, and learning the ropes.

Building a business on eBay is also a lot of fun. If you enjoy selling on eBay, then this is the greatest gig in the world. Not only have I made a lot of money on eBay over the past nine years, but I have had a fabulous time doing it. I have made dozens of online friends—many of whom I went on to meet in person. My wife, Karen, and I work together in the business and we still get as excited today watching the last few moments of an auction as we did when we entered an item in our very first auction more than nine years ago.

If you are already registered and have sold things on eBay, you might be tempted to skip through the first few chapters. I suggest that, at the very least, you scan them for new information. I frequently see items being auctioned on eBay by veteran sellers who are still making rookie mistakes. Clearly, they didn't set up their business for success right from the start.

To get the most out of this book, take the time to set up and organize your business correctly (chapter 1) before you start launching your first auctions. Work through the first few chapters to do the research and select the products you will sell. This is one of the most important decisions you will make. Then set your goals and write your success plan (chapter 12). Benjamin Franklin once said, "An investment in knowledge pays the best interest." Make the investment now to maximize your interest and dividends later.

BIZ BUILDER

As you read this book, you will come across Web sites for various companies and products. To save you the trouble of typing each link into your browser, I have set up a special Web page just for the readers of this book at www.skipmcgrath.com/3_weeks.

Here's a quick outline of how this book is organized:

WEEK 1 — GETTING READY TO SELL

In the first week we concentrate on setting up your business correctly, learning the keys to operating on eBay, researching and settling on the products you will sell, and learning how and where to find sources for those products.

WEEK 2 — PUTTING YOUR AUCTIONS TO WORK

Almost anyone can use the eBay interface to launch an auction, but the devil is in the details. Learning how to make your auctions stand out from the millions of others, how to maximize your bids and final values, how to promote your auctions, and how to build a strong feedback profile are the keys to long-term success.

WEEK 3 — BUILDING AND GROWING YOUR BUSINESS

There's no great trick to selling on eBay, but only a professional can make money doing it week after week. In the third week, we show you how to control your costs, save time with automation, deliver superior customer service, drive repeat business to your auctions, and open an eBay store, as well as steps you can take to expand your business beyond eBay to the rest of the Internet.

Here's to your success!

GETTING READY TO SELL

You are probably ready to jump right into selling on eBay, and I promise to get you there very soon. But, first, you need to take a few crucial steps to set up your business for the long term. If you have been buying on eBay or have sold a few items, you already may know some of this information or you may have performed some of the important tasks spelled out in the Week 1 chapters. Still, I would advise you to read through each chapter, looking for something you may have missed or for changes you may want to make to improve your current practices.

Strategies to help you conduct product research (chapter 4), select the right products (chapter 5), and figure out how to get products (chapter 6) are critical to your long-term success, and forgoing them makes most new eBay sellers wonder what is going wrong. Doing the research and going through the processes outlined here will help you avoid costly mistakes, and will make your first selling experience much more enjoyable—and profitable.

In Week 1, we will cover setting up and organizing your business, finding your way around eBay, and researching, choosing, and sourcing products to sell. In addition, we will explore the different types of auctions—and which may be right for your specific product—and then walk step-by-step through the process of launching your first auctions on eBay. Finally, we'll examine listing and pricing strategies, ways to quickly build positive feedback, and then tie together everything you've learned in a targeted business plan that will ensure your success.

At the end of each chapter is a short checklist of actions for you to take. Some of these actions can be done within a few hours, while others might span a few days. You may opt to carry out each task right away, or you may want to keep reading and come back to certain ones later on. If you choose to return to some of them later on, make a list of the tasks you're setting aside, be sure to do each one at some point, and check it off as you complete it. Don't be intimidated if your list looks long. None of the tasks are that difficult or time-consuming—and many are actually fun. Just take them one at a time and you will see progress every day.

I also find it helpful to keep a three-ring binder near my computer so I can print out information as I come across it, punch three holes in the sheets, and file it for easy reference. You can organize the notebook into sections: one section for eBay information, and one for research and products. Once you begin launching auctions, you will want to add a section for storing printed-out copies of the results of your auctions. This way you can review and critique your auctions and make notes right on the auction copy. I started doing this nine years ago and still do this for new items or if I change my listings. I now have several very full binders next to my computer and often refer to them to see which ideas worked and which did not.

CHAPTER 1

✦ SETTING UP AND ORGANIZING ✦
YOUR BUSINESS

TO START SELLING ON EBAY, there's only one step that's absolutely required: register-ing an eBay selling account. However, following a number of other steps will make your path to success much smoother.

This chapter will walk you through how to register and set up your eBay and PayPal accounts, as well as how to create your About Me page, so that prospective bidders can learn about you and your business. Keep in mind that before learning how to sell on eBay, you need to understand the entire eBay process—both buying and sell-ing. So we will first take a look at *buying* on eBay—how to gain experience, earn your first feedback ratings, and use your My eBay page to track your activity. Finally, we will address the issue of business licenses and explain how to get a state sales tax number, so you can buy inventory for resale from wholesalers and other distributors.

SETTING UP YOUR EBAY ACCOUNT

If you do not yet have an eBay account, the first thing you need to do is register as a buyer on eBay. You can do this by clicking on the link that says *Register* on the eBay homepage at www.eBay.com.

eBay will ask for your name, address, telephone number, and e-mail address; then you will set up a user ID (username), password, and secret question, and enter your birth date to confirm that you are over eighteen years old. Next, eBay will send you an e-mail with a link to click on and a confirmation code to enter. Once you do this, you are eligible to bid and buy on eBay. Note that when you create your eBay user ID, you cannot use any spaces. So, for example, *BidMoreOften* works, but *Bid More Often* will not be accepted. (However, you may use the underscore, as in *Bid_More_Often*.) You can click the *Check Your User ID* button to see if your chosen user ID is available before continuing with the registration process.

BIZ BUILDER

Give some thought to your user ID. Don't pick a name that will limit your business unless you will be concentrating on a specific niche. Something like *TheCameraDude* will work fine if all you plan to sell are cameras and photo equipment. A more generic name such as *HillsAndDales* or *SamsGreatStuff* will allow you to sell almost anything.

7

Next you need to register as a seller. Simply click on the *Sell* tab at the top of any eBay page (see Figure 1.1).

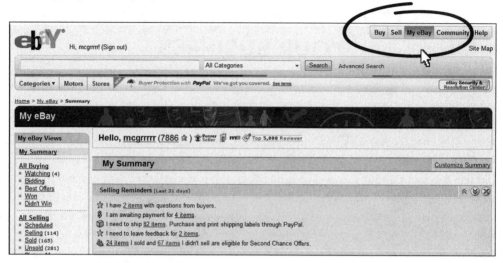

Figure 1.1 eBay Main Navigation Links

eBay will recognize that you are not yet registered to sell and will direct you to register. To register as a seller, you need to verify your identity by providing a credit or debit card and your checking account information. Both sets of information must match your registered name and address. Note that eBay will *not* charge your credit card or access your checking account unless you authorize the site to charge your eBay selling fees. You also have the option of paying your eBay selling fees by check or PayPal. (We'll discuss eBay selling fees in detail in chapter 21.)

Once you register as a seller, you also have the option to verify your ID. You will see a link in the site map that says *ID Verify* (see Figure 1.2). If you click on this link, eBay will ask you to enter your social security number. This prompts the software to pull an electronic credit report on you, and ask you two or three questions that only you could know the answer to, such as the following: What bank finances your auto loan? Or what is the amount of your monthly mortgage payment with such-and-such loan company? By answering these questions, you confirm that you really are Sally Jones from Moose Port, Michigan, and not Princess Motobuto from Nigeria or Sergei the Hacker from Russia. This doesn't affect your credit score as a "hit"; it's just an inquiry.

This verification service costs $5, but it's a very good investment. Once you are ID verified, eBay will place a little icon next to your name that tells everyone who looks at your auctions that you really are who you say you are. In addition to your feedback rating, credibility is very important to potential eBay bidders. If you are selling higher-priced items, many bidders will look for the *ID Verify* icon. Another advantage of becoming ID verified is that eBay will allow you to immediately sell using the fixed-price Buy It Now feature we will discuss in chapter 8. If you don't have a credit/debit card, or don't want to put one on file during the registration process, you can use ID Verify to verify your account for registration purposes, too.

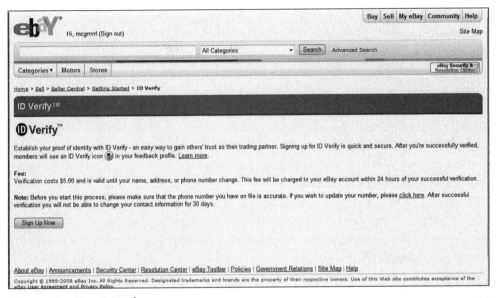

Figure 1.2 eBay ID Verify

OPENING YOUR PAYPAL ACCOUNT

The next step, if you haven't already done so, is to open a PayPal account. PayPal is the payment service owned by eBay. PayPal has a long record of reliability and service to eBay sellers. As a new seller, you are required to have a PayPal account and offer PayPal to your buyers. This is actually beneficial because well over 80 percent of eBay users are registered with PayPal. Since eBay went to electronic-only payments in 2008, even more buyers are switching to PayPal. (Currently a buyer's only other options are paying with ProPay if the seller is a Silver PowerSeller or higher, or with a credit/debit card through the seller's own merchant credit card processor.)

The Basic (Personal) PayPal account is free, but if you are going to receive funds on a regular basis (or are registered on eBay as a business seller), PayPal requires you to have a Premier or Business Account. To register, simply go to www.paypal.com. To link your PayPal and eBay accounts, you will need to provide the same information you did when registering with eBay, as well as your eBay user ID.

Once you are registered and you sign in to your account, you will notice a link at the upper left-hand corner of your account homepage that says, *Verify Your Account*. When you click on this link, PayPal will ask you to enter your bank name, routing number, and account number. PayPal will then make two small deposits to your bank account—both in pennies—such as $0.08 and $0.17. After that, PayPal will send you an e-mail instructing you to contact your bank and determine the amount of the two deposits. The e-mail will have a link to click on where you enter the information. If the information you supplied was accurate, you will now be PayPal Verified. This is very important because PayPal offers buyers fraud protection as long as they paid their money to a PayPal user who was verified.

When you buy something on eBay using your PayPal account, PayPal gives you several payment options. You can elect to use the credit or debit card you have on file, or you can write an e-check from your bank account. Of course, if you have cash in your PayPal account—which you will as soon as you become a seller and people start paying you—PayPal will first access the cash in your account whenever you authorize a payment. If you have both a credit card and a bank account on file with PayPal, you qualify for Instant Transfers. This basically works like an e-check, except there is no waiting period for the transfer to clear from your bank account. PayPal sends the money to the seller instantly (as if you had the funds already in your PayPal account) and then debits it from your bank account. If the funds are not available in your bank account, PayPal then charges the amount to your credit card. This gives you the convenience of e-checks without the long wait for the checks to clear. PayPal will *never* debit your credit card or your bank account without your authorization.

There is no fee to purchase using PayPal; however, there is a fee for sellers. Every time you receive a payment from PayPal, 2.9 percent of the transaction amount is deducted, plus $0.30 per transaction. This may sound like a lot, but it is actually cheaper than the rates and fees charged by merchant credit card companies like Visa and MasterCard. Depending on the bank where you open a merchant account, rates may go from 2.5 percent to as high as 4 percent of the amount paid, plus transaction fees that can run as high as $0.40 per transaction. In addition to that, most merchant credit card companies have high setup fees and recurring monthly charges.

Not only is PayPal cheaper than merchant credit card companies, but it is the payment system eBay buyers prefer. Don't worry if one of your buyers doesn't have a PayPal account. You can still send him an electronic invoice via PayPal that allows him to enter his credit/debit card information.

SETTING UP YOUR PREFERENCES

One of the most important benefits of using PayPal as your payment service is the automation eBay and PayPal offer to help you collect money quickly when an auction ends. Once you open your PayPal account, you have the option to set up PayPal as your preferred payment method and to insert the PayPal logo automatically into your auctions. Click the tab marked *Profile* on your PayPal Account page, then click *Auctions* under the *Selling Preferences* heading (see Figure 1.3). If the word beneath *Automatic Logo Insertion* is currently off, click it (it's an active link) and you'll be given the option to turn it on. The same is true of the *PayPal Preferred on eBay* option. You should definitely turn both on because buyers expect PayPal and if they don't see the standard *PayPal Preferred* box they may think you don't offer it. Plus, there is a *PayPal Only* checkbox eBay buyers can use to narrow their Search Results to listings that only offer PayPal. If you don't have the PayPal preference set for your auctions, your auction will not come up in this kind of search, even if what you're selling is exactly what the buyer is looking for, and even if you have *PayPal Accepted* written in your auction description.

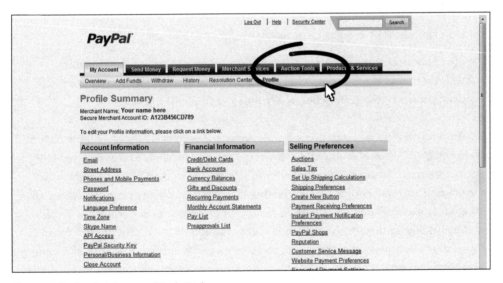

Figure 1.3 PayPal Auction Tools Link

The third option on this Auction Accounts page is *Customize End of Auction E-mail*. This allows you to have eBay send out a notice to the winning bidder of your auctions with a *PayPal* button embedded in the e-mail. All the winning bidder has to do is click on the button to pay you instantly via PayPal. You also have the opportunity to customize the e-mail by adding your own personal message.

GAINING EXPERIENCE

Now that you have a PayPal account, you are ready to buy and sell on eBay. Before you start selling on eBay, however, you should first bid on and win several auctions. *Don't skip this important step.* You can't really understand the selling process on eBay unless you become a buyer first. This way you learn how other sellers deal with winning bidders. For example:

* How do they communicate with you after the auction?

* How do they ask you for payment and what are their policies?

* How does PayPal work?

* How did they ship your goods, what did shipping cost, and how were the items packaged?

* Did the seller attempt an upsell—offering you a discount if you bought a greater quantity or a related product?

* How quickly did the seller post feedback for you, if at all?

* Just how smooth and comfortable was the process? Did you feel pleased with the transaction? If not, what could the seller have done better? If so, what aspect of the transaction really pleased you?

Bidding on (and winning) items from several different sellers is a valuable part of your education as a seller. If you forgo this step, you will certainly make mistakes you could easily avoid. Hundreds of ordinary products are for sale on eBay, things that you use every day, such as shampoo, razor blades, diapers, and beauty products. Many of them are less expensive on eBay than at your local drugstore or supermarket, so bidding on them and buying them to gain experience in working through the process doesn't cost you much—and may even save you some money. The other advantage of buying on eBay is that you can start building your feedback rating, which we turn to next.

FEEDBACK

We will discuss feedback in detail in chapter 11, but we need to introduce the concept here because it is related to several of the initial steps you should take as a seller. When Pierre Omidyar started eBay in 1995, most observers thought it was an insane idea. *People are just not going to buy products over the Internet from strangers* was the recurring critique from the Silicon Valley know-it-alls. However, Pierre embedded in eBay two major concepts, which no one at the time understood: eBay would become a community of users and the community would become self-policing. Indeed, eBay became a community because of the intimacy and the direct contact the platform provided—and, yes, because the idea was just quirky enough to attract the same kind of people who were attracted to chat rooms and playing games online. Self-policing came about through the concept of *feedback*.

Here is how feedback works: Every time an auction ends, each party—both buyer and seller—is encouraged to post a short comment about the other party. Those comments become a *permanent* part of the buyer's and seller's reputations on eBay. If you open any eBay auction, you will see the user ID of the seller followed by a number in parentheses—for example, *BidMoreOften* (74). The number 74 is the *feedback score*, calculated by tallying positive comments left for *BidMoreOften* (each worth +1) and negative comments (each worth –1). Before you bid on an item from a seller, you get to look at his feedback—what other actual customers have to say about their experience with that seller.

Figure 1.4 shows an example of feedback comments left for eBay user *McGrrrrr* (which is me, if you were wondering).

Feedback is an enormously powerful tool and has now been copied in various formats by many other auction sites and Web shopping portals. Imagine if you walked

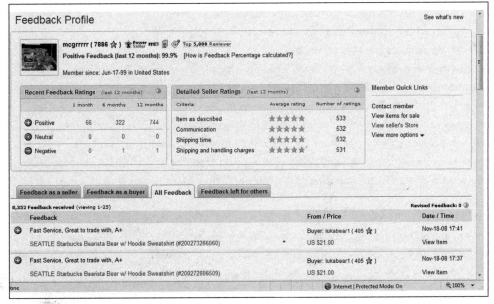

Figure 1.4 eBay Feedback Comments for Mcgrrrrr

into your local shopping mall and outside each store was a board where you could post comments about the quality of the products sold there and the customer service you received—and *the store was not allowed to remove those comments!* Don't you think the stores would work harder to provide good service? That is the power of feedback.

In addition to listing the comments from other eBay users, eBay also keeps track of the percentage of comments that are positive, which is called the *feedback rating.* Very few sellers have perfect feedback (100 percent positive), but over time eBay users have set the bar fairly high. A rating of less than 98 percent (two negatives out of one hundred transactions) is considered a yellow caution flag. Less than 95 or 96 percent, and you will find your bids dropping off substantially. So if you want to build a long-term business on eBay, protecting your feedback rating is critical to your success.

Another aspect of feedback is *Detailed Seller Ratings* (DSRs). Your DSRs are scores from one to five stars in each of four critical aspects of the transaction (item as described, communication, shipping time, and shipping and handling charges). Buyers can choose to leave these anonymous ratings in addition to a feedback comment. If any one of your DSR averages falls below 4.1, you will be prevented from listing any further items on eBay until the rating increases. It's based on your thirty-day DSR average so, provided your twelve-month average is above 4.1, you will only have to wait thirty days to start listing again; otherwise, it's a longer wait until the lower DSR ratings drop off (up to twelve months). A DSR rating of 4.2 or 4.3 will demote your items in the *Best Match* default Search Results order. Don't stress out too much about this. eBay reports that only 5 percent of regular sellers have ratings below 4.1.

This brings us back to the importance of buying on eBay before you start selling. You can only know how a buyer feels about each of those DSR points by becoming a buyer yourself. You also earn feedback comments (but not DSRs) when you buy; remember, both parties to a transaction get to leave feedback. However, only buyers can leave neutral or negative comments. When you start to sell on eBay, unless you have a feedback score of at least 10 to 15, it will be very hard to attract bids. Personally, I rarely buy from any seller with a score lower than 50, and at that low rating their feedback had better be 98 or 100 percent if they want me to bid.

ABOUT ME PAGE

Whenever you open an auction on eBay, you will see the seller's user ID prominently displayed in the top section of the auction. If the seller has an About Me page, you will see a little icon after his name that says *Me.* If you click on this icon, it will take you to the seller's About Me page (see, for example, Figure 1.5). This is a page that eBay allows you to create to tell prospective bidders about you and your eBay business.

There is no cost to set up your About Me page and it can help you to get more bids, especially when your are new and still have a low feedback score.

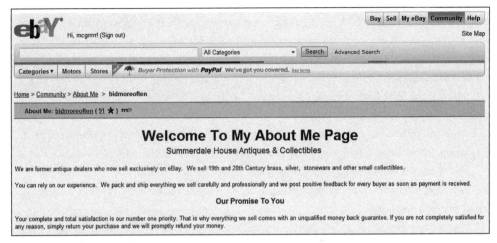

Figure 1.5 About Me Page

You can personalize the page any way you want. Some sellers use it to talk about themselves and where they live, often including photos. Others explain their policies and experience on eBay on their About Me page. Still others create an About Me page to help brand their business.

While eBay does not allow you to link to a Web site from your auction description, you *can* link to your personal or e-commerce Web site from your About Me page as long as you are not promoting items for sale there. In other words, you cannot say something like "Please visit my Web site to buy this item cheaper than I can sell it on eBay." In chapter 25 we look more closely at ways to use your About Me page to drive additional revenue to your eBay business.

MY EBAY PAGE

Once you register, you will automatically be set up with a My eBay page. A link to your My eBay page appears at the top of every eBay page you access; it's located in the navigation links. When you click on this, you will be prompted to sign in with your user ID and password, because your My eBay page contains links to your account and personal information.

The My eBay page has four main sections: All Buying, All Selling, All Favorites, and My Account. Under All Selling, the first thing you see is a list of all the items you are selling, the current price and number of bids, whether or not your reserve has been met (if you have one), and the number of people who are watching your auction. If you click on the *Sold* link, you will see a list of the items you have sold and their status, as well as actions you can take just by clicking on the button next to each item. These actions include *Send Invoice, Print Shipping Label,* and *Leave Feedback.* Later, we address the issue of automation as it relates to selling on eBay. eBay offers a program called eBay Selling Manager, which, once it's integrated into your My eBay page, allows you to automate a lot of sales-related functions, such as sending out invoices and shipping notices, and posting feedback. There is also a link on the My eBay page under My Account to your *Seller Dashboard,* where you can see your current DSR detail information and other information for sellers.

For the moment, just spend some time clicking on the various links on your My eBay page to become familiar with all the information that is available to you. Once you have some auctions launched and items sold, this page will become a useful tool for tracking your sold and unsold items, customer communications, payment and shipping status, and feedback.

Your My eBay page also includes an important link to *My Messages.* Whenever eBay or a potential eBay bidder sends you an e-mail, you will receive the message in your personal eBay account, accessible via your My Messages page. These e-mails are also forwarded to the e-mail address you registered with.

.... BEST PRACTICES ....

AVOIDING SPOOF E-MAILS

Be wary of spoof e-mails. These are messages that arrive in your e-mail inbox and *appear* to be from one of your bidders or buyers, often claiming that the buyer has not received an item he bought from you. The message will contain a link to sign in to your eBay account. *Never click on one of these links in an e-mail.* The link is bogus: It will bring up a page that looks just like the eBay sign-in page—however, it is really a fraudulent Web site designed to capture your user ID and password. We delve into the topic of spoof e-mails and other types of fraud in chapter 20, but since you may receive one of these messages shortly after signing up with eBay, you need to be aware of this scam right off the bat as a lot of new eBay users fall for this.

If you receive an e-mail relating to an eBay auction or a transaction purporting to be from eBay itself—or any message whose origin you are unsure of—just go to your My Messages page. If the message is authentic, it will also appear there. Remember: Neither eBay nor PayPal will ever send you an e-mail asking for your account details.

BUSINESS LICENSES

If you are running your business out of your home, you will most likely *not* need to obtain a local business license from your town or county. Typically, local business licenses are for businesses that have customers visiting the business location. If, however, you open an office or rent space in a commercial location, you may need to get a local business license. This license is usually inexpensive—under $100 in most towns and cities. You can apply for it at the city clerk's office.

SALES TAX NUMBER

If you live in a state that charges sales tax, you need a state sales tax number. Other states that do not charge sales tax, such as Oregon, typically issue a business-use tax number that serves the same purpose.

A sales tax number allows you to purchase merchandise for resale without paying sales tax to the vendor. Whenever you sell something in your state that is delivered to an address *in your state,* you must collect sales tax from the customer and remit the sales tax to your state's tax department. Most states require you to file and pay your sales taxes quarterly, although some states require you to do it monthly, often depending on the volume of sales generated by your business.

You *do not* have to collect, or pay, sales tax on orders that you ship *out of state.* However, if you live in a state with a large population, such as New York, Illinois, or California, most likely you will sell a lot of items on eBay to buyers in your state.

You should always collect and pay state sales tax, because state tax authorities are aware that many Internet sellers are skirting this requirement, and they are cracking down. Sometimes a state compliance officer, masquerading as a legitimate eBay bidder, will purchase something low cost from you, or just send you an e-mail pretending to be a bidder, and ask if you charge sales tax. If you don't collect the tax, you will be subject to some serious fines. In some states, you're liable for criminal penalties as well.

BIZ BUILDER

Luckily, eBay makes it simple to collect sales taxes on in-state transactions. On the Sell Your Item form, you can enter the name of your state and the percentage of sales tax to collect. When an auction ends, if the buyer is located in your state, eBay automatically adds the sales tax to the final selling price and the shipping amount. It also displays the rate charged and what state it applies to on the auction page. This alone can prevent you from being targeted by a state compliance officer.

INTERNET SALES TAX

Several bills are floating around the U.S. Congress, designed to change the federal law and allow states to collect sales tax on out-of-state Internet transactions (including eBay sales). One bill that several states have adopted does require Internet-based sales taxes to be collected and paid on out-of-state shipments; however, it exempts businesses that do less than $4 million in annual sales. eBay has been at the forefront of the fight against this kind of legislation. Each year, eBay selects fifty top sellers—one from each state—and they go to Washington, where they roam the halls of Congress meeting with legislators and lobbying against any form of Internet tax. In the United Kingdom, the government has not been successful at collecting value-added tax (VAT)—the UK version of sales tax—from individual eBay sales and sellers, but the government is now collecting VAT from sellers' eBay fees.

Most states require you to fill out a simple form once a quarter that lists all your taxable sales and mail it into the state with a check for the sales tax you collected. Later on, we'll look at a simple way to maintain these records and automate the process so it only takes a few minutes a week to keep track of sales tax collection and handle the payments.

Besides collecting and paying taxes, the other reason you need a state sales tax number is to purchase merchandise. Most legitimate wholesale companies simply will not sell to you unless you have a sales tax number.

It is very simple to get a sales tax number. In most states the fee is low, typically ranging from $25 to $100, although some states require new businesses to put up a deposit as high as $500. This is usually returned after one year of paying your taxes on time.

To get the lowdown on state sales tax, visit the Web site for this book, www.skipmcgrath.com/3_weeks, and click on the navigation link *State Sales Tax*. This takes you to a page where you can link directly to the Web sites of the tax departments in all fifty states. There you can get all the information you need and download the required forms. In most cases you can apply for a number online.

When you get your sales tax number most states allow you to register a business name. This can be any name you choose as long as it is not already in use or trademarked. I usually recommend people select a general name as this allows you to buy and sell different types of merchandise. Later when we talk about dealing with wholesalers we will discuss the importance of having traditional business identification such as business cards and letterheads, so take a few minutes to give some thought to naming your business. It does not have to be the same as your eBay username, but it can be.

COMMERCIAL CHECKING ACCOUNT

Since you are probably going to buy from wholesale companies, you will want to open a commercial checking account in the name of your business. Most legitimate wholesale companies and distributors prefer to deal with businesses, rather than individuals. They require you to have both a state sales tax number and a business checking account to do business with them. Later on, we give you tips on how to get into wholesale trade shows and merchandise marts, which also require this proof of business status. When you apply for a state sales tax number, you can register a business name at the same time. Simply take your certificate with the business name to your local bank and ask to open a commercial (or business) checking account. Most banks will do this for a minimum deposit of $100. At this time you should also apply for a credit or debit card for the account. You will be making wholesale purchases on the Web and paying online for different services, including your eBay fees. This way all your business expenses are handled through one account— and you will simplify both your record keeping and your taxes at the end of the year.

POWER MOVES

- ❑ Register your eBay account and sign up for a PayPal business account.

- ❑ If you haven't ever purchased anything on eBay, gain some experience by bidding on and winning a few items so you can learn about and get a good grasp of the process.

- ❑ As you are bidding and buying, be sure to look at each seller's feedback rating. When you win an auction, post feedback for the seller and make sure the seller posts feedback for you. E-mail the seller a polite request if she forgets to do this.

- ❑ Set up your About Me page.

- ❑ Explore the resources on your My eBay page.

- ❑ Apply for a state sales tax number.

- ❑ Open a commercial checking account and sign up for a business credit or debit card.

CHAPTER 2

✦ FINDING YOUR WAY ✦ AROUND EBAY

BESIDES THE MY EBAY and About Me pages, there are many more resource pages on eBay. As a seller you need to become familiar with pages that allow you to manage your items for sale, revise your auctions, end a listing early, and handle disputes from nonpaying bidders. You may not need to access these pages for your first few auctions, but if you do, it is imperative to know what actions eBay allows you to take and how to quickly find the tools you need.

SITE MAP

eBay's site map is the best place to start investigating the tools available to you. Table 2.1 shows the most important links for sellers.

As a seller, the middle column of the site map, Selling Activities (see Figure 2.1), contains several links you will be using often.

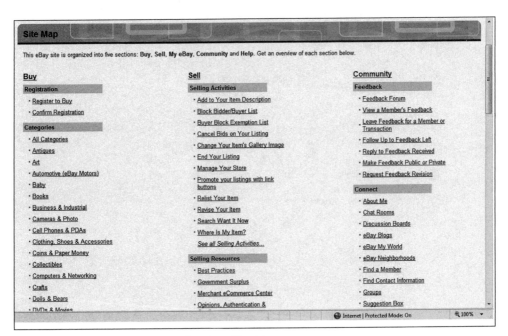

Figure 2.1 Selling Activities on the eBay Site Map

Some of these links are quite valuable and you will refer to them often, so you will want to bookmark them (add them to your Favorites). To access the others, you can just refer to the site map when you need them.

Table 2.1 Useful eBay Links

REVISE YOUR ITEM	Like all of us, you will occasionally make a mistake in one of your listings. This link allows you to fix any mistakes you made or add new information.
CANCEL BIDS ON YOUR LISTING	If you need to end an auction, you will first have to cancel any bids on your item. This is a page where you can do that.
END YOUR LISTING	You can end your listing at any time, but if there are bids, you must cancel them first (see above).
DISPUTE CONSOLE	This is where you can report buyers to eBay who have not paid for an item, or sellers who failed to ship an item that you purchased. You can also link to the Dispute Console from your My eBay page.
BLOCK BIDDER/BUYER LIST	This is where you can block certain bidders from bidding on your auctions. If a bidder leaves me negative feedback, I always block him from bidding on my future auctions.
POWERSELLERS	Once you are a PowerSeller, bookmark this page because this is where you can access special tools for PowerSellers and communicate with the PowerSeller support team.

SELLER CENTRAL

Further down the middle column of the site map is a heading titled Selling Resources. Under this heading is a link to *Seller Resources*. Seller Resources contains many valuable resources for eBay sellers, including:

* **BEST PRACTICES**: These are listings of strategies and techniques developed by eBay PowerSellers to help you increase sales. I strongly recommend that you read them after you have read this book. Some of them might not make a lot of sense until you understand the context.

* **ADVANCED SELLING**: This section introduces you to some of eBay's advanced selling tools, such as eBay Keywords, the Trading Assistant program, and co-op advertising opportunities. Again, these are services best accessed after you have been selling for a while.

* **CATEGORY TIPS**: This is a very valuable section. The resources here include:

  > *Seller's Edge*: Strategies, features, and insights from the category managers and PowerSellers who specialize in the specific category.

  > *Seller Profiles*: An in-depth look at how successful sellers maximize their sales and profits on eBay.

  > *In Demand*: Lists of what's hot, with expert picks and top searches.

  > *Selling Guides/Zones*: An overview of the basics of selling in your category.

  > *Discussion Boards*: Your link to other sellers so you can share experiences and best practices.

  > *Contact Us*: A quick way to e-mail your eBay Category Management team.

* **NEWS & UPDATES**: Here's how you can keep up-to-date on all the changes going on with eBay—and there are a lot of them. If you are going to be a serious PowerSeller, you should get in the habit of checking the News and Announcements Boards daily. I like to do it first thing in the morning after I check my e-mails.

* **RESOURCES**: This is a great page to bookmark because it takes you to a site map of all the resources available to the seller, conveniently listed in one place. It is akin to a "sellers only" site map.

Farther down the site map page is a series of links under the heading *My Account*. You do not have to bookmark these links because they are all easily accessible from your My eBay page.

THE EBAY TOOLBAR

The eBay toolbar (Figure 2.2) is a toolbar you can download from eBay that installs automatically right below the URL window in your browser. At the moment it only works with Internet Explorer.

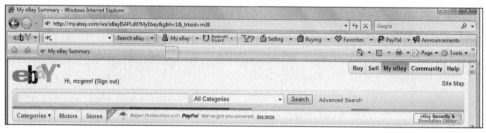

Figure 2.2 The eBay Toolbar

The eBay toolbar, which can be customized, contains a lot of useful features. There are instant links to the eBay homepage, My eBay, PayPal, new announcements, and the community message boards, as well as an alert feature that you can set to notify you of auctions ending soon. Probably the most important feature of the eBay toolbar is Account Guard. This feature can recognize if you try to enter either your eBay or PayPal passwords on sites that are not the official eBay or PayPal sites. Should you attempt to do so, an alert box will pop up, warning you that this could be a spoof site, potentially saving you from falling for an e-mail scam. You don't have to use Account Guard, but I highly recommend that you do.

EBAY COMMUNITY PAGE

eBay is a unique community. Its members have a long history (*long*, that is, in terms of the Internet Age) of helping each other out. You can connect to other members in several ways. On the eBay Community page (see Figure 2.3) there are four categories you should note:

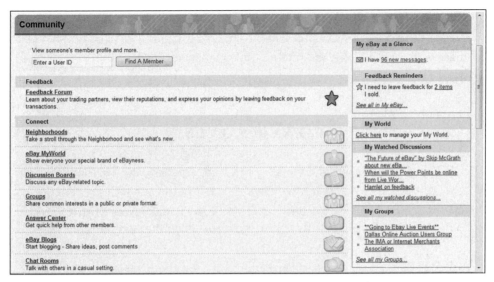

Figure 2.3 eBay Community Page

✳ **DISCUSSION BOARDS:** Here you can post and reply to messages on thousands of topics. Special boards are geared to PowerSellers and Trading Assistants; other boards focus on subjects like PayPal shipping and handling. Almost any eBay subject you can think of is covered here. And, if it's not, you can start a new board to discuss it.

✳ **GROUPS:** These are message boards arranged by category, so you can kibbitz with other collectors or sellers of merchandise in your category. Regional groups, by city and state, can be found here as well, so you can meet up online with folks in your local area.

✳ **ANSWER CENTER:** This is the place to ask any questions you may have, such as "How do I insert a photo into my auction?" or "How do I pack and ship a six-foot-long didgeridoo?" Other sellers and eBay employees will answer almost any question you pose. You can identify employees by the color of their user IDs—employee user IDs are always pink. If you see someone refer to a "pink," she is talking about an eBay employee.

✳ **CHAT ROOMS:** eBay hosts over one hundred different chat rooms. Unlike the message boards, where it can take hours to get a reply to a post, the chat rooms are active 24/7. Once again, there are category-specific and feature-specific chat rooms.

One thing to note about the discussion boards: There are unhappy or unsuccessful people in every community. While most posts are positive and helpful, there are always some posts from unsuccessful sellers or people who just love to complain. I take all of these with a grain of salt and rarely let them influence my decisions.

POWER MOVES

❑ Familiarize yourself with the eBay site map, especially the links under Selling Activities and Selling Resources.

❑ Bookmark important pages in a special eBay Pages folder, so that you can readily access important tools without searching through the site map every time.

❑ Visit Seller Resources and familiarize yourself with the resources and tools available to eBay sellers.

❑ Install the eBay toolbar on your desktop.

CHAPTER 3

✦ WHAT SELLS ON EBAY? ✦

WITH TENS OF THOUSANDS of categories and subcategories, you can sell virtually anything on eBay. But choosing what to sell can often be overwhelming. You should first examine your own professional experience, hobbies, and interests. If you currently own a small retail store, gallery, or antiques shop, experiment to figure out which of your products would sell well on eBay.

If you want to start an eBay business from scratch, then you have to decide what business you are going to be in and what kind of products to sell. The biggest mistake new sellers make is jumping from product to product, trying to find the latest, hottest-selling gadget. If you are going to launch a sustainable business, you will have to specialize in something—preferably something where the competition is minimal, or you have a distinct competitive edge.

In this chapter, we'll explore which products sell consistently well on eBay, and what categories might be right for you. We'll also focus on several product areas that are fairly easy for any eBay seller to enter. I am not suggesting that you choose one of these areas. Instead, I am trying to show you that there are plenty of categories where people can still make money, even with competition. Perhaps reading about some of the possibilities in this chapter will inspire some ideas of your own.

.... BEST PRACTICES ....

YOU CAN'T SELL *THAT* ON EBAY!

While you can sell anything from your kitchen sink to your pet rock collection on eBay, certain items are prohibited. Items you can't sell on eBay include human body parts; merchandise that has been recalled by the manufacturer; counterfeit brand-name goods, such as knockoff Rolex watches or Gucci handbags; live pets; any tobacco product; electronic surveillance equipment; animals and wildlife products; drugs and drug paraphernalia; firearms; bootleg recordings; and satellite or cable TV descramblers.

The complete list is quite long. In addition to prohibiting the sale of certain merchandise outright, eBay also places restrictions on other items, such as travel, real estate, paintball and Airsoft guns, and others. To find out more about prohibited and restricted items, click on the *Help* tab at the top of any eBay page and type *prohibited items* into the search box.

CONSIDER YOUR INTERESTS

If you worked as an audiovisual technician, then you have the knowledge to sell AV equipment. Do you love cooking? Then get into cookware, restaurant equipment, or gourmet food items. Do you collect sports memorabilia? If so, start there. Perhaps you love to read and you always wanted to own a small bookstore, but you could never afford the overhead. On eBay, you can start with only a few dozen books and build your business from there. The same goes for art. You can buy art posters or prints wholesale, just a few at a time. Thousands of art prints and posters sell every day on eBay.

If you are a computer or software whiz, look to the computer area for items to sell. Better still, write your own software or build a computer-related product or accessory and sell it on eBay.

Your business and product ideas are limited only by your imagination, but make sure there is a market for the products and/or services you love and plan to sell. (In the next chapter, we'll discuss researching a product to determine if there is a market for it on eBay, and what kind of prices you can realistically charge.)

Whatever you decide to sell, work to become an expert at it. Go to the library and read up on your products, talk to other merchants and collectors, research your competition, learn something about the history of your product, and study the manufacturers. Knowing your product category in depth will pay many dividends down the road.

If you don't believe in what you're selling, and you aren't willing to stand behind your product, your online business will most certainly fail. You should never sell a product you aren't enthusiastic about. If you wouldn't buy the product for yourself, or strongly recommend it to a friend or family member, then do not sell it to unwary consumers. (See chapter 11, "Building Great Feedback," to understand how important this logic is.)

Certain items definitely outsell others. Information and software products are particularly hot sellers. Why? Because everyone buying on eBay already owns a computer. And using a computer means they need hardware and/or software. Therefore, almost anyone buying on eBay is a potential customer for computer hardware, software, or accessories.

Software is a huge seller on eBay. Here's why: If you wrote a highly specialized application, you would have a difficult time selling it to a software company. Such companies are not interested in a product unless it can generate millions of dollars in sales. But *you* could probably make a lot of money selling a few hundred or a few thousand copies on eBay and the other auction sites. Trading cards–collecting software has become very popular (although there is so much of it around now that the price has fallen drastically). Or perhaps you have figured out a way to automate an eBay function.

You can apply to work with the eBay Application Program Interface (API) and write (and sell) a software program for eBay users.

Computer games are also big with eBay buyers. Just make sure you are selling a popular game and not one that is considered passé. Yesterday's hot game that sold for $49.95 in the stores can be bought from closeout dealers for $5.00 each. (You could still make this situation work, because there are people willing to buy old games for up to $15.00 each. Just don't expect to sell them for much more.)

A CPA with a large accounting firm here in Seattle collects sports memorabilia. He spent hundreds of hours scouring eBay for bargains. He realized right away that the market for common sports memorabilia was saturated and profit margins were too small for him to make much of a profit. So he decided to specialize in oddball and unusual items. He purchased a lot of five hundred unused tickets from the Ali–Frazier fight (the "Thrilla in Manila"), and began auctioning them off on eBay one ticket at a time. The last time I saw him, he was still selling them at up to $40 each. I believe he bought the whole lot for under $200.

My wife and I used to sell antiques. We worked through one of the largest antiques malls in upstate New York. The mall had a common Web site shared by all the vendors, and I ran auctions for the dealers. This gave us the image of being one large dealer with a high feedback rating. Whenever customers purchased from us, we would then introduce them to our Web site. Customers would link to our Web site over and over again because of the large variety of items available there.

At first I tried to use eBay to unload our slow-moving items. It didn't work! Slow-moving merchandise moves slowly for a reason; there isn't much interest in it on eBay, or in the store. After a few tries, I switched to selling our higher-quality, more expensive items. Our sales took off and we were getting bids 10–30 percent higher than we were selling the items for in the store.

Whatever your interest—clothing and fashion, sports, cars, cooking, high finance, antiques, art, books, collectibles—there are products you can sell on eBay and other auction sites. And, yes, eBay fortunes have been made on Furby toys, Pokémon cards, and Beanie Babies! Lately, anything related to Webkinz, Star Wars, or Dora the Explorer/Diego will be a big seller. Next year it will be something else—guaranteed.

TARGET EBAY SELLERS

Another excellent sales strategy is to sell supplies to other eBay sellers. Bubble Pak envelopes, printer ink cartridges, and packing tape are big sellers on eBay. You can also sell supplies to collectors. Card collectors buy card holders and software to catalog their cards; doll collectors buy display cases; coin collectors buy coin holders; and so on. Look at a current fad and try to find some way to supply every collector with something he can use to give his collectibles extra value—instead of selling the collectible itself.

A WORD ABOUT POPULAR CONSUMER GOODS

I always get e-mails from eBay sellers who want to sell the latest digital cameras, DVD players, stereo equipment, computers, games, or hot apparel items. Beware: *This is a very difficult business to enter.* First of all, the wholesale distributors for these products will not even talk to you unless you have a minimum $250,000 line of credit and can place orders of at least $50,000. I once spoke to Apple Computer's distributor about selling iPods online. The distributor's representatives were happy to sell the product to me at a wholesale cost of $122 for the $199 retail unit. However, I had to prove that I had a $200,000 line of credit and purchase 100 units at a time.

If you have the kind of money it takes to place large wholesale orders and you want to find these goods, the best strategy is to contact the manufacturer of the product you wish to sell and simply ask for the name and contact information of the company's wholesale distributor in your area. As long as you can meet the distributor's buying criteria, you can place an order.

The other issue is competition. If you are selling any hot or high-demand product, then so are hundreds of other sellers, and the profit margin on these products tends to be very low—sometimes so low that a small seller just can't compete.

USED GOODS

Hundreds of eBay sellers (many of them PowerSellers) sell used goods they pick up at flea markets, garage sales, estate sales, and thrift shops. Almost any product you can think of has been sold used on eBay. Some of the best-selling products are children's clothing, women's plus-size clothing, cowboy boots, ice skates, used athletic equipment, old cameras and any type of photo or darkroom equipment, old computers (that is, pre-1990), small appliances (such as Juiceman juicers, pasta machines, food processors, and mixers), and, of course, used watches and jewelry.

Used electronics, including vintage hi-fi equipment (pre-1980s), early computers, reel-to-reel tape decks, and 8-track tape players and cartridges are excellent products—always in high demand on eBay. Because many eBay users consider themselves at the cutting edge of technology, used electronics often have a quaint appeal. So do old film cameras and darkroom equipment. I recently learned that there is a good market on eBay for old flashlights—even those are now collected.

If you decide to sell used goods, you must first research what is selling. So before you buy that Juiceman at your local thrift store, check out the ones selling on eBay to make sure it's a desirable model and is going for a price that allows you to make a profit.

Only buy items that are in good-to-excellent condition. Don't attempt to sell anything defective or broken unless you are selling it for parts—and be sure to say this. If you sell anything used, it is critical that you completely and accurately describe its condition. In addition, you should take good photos and be sure to point out any defects. People will readily buy used goods with defects or blemishes as long as they understand the product's condition upfront.

USED BOOKS

Used books are big sellers on eBay, and this is a very easy business to start. There are hundreds of eBay sellers making over $1,000 a week selling used books.

Unless you are an expert bookseller, forget about novels, literature, or rare expensive books. Any used bookstore owner will tell you that her daily bread and butter are nonfiction books on art, photography, crafts, cooking, history, sports, cars, trains, motorcycles, and music, as well as children's books. The same is true on eBay. You can buy plenty of these books at garage sales, flea markets, and thrift stores, and resell them on eBay for markups as high as 100–500 percent.

The easiest books to sell are the large "coffee table" editions on art, photography, transportation (trains, boats, cars, etc.), and sports. I recently purchased a beautiful history of Porsche motorcars at a local thrift shop for $1.00. It sold on eBay for $29.00. I was browsing the closeout table at Barnes & Noble just after Christmas and bought a brand-new, marked-down *History of the Superbowl* for $5.99. The cover price was $29.95, and it sold on eBay for $17.50. I once purchased a set of Ansel Adams photography books at a garage sale for $15.00. I sold them individually on eBay for a total of more than $90.00.

Cookbooks can be excellent sellers. Look for cookbooks by big-name authors, such as Julia Child, Rachael Ray, Emeril Lagasse, and Bobby Flay, as well as classics like *The Joy of Cooking* and *The Saucier's Apprentice*.

Children's books are great sellers, if they are in very good condition. Any pop-up book is highly sought after. Children's pop-up books can be found for a buck or so at garage sales and will sell on eBay for prices up to $50 if they are in excellent condition. If you are selling low-cost books, such as cookbooks or children's books, group them into sets of three-to-five books each so you are not running a lot of small, individual auctions and you save on listing fees.

Another great category is old law and medical books, especially anything pre-1950s. It is amazing how many of these turn up at garage sales. Some of them, such as an early edition of *Black's Law Dictionary*, can go for huge amounts of money on eBay.

Finally, look for books on fine woodworking, as well as woodworking magazines. And while I recommend that you stay away from general "how-to-fix-anything" books, books that contain plans for building objects tend to sell readily.

Stay away from book club editions and series books, such as the Time-Life books, unless you have a complete set in perfect condition. I once found the complete Time-Life Photography series at a used bookstore for $65. I sold it on eBay for $122—less than I hoped to get, but still a nice profit. Reader's Digest Condensed Books show up at garage sales and thrift shops in great numbers and should be totally avoided as these rarely sell.

Only buy books in good condition, preferably with intact dust jackets. Never pay more than 30 percent of what you think the item will sell for, and no more than 25 percent of the cover price. You can find plenty of books at garage sales for less than $2 that will sell on eBay for $10 or more. Stay away from books that would sell for less than $10; otherwise, you will have to sell dozens of books every week to make a decent income.

A great way to find books to sell is to place a small classified ad in your local paper like the following:

> *Local dealer will pay top dollar*
> *for nonfiction books in good*
> *condition. Call Kathy, 666-555-1111*

If you are interested in selling used books, the special Web page for readers of this book at www.skipmcgrath.com/3_weeks has some free resources and additional information on this topic.

CLOSEOUT MERCHANDISE

Closeout merchandise is new merchandise that a retailer couldn't sell, or surplus goods left over at the end of a season. You can make good money selling closeout goods, but beware of some pitfalls in this area. We will cover buying closeout merchandise in great detail in chapter 6. In the meantime, the following surplus items sell well on eBay and are worth considering if you want to go this route.

Clothing

Brand-name surplus clothing is readily available from a number of wholesale dealers. The key words in the last sentence are *brand name*. Non brand-name clothing may sell on eBay, but it will not bring the prices you need to make a profit. We will show you how to find unlimited supplies of brand-name clothing in chapter 6.

Surplus Electronics

As noted earlier, it is both difficult and expensive to get *new* consumer electronics to sell. However, you can find tons of surplus electronics—goods that stores couldn't sell and must now unload to clear shelf space for new models—and these are strong sellers on eBay. Make sure you are buying surplus goods and not *returns*—products customers brought back because they didn't work or there was some other problem with them. For ideas on how to acquire this merchandise, see chapter 6.

Remanufactured Electronics and Consumer Goods

Manufacturers of almost all sorts of expensive electronic and mechanical merchandise offer "remanufactured" or "refurbished" goods. These run the gamut from computers and digital cameras to stereo and television equipment, and home appliances. Remanufactured equipment and merchandise are generally goods that were returned by consumers and, although not used, could not be sold as new because the package had been opened or some of the items had been assembled. In some cases, refurbished items are warranty returns. Typically, the manufacturers run these items through their normal quality-control process and repackage them. These goods are almost always offered with a full warranty. In the case of subsequent warranty returns, the items are repaired and once again run through the quality-control process.

Some large manufacturers, such as Sony, actually have outlet stores where they sell this merchandise directly to the public. For example, I once bought a Sony digital camera at the company's outlet store in Dallas at one-third the cost of retail. I used it for almost a year and then sold it on eBay for almost double what I had paid for it. You can shop Sony's outlet online at www.sonystyle.com (click *Shop Outlet* from the homepage). You can also find a list of Sony's brick-and-mortar outlet stores on this Web site.

These remanufactured goods can be great items to sell on eBay. How do you find them? The best way is to visit the manufacturer's Web site and see if there is a link to an outlet for these goods. If not, then e-mail the manufacturer and ask how and where the company sells its refurbished items. As a last resort, you can call the company and ask for the purchasing department; a representative will usually tell you how you can access these products. In chapter 6, we will discuss specific Web-based closeout dealers offering remanufactured goods.

CLIPPINGS

Do you have teenage or preteen children? If so, selling magazine clippings could be a great business for you. Go to eBay and type the word *clippings* into the search box. You will get hundreds of auctions listed that sell magazine clippings of famous sports, music, and Hollywood stars. Each auction represents dozens, or even hundreds, of clippings people have assembled from magazines and sold as a lot. Here are examples of recent sales on eBay:

Elizabeth Taylor	217 clippings	$575.00
ABBA	200 clippings	$304.00
Madonna	113 clippings and magazine covers	$223.00
Michael Jackson	149 clippings	$192.00

Clippings of more contemporary celebrities can also be profitable on eBay:

Cal Ripken	117 clippings	$121.00
Dalida	107 clippings	$108
Johnny Depp	77 clippings	$79.00
Mira Sorvino	80 clippings	$55.00
Jude Law	127 clippings	$41.00

The older the star, or the older the clippings, the greater the value.

You can find old magazines at garage sales, thrift shops, small-town auctions, and many more places. Just put your kids to work, clipping the magazines and arranging the pieces into file folders or envelopes. Pay them a penny or a nickel a clipping. Once you collect a large number of clippings on a specific celebrity, put them up for sale on eBay—you'll make about 1,000 percent on your investment. Your kids can even make money by paying their friends to find and collect clippings for them. There is one lady in South Carolina who has an entire neighborhood of children collecting clippings and selling them to her. One local kid brought her a pack of fifty Dale Earnhardt, Jr., clippings. She paid the young boy $5 and sold them on eBay for over $75.

I was attending a small, local auction recently, and a box of old magazines came up from the 1950s and 1960s. The box sold for $30. I spoke to the woman who bought it, and she told me she could turn these old magazines into over $1,000—just by selling the clippings on eBay.

COLLECTIBLES

There are all kinds of collectibles you can sell on eBay. Almost anything you can think of is collected by someone. Did you know, for example, that people collect and pay big money for old eyeglasses? "Great—where do I find old eyeglasses?" you may ask. You will probably never see them at a garage sale. However, if the people putting on the sale are over fifty or are wearing eyeglasses, try asking them if they have any old eyeglasses or even old sunglasses lying around the house. You will be amazed how many people will come up with them. Antique or vintage eyeglasses, both prescription and nonprescription, sell on eBay in the $25–$200 range.

The same is true of many more collectibles. Everyone knows that Elvis and Beatles memorabilia is highly collectible. The trick is to find the lesser-known items that most people don't think of. I have a friend who sells nothing but old fishing equipment and lures on eBay. He brings in more than $2,000 a month. That doesn't sound like much money, but he usually gets a 500 percent to 1,500 percent markup. He can buy an old fishing reel at a garage sale for $5 and sell it on eBay for $75. Other sellers do the same thing with vintage stereo equipment, old computers and cameras, old golf clubs and tennis rackets, and so on. You just need to do the research to see what is selling.

EBAY MOTORS

eBay Motors is a huge marketplace. More vehicles are sold on eBay Motors than on all the other automobile sales Web sites combined. For example, according to eBay, a Ford Mustang sells every seventeen minutes. Selling cars may be problematic, because most states have regulations that prohibit you from selling more than three or four cars a year unless you have a dealer's license. But most states exempt vehicles under three thousand or four thousand pounds (1,360–1,820kg) from that requirement. This covers motorcycles, motor scooters, Airstream trailers, pop-up camper trailers, boat trailers, car engines and parts, and all types of automotive accessories and after-market products.

The husband of the manager at my local Starbucks has developed a great business buying old cars, breaking them up, and selling the parts on eBay. For a few hundred dollars, he can buy an old Plymouth from the '50s or '60s that's in such bad shape it can't be profitably restored, and make several thousand dollars selling everything from the brake pads to the window winders on eBay. A single piece of interior hardware can be worth $50 to $100 to someone who is trying to restore an original car. A friend of mine had a British Triumph TR-7, one of the worst British cars ever made. He fully restored it and drove it for about a year and then tried to sell it. He had over $3,000 invested in the car and couldn't even get an offer of $2,000 for it. He ended up selling it for parts on eBay and made over $4,500.

Another prolific eBay seller scours the countryside for old Airstream trailers. If he finds one in good condition, he does some simple cosmetic repairs and can usually make 50–100 percent on his investment. If the trailer is in poor condition, he breaks it up and sells the parts, again always doubling his money.

One of the largest PowerSellers on eBay is a young man who started his business while he was a junior in high school, using his dad's eBay account. He started selling race car seats he got at a good discount from his local auto parts store. By the time he was a senior in high school, he was importing after-market car seats and performance parts from Asia and grossing over $20,000 a month on eBay. Today he is a large PowerSeller, someone who averages minimum sales of $25,000 to $150,000 a month on eBay.

CONSIGNMENT SELLING

When you sell something on consignment, you are selling an item for someone else as a service. This is the perfect eBay business. You do not need to purchase any inventory so there is no risk involved (except for the small amount you must pay in eBay listing fees). Someone gives you something to sell. You photograph the item, write a description of the piece, and put it up for sale on eBay. If it sells, you earn a commission—sometimes as high as 40 percent. Since the buyer pays for the shipping, whatever commission you collect is pure profit. If it doesn't sell, you simply return it to the consignor and you are only out a couple of dollars for eBay listing fees. In fact, many consignment sellers charge the fees to the buyer so they are not out anything except the time it took to research the price and list the item.

eBay actually has a program for consignment sellers called Trading Assistant. If you become a registered Trading Assistant, eBay will list you in its directory and help you promote your business in your local community with flyers, letters, business cards, and a co-op advertising program. These materials are available from eBay as Microsoft Word downloads. Simply enter your personal information (name, phone number, and so forth), and have them printed at a local print store. To attract customers (consignors), distribute your business cards to appropriate contacts and post the flyers on any free community bulletin board.

How much can you make as a Trading Assistant? When I was working on the manuscript for this book, I got a call from someone who saw my name in the eBay Trading Assistant Directory. He was trying to sell a vintage Indian motorcycle. I went to his house and took the photos, launched an auction that night, and within two days a buyer in San Jose, California, hit the *Buy It Now* button and bought the motorcycle for $13,500. My commission was 10 percent for about one hour's work.

We are going to cover eBay consignment selling in chapter 27 in great detail. But before you get too excited, this is a skill that takes some experience. You will want to have successfully completed at least a couple hundred auctions before embarking on consignment selling. (Don't worry. I am going to show you how to do that within a month or two.) While getting a consignment business up and running may take longer than three weeks, it's important to understand how this technique works from the outset. If you decide that you're interested in consignment selling, you'll want to work this strategy into the overall business plan you will develop as you read this book.

The Business & Industrial Category

Take a look at the Business & Industrial category on eBay. The subcategories include construction equipment, farm equipment, medical equipment and supplies, restaurant equipment, and much more. This is a great area for consignment selling. For example, you can contact doctors and hospitals looking to sell their used equipment, building contractors who are replacing tools and gear, and farmers looking to sell their farm equipment for top dollar rather than trade it in to a dealer for rock-bottom value. We will cover more of this in chapter 27 on consignment selling.

In this chapter, I only touched on a few of the categories of items that sell on eBay. As part of your research, I suggest that you spend a couple of hours surfing the various eBay categories and the many subcategories of products available on the site. Then look at the auctions in those subcategories to become familiar with all the items and services that sell on eBay. As you do this, you will see myriad possibilities and opportunities for areas to specialize in. In the next chapter, we are going to show you how to use eBay's powerful search engine to conduct product research.

WEEK
1

POWER MOVES

- ❏ In your notebook, make a list of your hobbies and interests.
- ❏ Next, brainstorm all possible products that fall into those categories. Don't rule anything out at this point.
- ❏ After reading the next chapter on product research, search on eBay to determine if there is a market for these products.

CHAPTER 4

✦ PRODUCT RESEARCH ✦

I AM OFTEN ASKED, "What is the secret to making lots of money on eBay?" It's not exactly a secret, but the answer to that question is simple: selecting the right product to sell. What makes something the right product? First of all, there must be a market for the product. You have to have something that other people want to buy. Second, you must find a product that you can buy for a price that allows you to make a profit reselling it. Last, the market for the product you're selling cannot be overly saturated. A moderate amount of competition is fine; you can always best your competition. Also, competition usually shows that there is a market for the product—otherwise, other sellers would not be selling it.

In chapter 3, we covered some of the popular selling categories on eBay. Here we'll explore how to dig into these and other categories to find products that are marketable on eBay and can earn you consistent profits as an eBay seller.

TYPES OF SEARCH TOOLS

There are three tools for searching out products on eBay:

* eBay Advanced Search feature
* Terapeak research
* HammerTap research tool

The eBay search engine is very powerful and, best of all, it's free to eBay members. Terapeak is a Web-based product that sells for $24.95 a month. HammerTap is a desktop-based product that sells for $19.95 per month. Both Terapeak and HammerTap give you access to important statistical data, such as a product's average selling price and the best day and time to list an auction for a specific item.

THE EBAY SEARCH ENGINE

If you want to know what something is selling for on eBay, you need to search Completed Listings. Looking at an ongoing auction will only reveal what the current bid is—you want to know what an item actually sold for.

At the top of every eBay page is an *Advanced Search* link. If you click on this link, you will go to eBay's search function page. Once there, look for another tab that says

Advanced Search. Here you will be presented with a list of options, including Completed Listings (see Figure 4.1). Check this box before beginning your search.

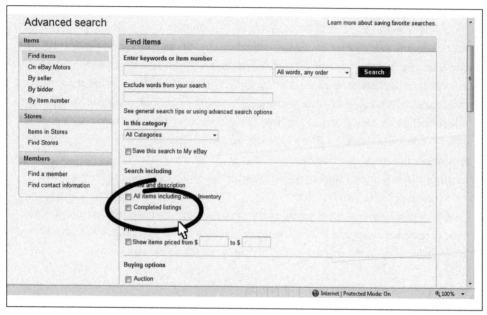

Figure 4.1   eBay Advanced Search Page

On the Search Results page, you will see a Sort By menu (the default will be Best Match). This allows you to sort by Best Match; Time: ending soonest; Time: newly listed; Price + shipping: highest first; Price + shipping: lowest first; Price: highest first; Distance: nearest first; Payment: PayPal first; and Category. When I am searching for a product I want to sell on eBay, I usually sort by Price: highest first. Because you are trying to determine what an item sold for, this gives you the results you are looking for without having to look through several pages of auctions that failed to close.

Another search checkbox is Title and Description. Do not check this box: It will bring up every auction that includes any of your keywords in the description, which could be thousands, depending on your keyword. For example, if you searched for old fountain pen, selecting this option would bring up every auction with the word old or fountain or pen anywhere in the title or the description.

A third search checkbox on the Advanced Search page is All Items Including Store Inventory. This will return all results on eBay, including those in eBay stores, which are usually excluded from Search Results.

Narrowing Your Search

Since using a single word for your search can return hundreds of auctions, you may want to narrow the search even further. For example, suppose you are looking specifically for Omega watches, as opposed to just any brand of watch. You can find exactly what you're looking for by simply entering *Omega watch*. This will return a list of all results with both the words *Omega* and *watch* in them, and exclude all that do not contain both words.

To narrow your search even further, look for items that include certain phrases or words that go together in a specific order. For instance, if you are searching for teddy bears, you can use quotation marks: *"teddy bear."* This will return a listing of all auctions with the words *teddy bear* in them. The word *bear* must immediately follow the word *teddy* or the listing will not come up.

Finding Auctions with Multiple Search Terms

If you are searching for listings that include any of several words, you can use the *or* keyword function in your search, indicated by a combination of parentheses and commas in the search field. For example, if you wanted to find all auctions that have in their title listing the words *cat* or *kitten*, then you would enter *(cat,kitten)* in the search field. This returns all auctions that have the word *cat* or the word *kitten* in their listing. Make sure you type the parentheses and *do not* insert a space between the comma and either search term. You can also include other keyword functions. For example, *(cat,kitten) crystal* will return all items that have *crystal* and either *cat* or *kitten* in the title, thereby narrowing your search to crystal figures of cats or kittens. (Note: There is a space between the parentheses and the search term.)

Eliminating Words from Your Search

eBay's search engine also locates auctions that include one word in the title but not another. For example, if you are looking for watches, but are not interested in Casio watches, you can use the *and not* keyword function, represented by a minus sign in the search field: *watch –Casio*. This will return all results whose auction titles include the word *watch,* but exclude the word *Casio.* (Note: There is no space between the minus sign and the excluded word.)

Spend some time playing with eBay's search feature until you are an accomplished searcher. This talent will put money in your pocket.

Search Completed Listings

You can also determine what items have actually sold for on eBay. After you do a search, look in the left-hand column and you will see a checkbox that says Completed

Listings. Check this box and hit the button that says *Show Items*. You will now see only Completed Listings. Listings that ended successfully will be in green. Now you can see what items actually sold for, instead of where the auctions are at the moment.

Learning from Listings

Besides discovering what a given product is selling for on eBay, there is much more you can learn from the eBay search feature. If you are about to sell a new product, look at all the auctions for that product and related products, and analyze them. What could you have done better? Could you improve on their listing titles? How do the descriptions read—could you write a better one? What about the photographs? Did successful auctions start with low or high bids? Compare two auctions for the same or similar products. Which one got the most bids? A little research at this point will pay huge dividends down the road.

Search and eBay Seller Resources

More than 80 percent of all people looking for products on eBay use the search feature. As we have just seen, you find products by typing in keywords. If you know the most searched-for keywords on eBay in any given category, you'll have a pretty good idea of what people are looking for. Knowing what people are looking for can help you decide what to sell.

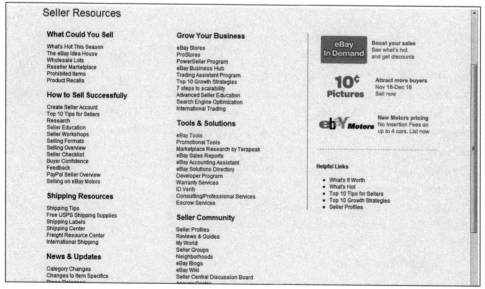

Figure 4.2 eBay Seller Resources

Sometimes you have a product to sell and you need to see if there is a market for your product on eBay. Other times, you may want to start your research by determining what hot products are selling on eBay, and then finding a product to fill a market niche. To do this, you need to know what other people are searching for.

Here's an easy way to find the most sought-after keywords on eBay. Visit eBay Seller Resources at http://pages.ebay.com/sell/resources.html.

On the Seller Resources page (see Figure 4.2), you can find all sorts of valuable information, including teaching tutorials, the What's Hot This Season report, shipping resources, and news and updates.

TERAPEAK

Terapeak is the most powerful and sophisticated research tool available today. All this power comes at a price: Terapeak charges $24.95 a month. Terapeak breaks its research reporting into four categories:

* Basic

* Listings

* Sellers

* Trends

Let's use *bird feeders* to look at each report Terapeak offers.

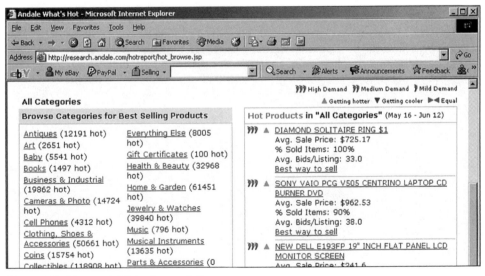

Figure 4.3 Terapeak Main Research Page

Basic Reports

Figure 4.3 shows Terapeak's Basic Research report. This report tells us quite a bit about how to sell bird feeders. This shot is only for one day; you can also pull a similar report for seven days, thirty days, or the current month-to-date. As you can see, there were fifty-three listings that received a total of sixty-one bids and a success rate of 73.58 percent. The total sales for all successful listings equaled $705.

Below these top-level statistics are the key ratios. Frankly, I don't find them that useful—with the exception of Successful Listings Per Seller. At .81 (81 percent), that tells me that almost any seller can sell a bird feeder if it is priced right.

Below the ratios are the Listing features. These are special features that eBay charges extra for. (We will cover these in detail in chapter 16.) Because these features have additional costs associated with them, it pays to scrutinize this information closely to make sure these add-ons are a good investment. In this example, no one used the Bold, Highlight, or Gift Icon features. However, 11.32 percent used the eBay Picture Services (which rotates and supersizes your photos). These sellers had a 100 percent sell-through rate. Another small percentage used the Second Category add-on, which lists your item in two categories, and the Scheduler, which schedules your auction to launch at a specific time. These sellers also had a 100 percent sell-through rate.

You can also see the pricing various sellers used. The highest starting price was $44.61 and the lowest was $5.00. The most common starting price was $9.99.

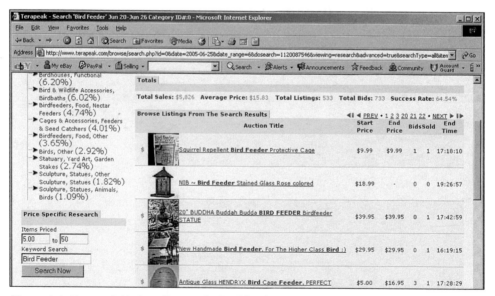

Figure 4.4 Terapeak Listings Report for bird feeders

Listings Reports

Let's switch to the Listings Report format (Figure 4.4). This shows you the actual listings on eBay. This is useful because you can look at the listings that have bids and see what the sellers' strategies are. What prices are they starting their auctions at? What features are they using? Which models and types are selling and which are not?

Sellers Reports

Next is the Sellers Report. This shows you how the top sellers for a specific product are performing. Once again, you should examine their auctions to see which products are selling and which techniques work best. We will discuss various listing, pricing, and selling techniques in later chapters, but the key here is to help you find a product that will sell on eBay. Figure 4.5, a snapshot of a Sellers Report for bird feeders, reveals two things: First, bird feeders are big sellers. Second, judging from the number of auctions, the competition is not that great. For example, there were about five hundred auctions listed for bird feeders during the week of this report. If you did a search for digital cameras, you would see roughly eight thousand auctions listed. If you narrowed the search down to one manufacturer, such as Sony or Nikon, you would still see several hundred auctions for each one.

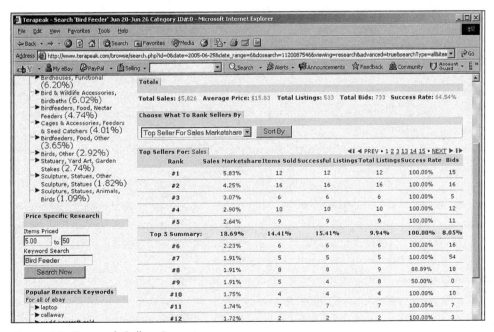

Figure 4.5 Terapeak Sellers Report

Trends

Finally, there is the Trends Report. This report shows you overall revenues and successful listings for a product over a specified period. Examine Figure 4.6, a snapshot of a Terapeak Trend Report for bird feeders. The graph reveals that Sunday, Thursday, and Friday are the best days to end an auction for bird feeders.

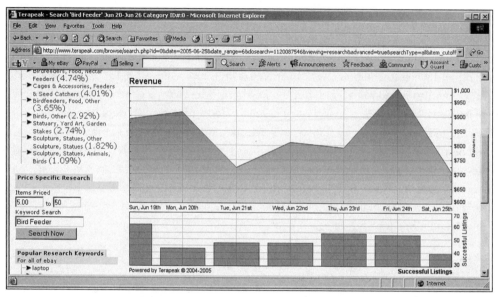

Figure 4.6 Terapeak Trend Report for bird feeders

As you can see, this is very useful data for helping you determine if a product you want to sell on eBay has a market. Once you begin listing your items on eBay, you can return to this report to click on the more successful (highest final value) auctions and determine which promotional features are most effective, and which days and times are best to list and end an auction for almost any product.

As you narrow down the list of products you want to sell—and discover new products as your business grows—continually return to and verify your research. Here is a quick way to do this: Open a Word document and list the items you want to sell. Now open the Terapeak research page in another window. Copy and paste products from your list of items one at a time into the Terapeak research box and perform a search on each one. Print out the basic report for each item and study it offline.

Once you have your printouts, for each product ask yourself the questions discussed in the next chapter, "What Should You Sell?" This research and analysis should help you to make an informed decision about which items would be best for you to sell.

HAMMERTAP

Earlier, we also mentioned HammerTap. HammerTap is a competitor to Terapeak and is very similar in the information it provides. HammerTap does offer a ten-day free trial, which Terapeak does not, so you may want to try HammerTap first to see if you like it. Personally I don't think there is very much difference between the two services—it is really a matter of personal preference. You can read more about HammerTap in Appendix C.

POWER MOVES

- ❏ Go to Terapeak (www.terapeak.com) or HammerTap (www.hammertap.com/skip), and read the features and benefits. Determine if you would like to sign up, and go through the necessary registration processes.

- ❏ Review your list of potential products to sell from chapter 3. For each product you are considering, use the eBay Advanced Search tool—as well as Terapeak or HammerTap, if you have signed up—to determine:

  - > Marketability

  - > Average selling price

  - > Best days and times to list

  - > Effective promotional features

  - > The best days and times to list the product for sale

  Be sure to keep detailed notes on your research, so that you can use this information when you begin listing items for sale.

- ❏ Based on your research, begin eliminating products from your list that do not appear to have a market, or whose average selling prices are lower than you are looking to charge per item. (You will narrow down this list further in the next chapter.)

CHAPTER 5

✦ WHAT SHOULD YOU SELL? ✦

YOU HAVE NOW GIVEN SOME THOUGHT to products you would like to sell, and you've learned how to research whether a specific product has a market on eBay. The key words in the last sentence are *on eBay*. There are plenty of products that might sell well in a specialty store or at your local mall, but cannot get any traction on eBay. This is why it is so important to take the time to research a product thoroughly before committing to purchasing a large quantity of merchandise.

We're about to move on to one of the most important topics in eBay selling: product acquisition (chapter 6). However, let's review in this chapter some final factors to consider before deciding which products and categories are right for you as a seller.

MARKET SIZE

First consider this: *Does the product you are thinking of selling have a viable market on eBay?* This question can best be answered by using the research tools we covered in the last chapter. If you searched for an item and found that only three items of its kind sold in the past month, that is not a large enough market to sustain a business.

COMPETITION

How much competition is there for the product you want to sell? Competition is a relative term. If thousands of items are selling in a given category, but there are only a handful of sellers, then the competition is low. On the other hand, when we were looking at bird feeders, we saw that only a few hundred of these items sold each week. It's crucial to examine the number of competitors very closely. A large number of sellers indicates a high level of competition. One clue as to level of competition is the average price the product is going for. If you are looking to sell an item, and you see that the average price for the item is ridiculously low, there is probably either too much supply or too many sellers.

PROFIT MARGIN

Can you source (buy) the product at a price where you can make money? We are going to cover how and where to buy products to sell on eBay in chapter 6. However, in evaluating which products to sell, you need to understand basic pricing and margin strategies.

If you are buying a product for $9.00 and selling it for $13.00, it would seem that you are making $4.00 on each product you sell. Four dollars works out to a 31 percent profit margin. That may seem fine at first. But remember: eBay listing and selling fees and PayPal fees are going to eat up about $1.00 of your margin. That brings your profit down to $3.00 per item. At $3.00 per item sold, you have to sell one hundred items a week to make $300.00. That is an awful lot of work for $300.00. If you are selling a $75.00 item and making a 33 percent profit, then you are grossing $24.75 on each auction before fees. Now you don't have to sell as many to make a decent amount of money. While there is no set rule for how much of a profit margin you should be aiming for, always keep in mind the following indisputable fact: The lower your selling price, the greater your margin must be to make a profit. If I am selling an item for less than $25.00, I want my margins to be much higher—closer to the 50–75 percent range.

SELLING USED VERSUS NEW ITEMS

Used, or vintage, products often have higher profit margins. Remember the topic of used books? You can often buy a book at a garage sale for $1 and sell it for $5 or $10 or more. But the drawback to selling any used or individual product is that you have to photograph and write a description on every item you sell. Whereas if you are selling a new product—say, you buy a case of identical birdhouses—you can simply create one listing and just keep relaunching it. Your profit margin will be lower, but so will your workload. Since time really is money, this is something every seller should consider.

INVENTORY

Do you have a reliable, continuing source of supply for your product? If you are selling closeout-type products or buying your products from a range of vendors, your inventory may become depleted and you might not be able to restock. Unless you are selling a broad category of closeout products, such as apparel, where there is always a large supply, you may want to pick a product you can source from a manufacturer or distributor on a regular basis.

UPSELLING

Does your product lend itself to upselling? An *upsell* (some people call it a *cross-sell*) refers to attaching a second product or a multiple quantity to the first sale. Let's look at our bird feeders, for example. When someone buys a bird feeder, he also needs birdseed. I could send the winning buyer an e-mail offering free shipping if he bought a package of birdseed, which I could ship with his order. If he agrees, I have only paid one set of fees to eBay, but I have made two sales.

Upselling is one of the keys to making huge profits on eBay. Whatever product you decide to sell, make sure there are compatible products that you can upsell the buyer at the time of sale. We will explain how to do this in detail in chapter 25.

EASE OF SHIPPING

Does this product present any shipping challenges? Shipping costs can be a big turnoff to your buyers. Large or unusually shaped products may require substantial shipping costs. I once had a great source of Australian didgeridoos. They weren't that expensive to ship, but a specialized box ended up costing me $11 each. The price I listed on eBay was attractive—until I tried to pass the extra $11 on to the customers.

BIZ BUILDER

Whenever I have a large item to sell that may be difficult to ship, I usually list it on Craig's List (www.craigslist.com), a free, local classified advertising service, partly owned by eBay. My wife recently decided to sell an old electric potter's wheel that weighed about 100 pounds (45kg). We put it on Craig's List and the next day there was a woman in my driveway with $400 who took it off our hands.

LONG-TERM VIABILITY

Does your product have legs? The phrase *having legs* refers to staying power. Is this a fad product, or does it have either a lasting or an evolving market? Millions of people bought Beanie Babies at the height of the craze and are still stuck with them today. I know one seller who bought the contents of a video rental store that was going out of business. He now has thousands of videotapes at a time when the rest of the world has moved on to DVDs and Blu-Ray.

SIMILARITY TO YOUR OTHER PRODUCTS

Is this a niche product that complements your other products? Does this item fit in to your current product niche, or will this represent a new direction for your business? If it's a new category, are there other products you can find to complement it?

If you ask yourself these questions before deciding which products to sell, you will avoid errors that many new sellers make. There is still no foolproof way to select a product. You may find a hot product, only to have a competitor come along and undercut you. This is why you should always be looking for new products and product categories. Both eBay and the Internet are highly competitive and fluid. If you are going to run even a small successful business, you must be on the lookout for new products and opportunities all the time.

POWER MOVES

For each item on your narrowed-down wish list of products, ask yourself the following questions:

- ❑ Is there a sufficient market for this product?
- ❑ How much competition is there for this product?
- ❑ What is the projected profit margin for this product?
- ❑ Is there a continuing, reliable source of supply?
- ❑ Does the product lend itself to upselling?
- ❑ Can this product be packaged and shipped easily?
- ❑ Does the product have a long-term market?

Based on the answers to these questions, eliminate any products from your list that do not appear viable at this time. You should now have a final list of products you would like to sell on eBay. In the next chapter, we will explore ways to source this merchandise quickly and economically.

CHAPTER 6

✦ PRODUCT ACQUISITION ✦

"WHERE CAN I FIND PRODUCTS at wholesale prices to sell on eBay?" is one of the most frequently asked questions by new eBay sellers. Learning how and where to acquire wholesale products can be intimidating. Yet it doesn't need to be. Successfully working with wholesalers is mostly a matter of learning their jargon and how the market works, as well as finding wholesale companies that will agree to work with small businesses.

In this chapter, we are going to learn just what *wholesale* means; in addition, we'll discuss the different types of wholesale suppliers, how to locate wholesale sources that will work with you, and how to deal with these suppliers once you are ready to buy. We will also introduce you to the specialized terminology of the wholesale world and some of the more common paperwork and forms used by wholesale suppliers.

DEFINITION OF *WHOLESALE*

First of all, you need to understand exactly what *wholesale* means. The term *wholesale* is a very fluid concept that loosely refers to the discounted amount at which you buy an item to resell at a (hopefully) higher price. Unfortunately, there is no such thing as a standard wholesale price or percentage. If I buy a pair of antique silver candlesticks at a local auction for $190 and sell them on eBay for $230, then $190 was my wholesale price. That is not a very large margin, but I did buy these candlesticks for less than I sold them, so my purchase price could be considered a wholesale price.

To better understand wholesale pricing, it helps to understand the different types of pricing used by resellers.

✳ **RETAIL PRICE:** Retail stores have very high expenses that include employees, rent, utilities, and inventory carrying costs. Most retail stores need to have a 100 percent markup on merchandise to make a profit over time. Therefore, retailers consider a wholesale price to be 50 percent (or more) of the suggested retail price.

✳ **QUICK SALE PRICE:** The quick sale price is the price bargain hunters are looking for. You find these prices in wholesale clubs like Costco and Sam's Club, at outlet malls, and on the sale tables in retail stores. Because people go to eBay to find a bargain, the quick sale price is often comparable to the eBay price.

✳ **DISTRESS PRICE:** Manufacturers, distributors, and retail store owners cannot afford to sit on nonperforming inventory: Such items tie up their cash and monopolize shelf space needed for newer products that will sell for higher prices. Once merchandise reaches this point, it is often sold to closeout or surplus dealers and ends up in dollar stores, at flea markets, and on eBay. Distress prices can be as low as ten cents on the retail dollar or half (or better) off the original wholesale price.

Retail stores typically buy from distributors, although some buy direct from manufacturers. When a retail store owner buys merchandise, he is looking to *keystone* the pricing, or set his retail price at twice what he pays for the item. So if you are negotiating with a wholesale distributor, she might say something like this: "Here are the retail prices. We give you the keystone discount on your first one hundred items and an additional 10 percent if you pay cash." If the retail price was $10.00, your price would be $5.00 each in quantities up to one hundred, and an additional 10 percent off the wholesale price ($5.00, minus 10 percent [$0.50], for a final per-piece cost to you of $4.50) if you paid cash, as opposed to getting thirty-day credit terms.

TYPES OF WHOLESALERS

There are several types of wholesalers, and we will explain shortly how to find these sources of merchandise. But first you need to understand who you are dealing with.

Importers

Importers may be large or small. A large importer generally sells in very large quantities, such as container loads or quantities of five thousand to ten thousand at a time. There are, however, many small importers who buy large quantities and break them down into smaller lots. These importers may sell by the case, by the dozen, or may require a minimum dollar order, such as $500.

Look in your local Yellow Pages under *Importers*. If you live in a small town or in the middle of the country, get a Yellow Pages directory from any large port city—such as New York, Philadelphia, Baltimore, San Francisco, Seattle, or Los Angeles—where you'll find a higher concentration of importers. You can use www.yellowpages.com or www.smartpages.com to locate importers as well.

Manufacturers

Manufacturers come in all sizes. The largest manufacturers, such as Sony, General Electric, Liz Claiborne, Revlon, and Cuisinart, will rarely deal directly with a reseller or retail outlet unless you are the size of Wal-Mart or Sears. Instead, these manufacturers rely on distributors.

There are, however, thousands of small- and medium-size manufacturers in the United States and overseas that will work directly with resellers. Some of them will even drop-ship to your customers. (We'll discuss drop-shipping in the next chapter.)

BIZ BUILDER

Whenever you buy from a manufacturer, you are as close to the source as you can get. This is always where the best pricing is.

Smaller manufacturers will often work directly with you, while others work through manufacturer's representatives, or manufacturer's reps. A manufacturer's rep is usually a one- or two-person business that represents both domestic and foreign manufacturers on a commission basis. If you are talking to a large manufacturer or a foreign exporter, ask if the company has a manufacturer's rep. This person will often sell goods to you at a lower price and in smaller quantities than a distributor will. Later in this chapter we will show you how to locate and contact both manufacturers and manufacturer's reps.

Distributors

There are two types of distributors—*master distributors* and *general wholesale distributors*. A master distributor is usually a sizable company that only distributes for one or two large manufacturers, or only distributes one product line, such as computers, apparel, furniture, or the like. Typically, a master distributor will not carry competing brands of the same product. For example, a master computer distributor might carry one brand of computers, printers, and monitors.

A general wholesale distributor buys products from various American and foreign manufacturers, and resells them to distributors. Some specialize in certain products, while others can, and often do, sell virtually anything.

Closeout or Surplus Dealers

Closeout dealers go by several names—closeout, liquidation, surplus, and overstock dealers—but they all do roughly the same thing. These dealers either buy distressed goods outright and resell them, or they act as consignment dealers for companies seeking to sell distressed merchandise. Remember that distressed merchandise consists of goods and products that a manufacturer, distributor, or retailer needs to get rid of quickly. Because of the subsequent low cost to resellers, surplus or distressed merchandise represents a large portion of new items sold on eBay. Buying from closeout dealers is an excellent way to find goods to sell on eBay that will allow you to make a healthy margin.

It is important, however, to understand some of the terms that closeout dealers use. *Surplus, overstock,* and *shelf pulls* refer to new merchandise that did not sell. These items will typically still carry the original store price tags. Be very careful that you are not buying *returns*. You want to avoid purchasing an item a customer returned because it was broken, didn't fit, or was the wrong color—or perhaps was an expensive dress someone bought to wear to a party one night and then returned to the store the next day. I generally do not buy returns unless I can physically inspect them, which is rare.

The other category of closeout merchandise to avoid is called *seconds*. These are goods that have some type of manufacturing defect. These can be real bargains if you know what you are getting. However, I recommend holding off on purchasing seconds until you have more buying experience, and can acquire and resell this merchandise effectively.

LOCATING WHOLESALE SOURCES

There are two basic ways to find the wholesale sources we've discussed so far:

* **THE INTERNET:** As each year goes by, more and more companies are listed on the Web.

* **OFFLINE:** It is also very easy to find sources close to you using traditional methods, like the Yellow Pages and business directories, and by visiting local wholesale merchandise marts or trade shows in cities near you.

Finding Wholesale Sources on the Web

There are several well-known wholesale search engines where you can perform a search online by product or manufacturer:

* **THE THOMAS REGISTER** (www.thomasnet; see Figure 6.1) lists virtually every manufacturer in the United States. If you know who makes a certain product, you can find the manufacturer—and often, the distributor's e-mail address, phone number, and other contact information—by typing the manufacturer's name into the search box. You can also search by product, which will bring up a list of manufacturers. Just click on a manufacturer's name, and the Register will direct you to the company's Web site, if there is one, or display the company's contact information if there isn't.

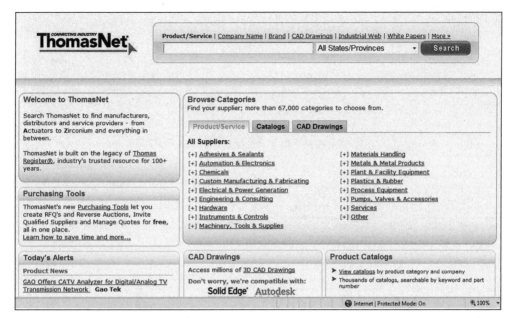

Figure 6.1   Thomas Register Web Site

✳ **GO WHOLESALE** (www.gowholesale.com; Figure 6.2) is one of the largest Web sites designed to help you locate dealers and distributors that sell to small resellers directly. You can search by individual products, such as shirts, cameras, or computers, or by brand name, such as Tommy Hilfiger, Nikon, or Dell. One minor shortcoming of Go Wholesale is that a search will often bring up retailers who sell at discounted prices and call themselves wholesale sellers. However, it is pretty easy to screen these retailers out by carefully reading the descriptions accompanying your Search Results.

✳ **GET THAT WHOLESALE** (http://www.getthatwholesale.com) is another great search engine where you can locate wholesale sources. In addition to offering a search feature, Get That Wholesale can connect you to dozens of major wholesalers who advertise on the site. Many of these advertisers are seeking eBay sellers to work with.

BIZ BUILDER

On the homepage of my Web site (www.skipmcgrath.com) is a link labeled *Web Wholesale Search*. This link will take you to a free wholesale search engine optimized for eBay resellers.

Figure 6.2 Go Wholesale Web Site

✳ **WHOLESALE CENTRAL** (www.wholesalecentral.com; Figure 6.3) lists several hundred wholesale vendors who pay to be hosted on this site. Its companion site, **CLOSEOUT CENTRAL** (www.closeoutcentral.com; Figure 6.4), hosts dozens of closeout and surplus dealers.

Figure 6.3 Wholesale Central Web Site

Figure 6.4   Closeout Central Web Site

✳ **ALIBABA** (www.alibaba.com; Figure 6.5) is a pay-per-click site where manufacturers from China, Taiwan, Korea, and other Asian countries list their products. (The manufacturers pay for each click or pay a monthly fee to be listed. It does not cost you anything to search this site.)

Figure 6.5   Alibaba Web Site

Alibaba is a very powerful search engine, where you can find thousands of products. Many of the companies sell only in large volume, but if you are patient and keep searching, you can find plenty of sources that will sell in smaller quantities, suitable for the average eBay seller. One word of caution:

Anyone can list products for sale on Alibaba, and there are many scam artists out there. If you click the *Buy Now* button at the top of the Alibaba homepage, you will then see a link to *Search Gold Suppliers by Product or Category*. Alibaba has certified these suppliers and confirmed their identities. I recommend confining your search to these "Gold" suppliers.

✳ **GLOBAL SOURCES** (www.globalsources.com; Figure 6.6) is a large, international pay-per-click Web site, similar to Alibaba. In fact, you will find many of the same companies listed on both sites. You can link to Global Sources directly from eBay. In 2005, eBay announced a strategic partnership with Global Sources, whereby the exporter works with several manufacturers to sell to eBay sellers in smaller quantities. These items will be placed for bid in lots in the eBay Wholesale, Large Lots category (see the sidebar titled *Wholesale on eBay* later in this chapter for more on how this works).

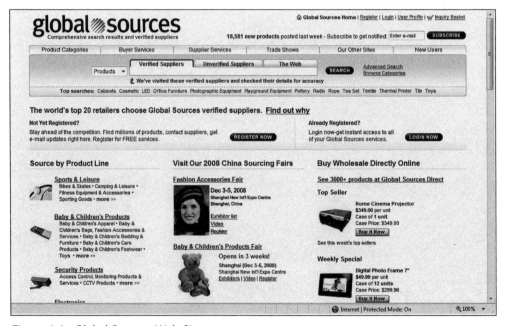

Figure 6.6 Global Sources Web Site

✳ **BUYLINK** (www.buylink.com) is an online merchandise mart for gifts, collectibles, and household accessories. Once at the site, you have to fill out a form to register before you can view any pricing. It typically takes about two business days for BuyLink to e-mail you with a password and user ID. Once you are registered on the site, you can see prices and specifications, and purchase online from more than five hundred wholesale sources.

Merchandise Marts

Almost every large city in America has a merchandise mart. A merchandise mart is a building where various wholesalers—including small manufacturers, manufacturer's reps, and distributors—rent showroom space. (If you live in a small town or a rural area, you will likely have to go to the nearest large city to locate one, although you can reach some by e-mail, telephone, and fax.)

These venues go by many names; some specialize in one kind of item, while others feature all sorts of general merchandise:

* A *merchandise mart* typically showcases a wide variety of products, but most tend toward the low end in price.

* A *gift mart* usually specializes in gifts, collectibles, kitchen and gourmet food items, and small decorator and household pieces.

* A *design center* sells furniture, rugs, lamps, and decorator items.

* Some cities, such as New York, Chicago, and Los Angeles, have *fashion centers* and *jewelry centers* that specialize in items of personal adornment.

Whatever the name and the type of goods they carry, all these markets have one thing in common: They are not open to the general public. When you walk up to the information booth at a merchandise mart or design center, you will often see a sign that reads, "Admission to the trade only." The word *trade* refers to retail stores, eBay and Web site sellers, and interior decorators. Depending on the venue, it can be somewhat difficult to gain admission. A few even insist that you own a retail store, although this is changing, as more and more companies conduct business exclusively on the Web.

You can locate a merchandise mart by doing a Google search for the term you are looking for: *merchandise mart, jewelry mart, design center,* and so on. This will usually bring up a list of markets by city. Just look for the one nearest you. You can often find local results by adding the name of the closest city to the end of the search, for example: *jewelry mart Chicago.*

When you approach the mart to go in, there will usually be a counter where officials are checking to see if you have a badge, which was issued in advance, or the qualifications to obtain one on site. To gain admission to most of these marts, you'll need to show proof of your business status, including a sales tax number, a registered business name, a commercial checking account, business cards, or company letterhead. If you followed our advice in chapter 1, you should have all of these. Once the person at the front desk examines these, he will issue you a badge that you must wear while you are inside.

Once you gain entry, a whole new world of wholesale products opens up to you. Merchandise marts, gift marts, and wholesale trade shows (which we discuss next) are the best places to find new merchandise to sell. You will find dozens, even hundreds, of products that you will not come across on a Web search. Each dealer has a showroom that is much like a retail store, displaying all her products. Unlike a retail store, however, you can't walk out with the items. When you enter each showroom, ask for a catalog and a price sheet. As you walk around the room, you can refer to the prices for any items you see.

Most dealers at merchandise marts have minimum-order requirements. Sometimes it will be a case or a dozen units; sometimes it will be a certain dollar amount, such as $250 or $500. Unless the dealers are selling expensive merchandise, like jewelry, the minimums will rarely be more than $500.

When you decide what you want to buy, return to the front desk and fill out an order form. You can pay by check or sometimes by credit card. Once you place a few orders with the same dealer, he will usually ship on credit.

Wholesale Trade Shows

Trade shows are just like merchandise marts, only larger. Trade shows move around the country, and there are different shows at various times of the year. Here in Seattle, where I live, the Seattle Gift Show is held every January and August. (If you go to the Web site for this book, www.skipmcgrath.com/3_weeks, I have posted links where you can find trade shows nearest your community.) Certain cities, such as Las Vegas, Los Angeles, Chicago, Dallas, Atlanta, and New York City, host dozens of specialized trade shows virtually year-round.

Getting into a trade show is much like gaining admission to a merchandise mart. The first time you register, the managers will want to see your business license or sales tax certificate, your business card, commercial checkbook, and so on. In many cities, once you register at the local merchandise mart, your name will be given to trade show companies coming into town, and you will automatically receive tickets in the mail.

You shop at a trade show the same way you do at a merchandise mart. Browse the merchandise and place an order when you see something you like. The goods will usually be delivered within a week or so, unless you are seeing samples of products that are not yet available. For example, shows that run from July to October will often show-case merchandise the vendor plans to release in time for Christmas. While you might place an order in August, the goods might not be shipped until early November. When this happens you will be asked for a small deposit with your order and you must pay the balance before it is shipped.

Most trade shows have a computer kiosk in the lobby as a convenience for the attendees. If not, there may be a "wi-fi hot spot" in the
convention center or hotel where you can boot up your laptop and
gain Internet access. If I see a product that interests me, I go out to
the kiosk and do a search on eBay to see what it's selling for before
deciding to buy. You can also do this right on the show floor with
many of the modern PDAs, an Apple iPhone, or a Web-connected
BlackBerry device.

Trade shows are an excellent way to see the newest merchandise on the market.
When the Texas Hold'em poker fad was just getting started, I found a dealer selling
complete Texas Hold'em poker kits, consisting of chips, cards, instructions, and the
table covers you see in the casinos. I purchased a couple of cases and sold them
quickly on eBay before everyone else jumped on the fad. They were so hot I was actually getting 50 percent over retail. Within a few months, everybody had them and the
prices had fallen to 20 percent below retail. You could still make money at that price,
but not nearly as much as when they were new.

Other Ways to Find Wholesalers

The final way to find local wholesale sources is through your local phone book or the
Yellow Pages. If you look up a product in your local Yellow Pages, the product will
usually be broken down by category. For example, if you looked up *cameras*, you would
see listings for *Cameras, Accessories; Cameras, Repair; Cameras, Retail;* and so on.
Typically, at the end of each product listing, you will see an entry for *Cameras,
Wholesale* or *Cameras, Wholesale Distributor*. This is true for almost any product you
can find in the Yellow Pages. If you live in a large city, there is often a special directory
for the business community, called the Commercial Directory or sometimes the B2B
Yellow Pages.

The Yellow Pages also has an online site for finding local wholesale companies
(see Figure 6.7).

Figure 6.8 shows Search Results for the term *wholesale* in the Pittsburgh area.
The Top Category Matches are simply the categories with the most results. By scrolling
down to *Related Categories,* you will see all the categories, including virtually every type
of wholesale manufacturer and distributor for the entire Pittsburgh region. When you click
on one of the category links, you'll get a list of companies. Click on an individual
company's name to find its contact information and a list of the goods the company sells.

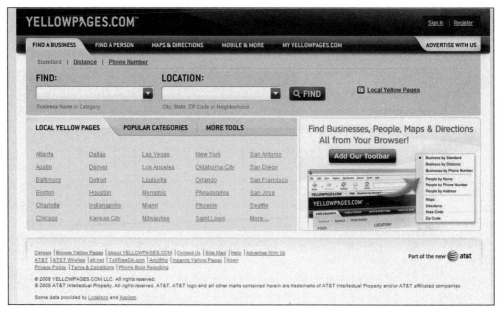

Figure 6.7   YellowPages.com Main Search Page

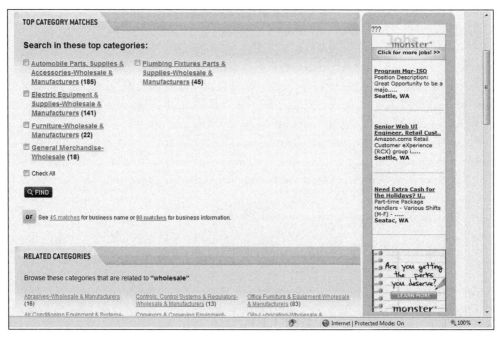

Figure 6.8   YellowPages.com Results for Wholesale Suppliers in Pittsburgh

Wholesale on eBay

The final place to find products to sell on eBay is on eBay itself. Almost every category on eBay has a subcategory called Wholesale, Large Lots. Here you'll find companies (usually overstock companies) selling wholesale lots to the highest bidder. Make sure the seller has a good feedback rating, that the company is located in the United States (goods from overseas are often knockoffs, and it can be difficult to get your money back from an overseas vendor), and that you get a thorough and accurate description of the products being sold.

I once bought a pallet load of 7 For All Mankind jeans and made a ton of money reselling them individually on eBay. But then a few weeks later I bought a shipment of Burberry golf caps that turned out to be fake. I did eventually get my money back, but it was a lot of trouble and I was still out the return shipping.

A final piece of advice: Don't be an impulse buyer. Whether you are shopping on eBay, on a wholesale Web site, or strolling through a merchandise mart or trade show, take the time to do some basic research to make sure there is a market for the product you are considering before placing a bid or an order.

POWER MOVES

❑ Once you select a product or product category that interests you, visit the various search engines mentioned in this chapter and run product searches to locate suppliers.

❑ Make a list of potential suppliers and begin contacting them to see if they work with small accounts. If so, ask about pricing and minimum-order requirements.

❑ If you live in a city with a merchandise mart or design center, visit it and register for admission.

❑ Call the convention bureau in your city (or the nearest large city) and find out if and when any wholesale trade shows are coming to town. Register to attend them.

CHAPTER 7

✦ WINNING WITH DROP-SHIPPING ✦

DROP-SHIPPING IS AN INTERESTING and potentially profitable business concept. In the drop-shipping business model, you locate a wholesale vendor who will agree to ship his products directly to your customer. In the models we've discussed so far, you purchase an item and then resell it on eBay. With drop-shipping, you first list the item on eBay, at a price that is higher than the drop-shipper's wholesale price. Once you make a sale and collect the payment and shipping fee, you then send a payment to the drop-shipper, who in turn ships the item directly to your customer.

The advantage of this business model is obvious. You do not have to risk any money buying products until the merchandise actually sells and you receive payment. Theoretically, if you found a vendor with hundreds of products to sell, you could list hundreds of auctions on eBay and, each time an auction closed with a winner, simply collect the money and send the payment and shipping instructions to the drop-shipper. At first blush it sounds easy—a sort of unstoppable money machine. It can work, and it does work for many people. But like many things in life, it is not as simple as it sounds.

EBAY DROP-SHIP SUPPLIERS

If you do a search on Google for the term *drop shipper*, or *dropshipper*, you will get several hundred results. There are dozens of companies that purport to have warehouses full of merchandise you can list on eBay—and then just sit back and collect the money, allowing them to drop-ship for you. When you visit their Web sites, you will usually see a sales pitch to sign up for a membership, although some of the sites offer free memberships if you register with them. These companies are often referred to as general drop-shippers. The problems arise when you start examining the merchandise and the pricing.

Disadvantages of General Drop-Ship Suppliers

True wholesale companies can only sell at low wholesale prices when they sell in bulk. Because their margins are much lower than a retailer's, they have to make a larger average total sale to make a profit. Most drop-shipping companies buy from wholesalers and then mark the price up somewhere between wholesale and typical retail. On top of this amount, they will usually charge a special drop-ship fee of anywhere from $2 to $5 per item, plus the shipping charge. When you compare their shipping charges to those of UPS, you will often see that they are making another few dollars on the shipping as well.

Once you determine the final price (including all the additional fees), search for the same product on eBay. You will often see the product selling for the same price or even less. This is because other eBay sellers are purchasing the same products from the importers, distributors, or direct from the manufacturers, and therefore can sell them at much lower prices than you can using a general drop-shipper.

There are other drawbacks when dealing with a general drop-shipper, even if you can find items to sell at a profit. The primary one is customer service. Unfortunately, you are at the mercy of the drop-shipping company. If the drop-shipper sends out the product late, ships the wrong product, or packs the product poorly and it arrives damaged, you are stuck with an angry customer who may leave you negative feedback. So even if you find a drop-shipper with products that allow you to make a profit, you must still manage the relationship very carefully to ensure that the drop-shipper is giving your customers the same customer service that you would.

Working with Drop-Ship Suppliers

Does all this mean you cannot make money drop-shipping? No, you certainly can, and many eBay sellers do—including myself. I have tried several of the general online drop-shippers without success. The only success I have with drop-shipping is working directly with small manufacturers or wholesale drop-shippers who specialize in one type of product. Mostly I find these companies at wholesale trade shows. Admittedly, it takes a bit of work and it may be hit or miss to find them—but they are there, and when you find them this is a really profitable way to work. Currently over 50 percent of my sales on eBay are from three small manufacturers that I work directly with. Two of them work with me exclusively.

BIZ BUILDER

Use the eBay search engine and research tools and methods we discussed in chapter 4 to determine which drop-ship products will sell and what price points are realistic.

The fastest-selling and most popular products will be the hardest ones to profit from because everyone else is selling them, too. The key is to look for those small niche or specialty products that very few people are selling. Instead of trying to sell digital cameras, for example, look for accessories, such as camera cases, batteries, flash cards, tripods, and so on. You will be far more likely to make money if you work around the margins than if you try to compete directly by offering top-brand consumer products.

I don't want to imply that you cannot make a profit working with general drop-ship companies. It is just that I haven't tried them all, and traditionally this industry has been plagued by upstart companies that don't last very long, as well as by a number of scams.

In addition to general drop-shipping companies, there are also specialty companies that will often drop-ship. Again, the best way to find these is with a Google search—but you want to add the product name to the search term *drop shipping*. For example: *drop ship books, drop ship Christian, drop ship china, drop ship art supplies*, and so on. This will usually bring up a list of companies that specialize in those products. Remember you are looking for manufacturers and specialty drop-shippers, not the companies that come up in the search results that sell thousands of different products.

DROP-SHIP MANUFACTURERS

You can also find thousands of small- and medium-size manufacturers that will agree to drop-ship goods for you. There are two ways to locate them: You can go through the Thomas Register (www.thomasnet.com) and contact the companies to determine if they will drop-ship, or you can pay someone to do this for you.

Worldwide Brands (www.worldwidebrands.com; Figure 7.1), an eBay-certified solutions provider, offers an online Product Sourcing Membership that costs $299.00 for life and locates manufacturers that will drop-ship. The listings in its online directory are updated weekly by a staff that researches the manufacturers and actually calls them on the phone to confirm if they will drop-ship and if they will work with eBay sellers.

Worldwide Brands currently offers the following information and services for the one-time fee:

* 8,000+ prescreened premium drop-shippers and wholesale suppliers

* Access to 8 million+ products to sell online

* Instant market and pricing research

* Video education for beginners and advanced

* Professional business advice

* Dedicated research team for your product requests

* Private access to the e-commerce forum community. They currently offer a $20 discount for readers of this book if you use the link www.worldwidebrands.com/skipmcgrath.

Figure 7.1   Worldwide Brands Web Site

I have been a member of Worldwide Brands for the past four years and can attest to the quality of the information. In just one hour of working with the Worldwide Brands directory, I was able to locate three manufacturers that would agree to drop-ship for me. I tried out all three of them. One manufacturer's product just wouldn't sell on eBay; another one sold sporadically (but at a nice profit margin); and the third product, a handmade steel barbecue grill, has been a steady producer of profits. We make about $90 on each one we sell and have sold as many as thirty in a single month. I have since found a line of digital photography lighting systems and accessories that are selling quite well. In this case, the small manufacturer readily agreed to drop-ship and he also gave me a semi-exclusive deal, so I would not face too much competition.

I am not going to kid you: Setting up these relationships can take a lot of research, testing, and hard work. But if you can make it work, drop-shipping really can be a money machine. Keep in mind, however, that in the long run you're much more likely to be successful with drop-shipping if you specialize in one category of product.

POWER MOVES

❏ If you are interested in drop-shipping, sign up with Wholesale Marketer for a three-week free trial offered to readers of this book at www.skipmcgrath.com/3_weeks. Find products that interest you and then see what they are selling for on eBay, using the Completed Listings search option.

❏ Use the Thomas Register to find manufacturers of products that interest you. Contact the manufacturers and ask if they will drop-ship for you.

❏ If you can afford the investment, give Worldwide Brands a try. Use their directory and research tools to find products that interest you and that you can test on eBay.

❏ As you explore Wholesale Marketer and other potential drop-shippers, maintain a list of products they offer that you believe you can sell for a profit. Once you are ready to begin selling, come back to this list and try listing a few of these items.

❏ Once you begin working with drop-shippers, evaluate each one in terms of competitive pricing, reliability of delivery, customer satisfaction, and ease of dealing with returns and other customer service issues.

CHAPTER 8

✦ TYPES OF AUCTIONS ✦

WHEN EBAY FIRST STARTED, there was only one type of auction. All auctions ran for a specified period and ended at a specified time. The highest bidder at the last possible moment was the winner.

Now eBay offers several auction formats, as well as Buy It Now and Fixed Price listings. Before you begin to sell, it is important for you to understand all the different formats available to you—and to familiarize yourself with the unique advantages and disadvantages of each one. Most sellers use several formats, depending on what they are selling. For example, if you are selling a high-priced antique or collectible, you may want to use a Reserve Price Auction (RPA). Alternatively, if you purchased a wholesale lot of inexpensive toys just before Christmas, there are advantages to offering your items in a Fixed Price format. In this chapter, we'll explore each of the selling formats in detail.

STANDARD AUCTIONS

A typical auction-style listing works this way:

- ✳ The seller offers one or more items and sets a starting price.
- ✳ Buyers visit the listing and bid on the item during the online auction's duration.
- ✳ When the auction-style listing ends, the high bidder buys the item from the seller for the high bid.

eBay uses a system of proxy bidding. Let's say a seller sets a starting price for an item at $1.00 and it's now been bid up to $9.00. eBay sets the minimum incremental bid at fifty cents ($0.50) for items priced between $5.00 and $25.00. Now assume that you are a bidder and you decide you would be willing to pay as much as $14.50 for the item being offered. You enter a bid of $14.50 and hit the button that says *Place Bid*. eBay now adds $0.50 to the current bid of $9.00, and displays the item's price as $9.50. No one else knows the top value of your bid—others can only see the current bid. Now another bidder comes along and bids $10.00. The bid price rises to $10.50 (her bid plus a $0.50 incremental bid from you), and she gets an immediate message that she has been outbid. If no one else bids, you will win the item for $10.50. As long as no one bids more than your $14.50 maximum, you are still in the running.

If someone bids more than your maximum, you will receive an automated e-mail from eBay that you have been outbid. You can let it go, or you can go back in and place a higher bid if you still want the item at a higher price.

RESERVE PRICE AUCTIONS

Some auctions have a reserve price—a hidden minimum price—for the item. This is done to allow a seller to start an item at a low price that is sure to attract attention, yet protect him from selling it at too low a price. A few points to keep in mind when it comes to Reserve Price Auctions:

* Buyers are not shown the reserve price, only that the reserve has not been met.

* The seller is not obligated to sell the item if the reserve price is not met.

* The winning bidder must meet or exceed the reserve price *and* have the highest bid.

When you're bidding in a Reserve Price Auction, bid as usual, entering the maximum amount you're willing to pay for the item. Watch the label beneath the current price to see whether the reserve price has been met. Until you see that the reserve price has been met, there have been no successful bids in the auction. Once the reserve has been met, the item will sell to the highest bidder when the auction closes. The Reserve Not Met label disappears once the reserve is met and future bidders will have no knowledge that it was ever a Reserve Price Auction.

If your maximum bid is the first to meet or exceed the reserve price, the bid displayed will automatically be raised to the reserve price.

BUY IT NOW AND FIXED PRICE LISTINGS

Buy It Now (BIN) is an option eBay created for people who don't want to wait for an auction to end to purchase an item. The BIN option allows you as the seller to set a price at which you are willing to end the auction immediately and sell the item to the buyer. One thing you need to know about the BIN option is that it usually disappears once an auction bid is placed. When you choose the Buy It Now option on a traditional auction listing (available for single quantity only), your item has two ways to sell:

* If a buyer is willing to meet your Buy It Now price before the first bid comes in, your item sells instantly and your auction ends.

* Or, if a bid comes in first, the Buy It Now option disappears. Then your auction proceeds normally. (In Reserve Price Auctions, Buy It Now disappears

after the first bid that meets the reserve; in some categories the Buy It Now price remains after the first bid.)

The purpose of Buy It Now (BIN) is to make immediate sales. You set your BIN price at the upper end of what you would like the item to sell for. For example, say you are selling a pair of cowboy boots (yes, these are big sellers on eBay) in a standard auction with a starting bid of $49 and you hope to get at least $75 for them. You could set your BIN price at $79 (or even higher). Now if someone comes along and really wants those boots and doesn't want to take a chance on getting outbid, she simply clicks the BIN button in your auction. The auction ends and she is taken to a page where eBay calculates the shipping and insurance and your buyer pays instantly with PayPal.

Another variation on Buy It Now is the Fixed Price listing. You list an auction with a starting price and a BIN price that are identical. In this case you are simply putting an item up for sale at a fixed price. If someone bids the starting price, eBay will realize that it is identical to the BIN price and will end the auction and declare that buyer the winner.

There is one more option that can be used in conjunction with Buy It Now. This is called Best Offer. The buyer can submit an offer lower than your BIN price for your consideration. You can accept it, reject it, or send a counteroffer. Most savvy buyers who see the Best Offer option will use it. They know that you're willing to sell the item for less than the BIN price or you wouldn't have added the option. You can have your settings autoreject any offers below a certain threshold so you're not wasting time on lowball offers. If you use Best Offer, you should decide what your minimum "accept" price will be and then adjust your BIN price accordingly. A buyer who sees a BIN price of $50 and is able to "talk you down" to $43 using Best Offer thinks he got a much better deal than if you'd just set the BIN at $43. This can help you get excellent feedback and repeat buyers.

SELLING MULTIPLE ITEMS

Depending on the type of merchandise you sell, you may want to use one of the formats allowing you to sell multiple, identical items. If you sell art, antiques, collectibles, or used books, this format generally won't work for you, because each item is different. However, if you bought a pallet of toys or games from a closeout dealer, you might find yourself with several or even dozens of identical items to sell.

There are two ways to sell multiple items on eBay:

* Fixed Price listing
* Lot listing

Using these methods can save you time and simplify the auction process. Let's explore how each one works.

Fixed Price Listings

In a Fixed Price listing you list multiple, identical items in one listing with a fixed price for each item. Buyers can choose the quantity they want and pay the set price.

For example: Suppose you have fifty flashlights that you'd like to sell for $9.99 each. You would list them with a *quantity* of fifty and a *price* of $9.99. Buyers could purchase any available quantity of your item at any time without waiting for an auction to end. Fixed Price listings run for thirty days and you can set them to renew automatically. The listing fee for Fixed Price listings is the same whether you list one item or one hundred.

With Fixed Price listings, eBay only permits multi-item listings in which the price times the quantity is less than $100,000. In order to sell with this format, you must:

* Be ID verified

Or

* Have a feedback score of 30 or above and be registered on eBay for at least fourteen days

Or

* Have a feedback score of 15 or higher if you have a PayPal account, and accept PayPal as a payment method on the listing.

Fixed Price listings have a different fee structure and they run for thirty days or are Good 'Til Canceled (GTC). See the eBay fee schedule for Fixed Price listing fees.

Lot Listings

In a Lot listing you sell similar items together in one listing to one buyer (such as a record collection, a lot of same-size clothing, or the like).

For example, suppose you have fifty baseball cards that you'd like to sell together to one buyer for an average price of $1.99 each. To list the cards as a lot, you would first click the *Lot* tab in the Quantity section, and enter *1* in the *Number of Lots* box and *50* in the *Number of Items Per Lot* box. You would set the price at $99.50. The winning bidder will win all fifty cards.

PRIVATE AUCTIONS

Sellers who don't want the items they've sold showing up on their feedback profile use private listings. Usually the item title and the selling price are displayed beneath a buyer's feedback comment, but in a private listing, only the term *private* appears. This tends to be used for items of an adult or sexual nature, or simply when the seller doesn't want potential bidders seeing what previous buyers paid for the same item, as it may deter them from bidding higher.

EBAY STORES

The final type of listing is the eBay store. An eBay store is essentially a Fixed Price listing, where you can list items for thirty days or autorenew your listings every thirty days with the Good 'Til Canceled option. The eBay store listing fees are lower than auction and Fixed Price listings. We cover eBay stores in detail in chapter 26.

I suggest that you stick with the regular auction format for your first few dozen auctions. Then, after you have read chapter 10 on listing and pricing strategies, I would start adding Buy It Now to your auctions and even putting up some Fixed Price Auctions.

·············· BEST PRACTICES ··············

ADULTS ONLY

eBay does not list adult items in the regular section of eBay and they will not come up in a search unless you log in to the category titled Adults Only (located under the main category Everything Else). When you log in to this category, an agreement will come up on the screen asking you to confirm that you are over eighteen, will abide by the rules of the community, and will not hold eBay responsible for material you purchase in this category. You must have a credit card on file to prove that you are over eighteen to access this category. Also note that you cannot use PayPal or ProPay to pay for any items in the Adults Only category. Personal checks and money orders are the only accepted payment methods for this category.

POWER MOVES

❑ Spend some time on eBay looking at the various types of auctions. Analyze which types of auctions seem to be most popular/successful for different products.

❑ Think about the products you plan to sell, and which type of listing is right for each one. In your notebook, note which formats your competitors used, and which appear to have been successful.

❑ If you plan on selling multiple, identical items, study various multiple-item listings until you become comfortable with Fixed Price listings and Lot listings. Make a list of what worked and what failed for other sellers.

CHAPTER 9

✦ LAUNCHING YOUR FIRST AUCTIONS ✦

YOU'VE GONE THROUGH THE PROCESS of bidding and buying on eBay, you've figured out how feedback works, you've seen how to pay and get paid, and how different sellers package and ship their goods. Now it's time to try selling. You are going to learn a lot more about selling techniques in the following chapters, but first let's try launching a few auctions to get your feet wet. Throughout this chapter, I point out that we are going to cover some tasks, such as writing headlines (auction titles), in greater detail later on. You may wonder, "Why don't we do that first?" Here's why: I have found that actually going through the selling process a few times, even if you don't fully understand all the techniques, makes these methods easier to understand when you study them in detail. These first few auctions are like learning to ride a bike with the training wheels on. When you take the training wheels off, you will be glad you had the experience.

FINDING SOMETHING TO SELL

If you've been following my system, you have researched products to sell and are well on your way to sourcing and/or ordering those items. However, for the purpose of this exercise, walk around your house, look in your garage and attic, and find a few items to sell that you don't need anymore. If you cannot find anything to sell around your house, then stop by a few garage sales this weekend.

Look for old golf clubs, nonfiction books in good condition, and small working appliances, such as espresso machines, coffeemakers, bread makers, pasta machines, and so on. Try to find machines that are still in the box and have the instructions with them. These sorts of products are reliable sellers on eBay.

If you have small children, you probably have some clothes that no longer fit them. Assemble the clothes into a set of the same size and gender—for example, two pairs of trousers, a jacket, and two shirts in Boys' size 3; or two dresses, two

Figure 9.1   eBay Main Navigation Links

pairs of trousers, and two sweaters in Girls' size 4. Sets of used children's clothing sell extremely well on eBay, and you can realize far greater profit on eBay than you would at a garage sale. Make sure the clothing is clean and in good condition. Don't sell clothing with rips, tears, or excessive wear. In general, name-brand items, from manufacturers such as the Children's Place, Gymboree, the Gap, or Old Navy, outsell house-brand clothing.

Another good category is used sporting, hunting, camping, and fishing equipment. For now, avoid large items like skis or hockey sticks that could be difficult to ship.

PREPARING YOUR ITEMS FOR SALE

The next step is to take some digital photos of your items, and upload them to your computer's hard drive. Make sure you take sharp, properly exposed photos, and that you shoot the objects without a lot of background clutter. (See chapter 15, on taking effective auction photos, if you need some help in this area.)

Whenever you are selling something used, be sure to inspect it carefully and clean it. People know they are buying a used item, but they don't want it to arrive covered in greasy fingerprints or caked with dust and grime.

Once you have your items assembled, you need to weigh them and precalculate the postage. Forget UPS for now; instead, visit www.usps.com and look for the U.S. Postal Service's postage calculator. Type in the weight and a zip code that is at least halfway across the country (four zones away). Whatever cost you come up with, add 20 percent to cover the cost of your handling, shipping, and packing materials. If the postage comes to $3.90, you would add $0.78 (3.90 × .20) for a total of $4.68. When you enter your shipping amount into eBay, you might want to round up to $4.70. (We will deal with Calculated Shipping and other shipping methods, such as UPS, later on.)

The reason we chose four zones is that there are eight postal zones in the United States. If you live in the middle of the country, you will seldom ship farther than four zones from your current location. If you live on either coast, you will sometimes ship close to your zone—so you will make a few cents—and you will often ship more than four zones away, thereby losing a few cents. Overall, it will average out. Fixed shipping (as opposed to Calculated Shipping) is much easier for both the buyer and seller to deal with, so let's stick with that for now.

LAUNCHING YOUR FIRST AUCTION

Go to any eBay page and click on *Sell* at the top of the page (see Figure 9.1). Now click on *Start Selling*.

Step 1: Selecting a Category

You will be asked to enter at least three keywords about your item to help select a category. In this example, I am going to sell a Starbucks coffee mug that I picked up at the Pike Place Market in Seattle. Seattle is the home of Starbucks and the Pike Place Market store is where Starbucks first started. These mugs are highly sought-after. I paid $9.95 for this particular mug, which has been discontinued and is no longer sold. So my keywords might be *starbucks pike place coffee mug*.

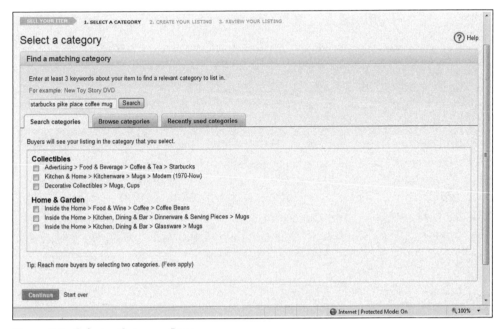

Figure 9.2   Select a Category Page

eBay uses the main category as a heading, and then shows you all the matching subcategories beneath it. In Figure 9.2, the main categories are Collectibles and Home & Garden. Select the category and subcategory that most closely fits the item you are selling. Once you select a category, a link will appear at the bottom of the page to See Sample Listings to make sure you made the right choice.

If you already know the category you want and it's not listed, you can use the *Browse Categories* tab to select each level of subcategory manually. Figure 9.3 shows how you would get to the same category we selected above using the *Browse Categories* tab.

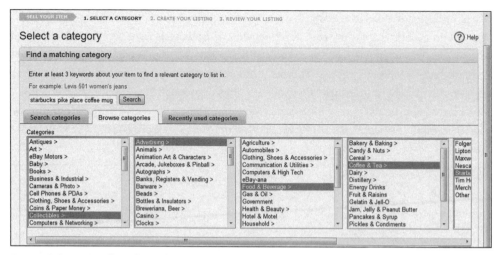

Figure 9.3   Manually Selected Category

You can select up to two categories. This List in Two Categories special feature costs a little extra. There are some situations where you will want to use this option, but let's ignore it for now. (We will cover this feature in detail in chapter 13.)

Step 2: Title, Pictures, and Description

After you hit *Continue*, you will be directed to the Create Your Listing page (Figure 9.4).

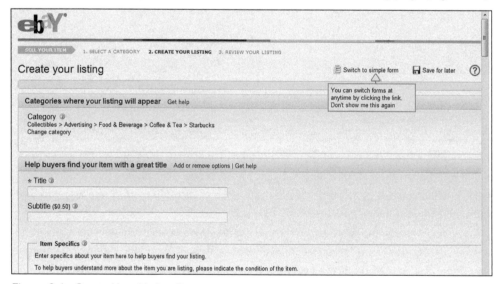

Figure 9.4   Create Your Listing Page

You have the option of switching to the Simple Form, but I strongly recommend that you stick with the full version. You lose a lot of options if you go to the simple form.

First, you must write a title for your listing. Writing effective eBay titles is a real art, and one that we are going to spend some time on in detail in chapter 14. But for now, let's just go with a straightforward description: STARBUCKS PIKE PLACE, FIRST STARBUCKS STORE MUG. Write a title that simply and accurately describes what you are selling. If the product has a brand name, be sure to include it. And keep in mind that you only get fifty-five characters, including spaces. Here are some examples:

- LOT OF SIZE 6 GIRLS TOMMY HILFIGER CLOTHES
- HAMILTON BEACH BREAD MACHINE IN GOOD CONDITION
- PEG PEREGO DUETTE, DOUBLE TWIN STROLLER, Excellent Cond.
- PAIR OF HARLEY DAVIDSON ROAD KING SADDLEBAGS
- COMPLETE SET OF OLD WOODEN WILSON GOLF CLUBS WITH BAG

Punctuation marks, like commas and long dashes, may be used in these titles as well. Just remember that punctuation marks count as characters in each title's fifty-five-character maximum.

BIZ BUILDER

I like to use all caps in my titles, because it helps them to stand out from the other auction listings. Using all caps in eBay titles is not considered "shouting," as it is in Internet parlance. However, adding a few words in lowercase to an otherwise all-caps title can make that information stand out.

Right below the title box you will see a box that says Subtitle ($0.50). This is another eBay option, and a somewhat expensive one at that. I only use subtitles for very expensive items.

Now that we have our title, let's move on to Item Specifics. The options vary by the product you select. It is vitally important to complete the Item Specifics because they are used when buyers narrow down their Search Results. Also, if a buyer searches for a term you didn't put in the title, but it matches based on your Item Specifics, your listing will still come up in the buyer's results.

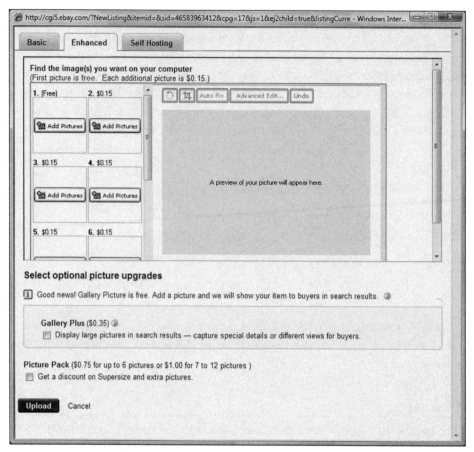

Figure 9.5 Enhanced Picture Services

Next you need to add your pictures. Start by clicking on the *Add Pictures* button; this will install the enhanced eBay Picture Services program (see Figure 9.5). From here, click on *Add Pictures* to select a photograph from your hard drive. The top-left picture will become your Gallery thumbnail picture on the Search Results page.

Repeat this process with any other photos you have. I always suggest including at least two and up to four photos of an item. The more you can show a prospective bidder, the better. Below your photos you will see options to add a Picture Pack, which is a discounted rate for when you use lots of photographs and also includes a free supersize for your pictures. The other option is Gallery Plus, which makes it possible for the buyer to view an enlarged version of your Gallery picture right on the Search Results page. These are expensive add-ons I only use when selling high-priced items.

Next, scroll down the page to the Item Description box.

If you look at Figure 9.6, you will see a box where you can enter text. Above it is a toolbar that looks similar to a Word document toolbar. Here you can select font and type size, as well as special formatting, such as bold, italics, underline, bullets, and numbered lists. This box is an HTML generator: You type in normal text, and it generates the HTML code necessary to present your text as you wish it to appear on the Internet. There is no longer any need for eBay sellers to know HTML in order to change paragraphs, format text, and so on.

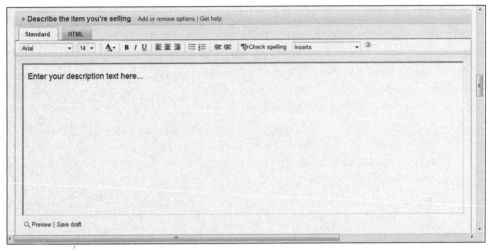

Figure 9.6   Description Box

Type your description into the box. Use a series of short paragraphs instead of one long one, since that's easier for customers to read. If you have specifications to list, then use the bullet list or number list feature. Although eBay's Sell Your Item form has an HTML editor that works like a Microsoft Word document, I prefer first to create my listing in Word, and then to copy and paste the description into the editor. This way I have a backup should anything go wrong, as well as a record I can use again in future auctions.

When you're selling a collectible or a used item, your description should contain as many specifics as possible. These might include:

※ The year and provenance of the item

※ Item size (length, width, height, weight)

※ Brand (such as John Deere, Coca-Cola, or Hard Rock)

※ Name of series set, special edition, or collection (for example, Coca-Cola Holiday Collection)

* The condition (new in box, mint, etc.), including possible flaws or scratches

* Material (such as porcelain, wood, or tin)

* Product type (sign, bottle, box, etc.)

So let's take a stab at describing my Starbucks mug.

> *This is a brand new—never used—Starbucks mug from the first Starbucks store in the world-famous Pike Place Market in Seattle. This is where Starbucks started and the store is still there today. It is one of Seattle's most popular tourist attractions and one of the busiest Starbucks stores in the world.*

> *The mug is four inches high, three inches across and holds 12 ounces. There is a beautiful printed scene of the Pike Place Market printed around the mug with the words Pike Place Market and Starbucks Coffee Co. printed over the scene. Inside the rim of the mug is the legend: The Birthplace of Starbucks Coffee.*

> *This mug is from the Skyline Series, the most collected series of Starbucks mugs since they were introduced in 1995. This mug was introduced in 2002 and discontinued in 2004. This mug is very hard to find and has sold for as much as $75 on eBay.*

> *These mugs do not come up on eBay very often. Don't lose out to a last-minute sniper. Place your best bid now.*

> *Shipping and handling is $5.90 via Priority Mail to any U.S. destination. Please e-mail me for shipping costs to Canada and overseas.*

> *I accept PayPal, or credit/debit cards directly via phone. I guarantee this item to be exactly as described or you can return it for a full refund. I will post positive feedback for all buyers as soon as payment is received.*

> *Thank you for looking at my item. Please e-mail me with any questions.*

Notice that at the end of the description I specify my shipping cost, payment options, return policy, and feedback terms. The Sell Your Item process provides other opportunities to enter this data, but I always like to place it in the description as well.

Next you'll encounter eBay's Listing Designer feature (Figure 9.7). This is a template that can add borders and background art to your auction listings. Since this only costs ten cents, you may want to use it. As you can see, I have selected a template for my listing. You can scroll down the list and select a frame that complements the category where you are selling.

Finally, at the bottom of the section, you can select the design of the visitor counter (often known as a "hit counter") you want to use. The hit counter will appear at

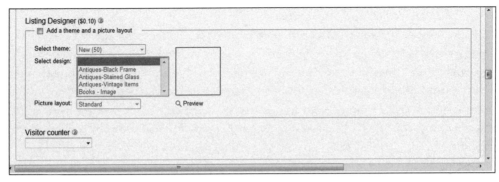

Figure 9.7   eBay Listing Designer

the bottom of your listing and will tell you how many people have opened your auction. You should always select a hit counter, because this information is very useful when you are testing titles and auction listing strategies.

Step 3: Pricing and Item Details

Enter your starting price. As you can see in Figure 9.8, I have entered $9.99, which is what I paid for the mug. If you are selling a used item, make a low estimate of the value and use that as a starting price. In general, the lower your starting price, the more bids you will attract. Brand-name items usually attract a lot of attention and bids.

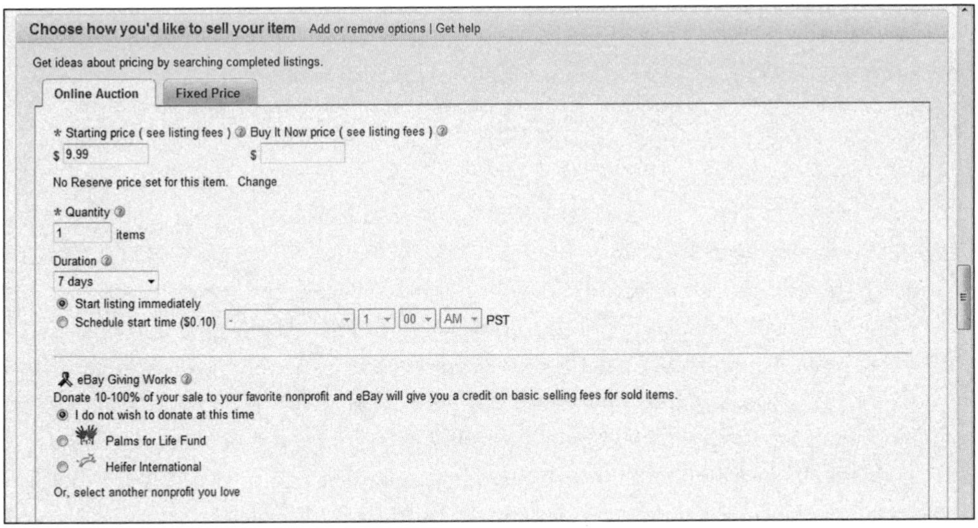

Figure 9.8   Pricing Your Item

If you are selling something obscure that has a high value, you have two options: You can set a low starting price and use a reserve, or you can set the starting price at the minimum you will accept for the item. We are going to cover listing and pricing strategies in great detail in the next chapter, so if you are unsure about what starting price to set, you may want to read ahead a little. Remember, however, that for now you are simply trying to gain some experience—not necessarily make a ton of money. You should be selling relatively low-cost items from your garage or attic. So I would suggest that you just go with a low starting price in hopes of attracting bids.

Looking again at Figure 9.8, you'll see that eBay offers two additional options: selecting a Buy It Now (BIN) price and donating a portion of your proceeds to charity. Again, let's ignore these features for now; we will cover them in greater detail later on.

Below the starting price is a place to enter your item quantity. Our quantity is 1.

Next you are asked to set the duration for your auction. A drop-down menu offers several choices: one, three, five, seven, or ten days. We will use a seven-day auction for this example.

Now you are given the option of starting the listing immediately, or scheduling it to start at a later time. Unless you happen to be uploading at the optimal time for your item (we'll talk about this later), I strongly suggest you pay the ten cents for Scheduled Listing. With this option, you can select the time and date you want your auction to start.

The next box is about Skype. Skype is a voice-over-Internet-protocol (VOIP) system that eBay purchased. You can choose to allow buyers to call you using Skype, or just select your e-mail address, or allow them to contact you through Skype's instant messenger. It's entirely up to you if you want to offer this. If you only have a few auctions up this is a handy service. But I had to turn it off because I had so many auctions running and I was getting interruptions from a lot of people who just wanted to chat as I tried to work.

Step 4: Payment and Shipping

The next page addresses the Payment Methods you will accept (see Figure 9.9).

All new eBay sellers are required to offer PayPal. Your other additional options are ProPay or accepting a credit/debit card through your own merchant credit card account. At least 80 percent of buyers will pay via PayPal, either using their bank account or using their credit/debit card through PayPal's payment processor. eBay payments are all electronic to help curb fraud issues and also so buyers will get their items faster (waiting for a check to clear can be frustrating). So checks, money orders, Western Union, MoneyGram, and so forth are not allowed on eBay.

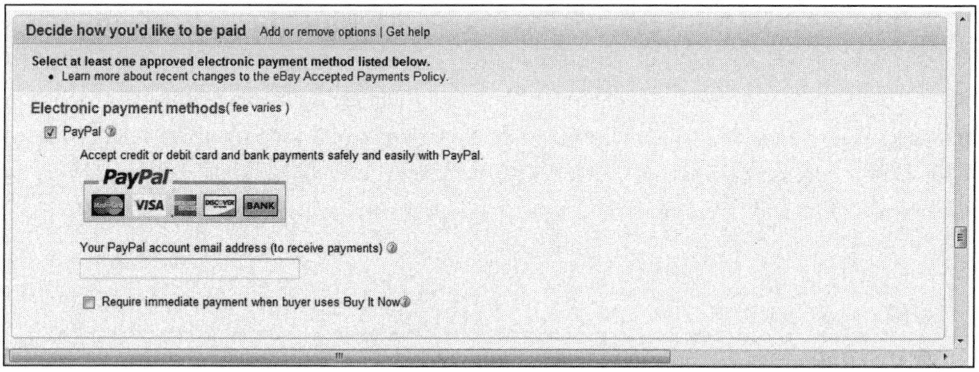

Figure 9.9   Selecting Payment Methods Accepted

The next section on the Sell Your Item form is your shipping information (see Figure 9.10). If you want to offer international shipping, you will need to add that to the form. Click on *Add or Remove Options* next to the section title, select the checkbox for *Show International Services and Options*, then click *Save*. Now you will see an international shipping box beneath the U.S. Shipping section. There are several issues involved in international shipping, which we will explore later on. For the time being, I suggest that you stick to shipping to the United States and Canada.

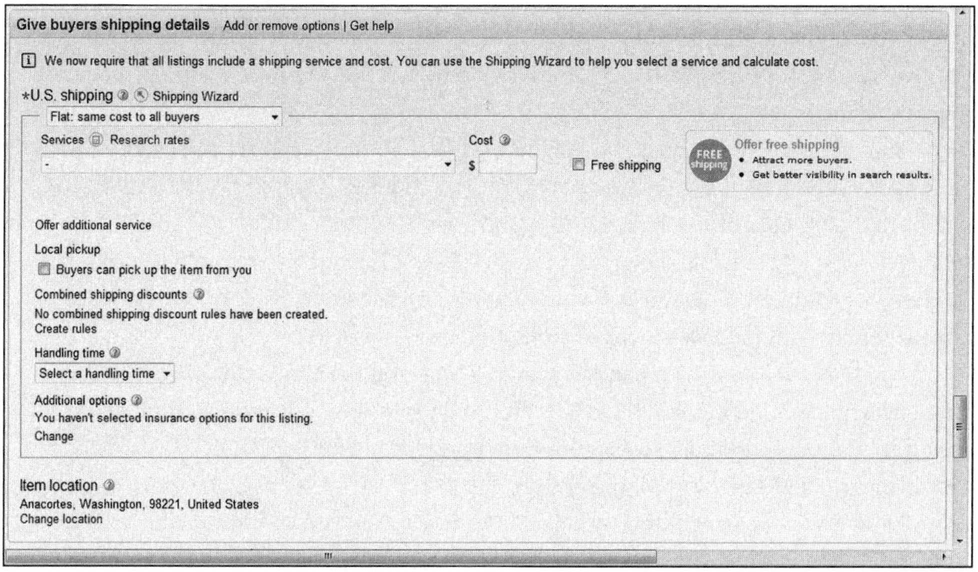

Figure 9.10   Entering Shipping Information

Using the drop-down menu, you may select either flat-rate or Calculated Shipping. There are times when I use Calculated Shipping, but most eBay PowerSellers prefer to use fixed shipping amounts for reasons of economy and convenience, both for the buyer and the seller. It also means your shipping price shows up on the Search Results page even if the buyer isn't signed in (because it's not based on where he lives). This can be a big bonus if you offer lower shipping rates than your competitors.

BIZ BUILDER

If you select *calculated shipping*, eBay inserts a box in your auction where a bidder can enter her zip code, and eBay will calculate the shipping cost to her location. If you select *fixed shipping*, you set the shipping price and enter that amount into your listing.

You can use the Shipping Wizard to determine your shipping cost. This can be useful if you use Calculated Shipping; you can add a handling fee and the buyer won't see it separated from the actual postage cost.

Use the *Offer Additional Service* link to add more options. Always put the cheapest shipping method at the top because this is the one eBay will use on the Search Results page. I've seen many sellers list the fastest (and therefore most expensive) shipping method first, which makes it look to buyers as if the seller is gouging on shipping. They never get as far as clicking on the auction to see that there are actually cheaper shipping options available.

You can also set up combined shipping rules. You may choose to discount $1.50 from each additional item's shipping cost, or you could go the other way and charge the full shipping cost of the highest item and then $2.00 per additional item. Make sure whatever rules you set still allow you to cover your shipping! You can offer combined shipping without setting up rules; simply mention this in your description and have buyers contact you directly to get a combined shipping quote.

Next you must select a handling time. This is the time between when the buyer pays and you mail the item. Typically, it should be one or two business days; any more than that and your feedback will suffer. Personally, I say that I will ship the same or the next business day upon receiving payment.

Finally, you are presented with *Seller Location*. You can either type in your zip code, and eBay will display your city and state, or you can enter a short custom message, such as "Proud Seller from the Show Me State."

Step 5: Buyer Requirements and Return Policy

Your Buyer Requirements are automated blocks you put in place to prevent certain buyers from bidding or buying your items. These can be very useful, but are also limiting, so use them wisely. Click on *Change Buyer Requirements* to set up your rules (see Figure 9.11). These will apply to all your listings.

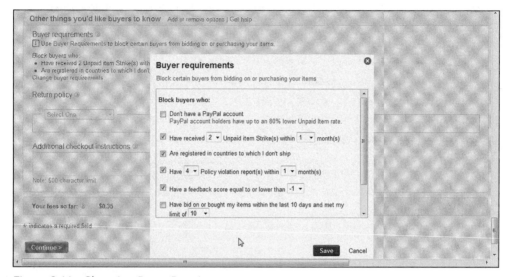

Figure 9.11   Changing Buyer Requirements

You may choose to block buyers who:

* Don't have a PayPal account

* Have received X unpaid item strikes against them within X months

* Are registered in countries to which you do not ship (this is a very useful option if you don't offer international shipping or don't want to ship to certain countries)

* Have X policy violation reports within X months

* Have a feedback score equal to or lower than X

* Have bid or bought your items within the last ten days and met your limit of X

For each of these, the X refers to a drop-down menu where you can select from a list of applicable numbers.

You can always exempt a specific buyer from these requirements if you want to. For example, if someone is registered in the UK but is visiting family in the United States and wants to buy from you, your Buyer Requirements may block him because he's registered in a country to which you don't ship. However, since the buyer wants you to ship to his family's address in the United States, you could choose to unblock that particular buyer while keeping the Buyer Requirements set for all other buyers. You do this using the *Buyer Block Exemption List* (http://pages.ebay.com/services/buyandsell/biddermanagement.html). It's also a prominent link in the Sell section of the eBay site map.

After your Buyer Requirements comes your Return Policy. You must select either *Returns Accepted* or *Returns Not Accepted* from the drop-down menu. If you identify that you do accept returns, you will then be given extra options to select the specifics of your return policy (see Figure 9.12).

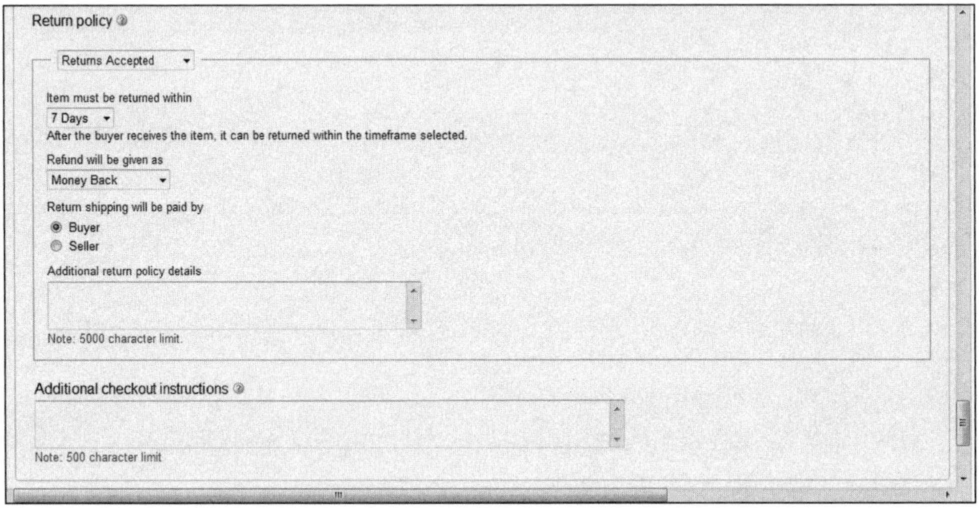

Figure 9.12   Entering Your Return Policy

Select the time frame in which returns are accepted, who pays for return shipping, how you will refund the buyer's money, and any other details you want to specify. Once you enter data in these fields, this information will be saved for all future auctions. So if you are selling something that will follow a different policy, be sure to change your standard return policy before launching the next auction.

Beneath this box is *Additional Checkout Instructions*. This is where you enter any other specifics not already covered.

Step 6: Promotional Add-Ons

Once you click *Continue*, you will go to the final page of the Sell Your Item form. Here you are given the opportunity to select from one of several eBay promotional options under the heading *Make Your Listing Stand Out*. Some of these options can get very expensive. We are going to cover all the eBay promotional features in chapter 16, but for now let's look at just Bold.

Bold costs $2. When you select this option, your listing's title appears in boldface in bidders' Search Results pages. eBay offers strong statistical evidence that using the Bold feature increases the number of hits a listing receives, the number of bids submitted, and the final price the item commands. If you are auctioning something likely to sell for $25 or more, this option will usually pay for itself. If you're anticipating less than that amount, I would not use it.

Next, eBay will show you its suggestions for how to make your listing more successful (add a picture, add a subtitle, etc.). If you've followed my advice in this book, you can ignore this section. This is eBay's way of trying to upsell you to more features with higher fees.

Step 7: Review and Submit Your Listing

After you have launched dozens of auctions, you'll be able to review your listings very quickly. For now, take your time as you review each part of your auction for accuracy (see Figure 9.13). Read your description carefully for any errors.

Be sure to examine the fees eBay will charge you. In this auction, my fees came to $1.00. If you recall, the cost of this mug was $9.95; if I add $1.00 to that, I get my

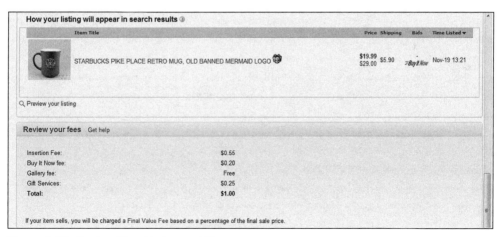

Figure 9.13   Review Your Listing and Fees

true cost for launching this auction on eBay: $10.95. If the mug sells, there will also be a final value fee of 8.75 percent (for the first $25.00, plus more for any value above that). Because I expect this mug to sell for at least $25.00, the final value fee should be somewhere around $2.19. This brings my total cost to $13.14. If the mug sells for $25.00, my profit will be $11.86. It took about ten minutes to create and launch the auction, and it will take another fifteen minutes or so to communicate with the seller about payment and pack and ship the box.

If this were an item you always carried in stock and were selling repeatedly, we would show you how to store your auction so you could launch identical auctions in less than a minute. In chapter 23, we are going to show you how to use outside services to automate your auctions and lower your eBay fees.

Click on *Preview Your Listing* at the bottom of the page to see how your auction will look. Click *Edit Listing* if you notice anything that is wrong. This will take you back to the previous page of the Sell Your Item form without losing the options you've selected on this page.

Once you are satisfied, hit the *List Your Item* button and give yourself a pat on the back. Now the fun starts.

THE LIFE OF YOUR AUCTION

Don't be surprised if your auction receives few bids—or even no bids at all—the first few days. This is normal. Auction listings typically see the most activity on the final day and in the final four hours, with furious bidding in the last few minutes. The advantage of having your auction up for seven days is that a lot of people will have a chance to consider your merchandise. Those who are interested will add the auction to their Watch List, waiting until the right moment to place their bid. Other sellers use automated programs, called sniping software, which will not place their bids until thirty seconds before the end of the auction.

Don't be surprised if your used household items bring far more money than you would have expected. If you are selling an old pasta machine at a garage sale, you might have thirty or forty people look at it during the day. On eBay, the keyword *pasta machine* is searched more than two thousand times a day. I was cleaning out some old boxes in the attic last year, and I came across an RCA transistor radio from the early '70s. I think it cost about $25 when it was new, which was pretty expensive in those days. I put fresh batteries in it and it worked! I know people collect old radios, and I thought I might be able to get $30 or $40 for it on eBay. I placed it on eBay in a seven-day auction. It received over fifty bids and sold for $212!

And the Starbucks Pike Place Mug? I just sold my last one for $78.

POWER MOVES

❏ Locate a few items from your attic or garage that you can use for your first listings. Make sure to clean them so that they're in good shape for selling.

❏ Take some digital photographs of your items. See chapter 15 if you need advice on how to do this effectively.

❏ Determine a price point for your merchandise. Do some research on eBay to determine the average selling price for your products.

❏ Follow the steps outlined in this chapter to launch your first auctions. Take note of any questions that arise regarding titles, descriptions, pricing, and so forth. We'll cover these topics in greater detail later on in the book.

CHAPTER 10

✦ LISTING AND PRICING STRATEGIES ✦

HERE'S AN INDISPUTABLE FACT about eBay: Low starting prices attract more bidders. The typical eBay bidder scans the category and Search Results pages for two things: low prices and items that already have bids. So getting that first bid is all-important, because it drives more traffic—and, therefore, more bids—to your auction. (We'll discuss the reasons why in a moment.) Therefore, where you set your starting bid is a critical decision, fraught with anguish and uncertainty. In this chapter, we'll go over different pricing strategies for different types of auctions, as well as the best days and times to begin and end your auctions.

GENERAL PRICING STRATEGIES

The risk in setting your bid price too low is that, if you don't get many bidders, you may end up giving your treasure away for a song. Conversely, if you set the price too high, you may not attract any bids at all. Setting the opening bid price is something of an art. This is a decision that takes some experience and research. If you are selling hot or popular items that routinely attract a lot of bids, it is usually safe to set a low minimum bid. If you are spending money on eBay's optional features to attract attention to your listings (we will cover these features in the next section), it is probably safer to set a low starting price, so that your auction will receive more hits.

The problem arises when you are selling an item that is not well known or does not have a popular brand name.

Remember: The starting bid is only important to attract those first few bidders. Once the bidding starts, the current bid price will appear next to your title on the Search Results page. eBay's research shows that a sizable percentage of sellers will scan the Search Results page looking for items that already have bids on them. For some reason, buyers feel more secure bidding on an item that has already received at least one bid. In response to this buyer behavior, some unscrupulous sellers will have a friend place a bid on their item, just to record that first bid. This is a prohibited practice called *shilling*, and can get you banned from eBay permanently.

One school of thought holds that you should start all items at $1, with no reserve. In theory, this practice works well most of the time, although you can get burned occasionally. Many experienced PowerSellers list their items at cost. Their reasoning goes like this: Their cost is lower than the item's value, and therefore will attract bids. At worst, they will recover what they paid for the item and only lose out on the eBay listing fees.

Other sellers argue that you should set the opening bid at the minimum price you will accept for the item. However, this strategy has a drawback: A smaller percentage of your auctions will actually receive bids. You'll eventually get killed by eBay's listing fees, which can add up pretty quickly.

Personally, I set a $0.99 starting price with no reserve only when listing popular, name-brand items that I know will sell. The low starting price minimizes my eBay listing fees. However, unless the item is very popular and a sure seller, I usually use my cost as the starting price.

RESERVE PRICE STRATEGIES

We covered the basics of Reserve Price Auctions (RPAs) in chapter 8. An RPA is an auction where you start the bidding at a low price but establish a hidden reserve price—the minimum amount for which you are willing to sell the item. eBay charges special fees for RPAs. Table 10.1 presents a summary of these fees.

Table 10.1 **Reserve Listing Fees**		
RESERVE PRICE (US$)	$0.01–$199.99	$200.00 and up
FEE (US$)	$2.00	1% of Reserve Price (up to $100)

I rarely use RPAs for items under $50. But I almost always use them when listing an expensive item (over $200)—unless I'm selling an extremely popular product, like an Apple iPod, which is likely to attract many bids and reach the desired price without a reserve.

Reserves are controversial on eBay. If you visit the message boards, you'll see lots of negative comments about them, mostly from buyers who have no experience with selling. While no one keeps official statistics on things like this, there is plenty of anecdotal evidence suggesting that a large percentage of eBay members will not bid on an item with a reserve.

Personally, I have not run up against this kind of resistance in my auctions. In fact, I sell several items in the $200–$500 price range, and I have actually garnered more sales with reserves—not fewer.

BUY IT NOW PRICING

Buy It Now (BIN) is an eBay feature that allows a bidder to end an auction immediately by bidding at a fixed BIN price. The Buy It Now price is usually only displayed until the first bid is placed, and then it disappears. On Reserve Price Auctions, the BIN price is available until the reserve is met. In some categories, the BIN price will remain even past the first bid or after the reserve is met. BIN auctions exist to attract impulse bidders or to capture that one bidder who must have exactly what you are selling and cannot risk losing it to a higher bidder. Table 10.2 specifies the special fees to use the BIN option.

Table 10.2 Buy It Now Fee Schedule

BUY IT NOW PRICE (US$)	$1.00–$9.99	$10.00–$24.99	$25.00–$49.99	$50.00 or more
FEE (US$)	$0.05	$0.10	$0.20	$0.25

If you list a BIN price, avoid starting the auction too low. Otherwise, someone will simply bid a very low price, and the BIN option will disappear. One benefit of BIN is that it works to establish a value in a bidder's mind. I like to set my BIN price slightly above the item's value. If I start an item at $19.99 that I think will sell for $29.00, I usually set the BIN price a little higher, say, at $33.00.

Another way to use Buy It Now is to create a Fixed Price listing. This is a set price and there is no bidding. If you have multiple identical quantities, you can list all of them for one fixed listing fee. In a Fixed Price Auction, either the bidder buys the item at the price you specified or she doesn't. The advantage of Fixed Price listings is they can run for up to thirty days and can be renewed automatically. This gives you maximum exposure for your item. An optional add-on for a Fixed Price listing is Best Offer. This gives the buyer the option of making an offer lower than the BIN price. You have the option to accept, reject, or counter that offer. So, in effect, you get to haggle online. If I use Best Offer, I list my BIN price higher than I expect to receive because I know most of the potential buyers will make me a lower offer, and accepting it makes them feel as if they got a better deal. You can set your options to autoreject any offers below a certain amount, so you don't need to waste time with ridiculously lowballed offers.

THE SECOND CHANCE OFFER

eBay offers another useful feature that can really add to your profits. It is called the Second Chance Offer (SCO). Whenever an auction ends with a winner, if you look at your auction listing, you will see a link to *Send a Second Chance Offer*. This feature allows you to offer identical items to losing bidders after your auction ends, either because the winning bidder was unable to complete the transaction, or because you have more than one of a specific item available for sale.

Consider the following example: I've successfully sold a fire pit for $255. That is $36 over my target price of $219, the minimum price at which I will make a profit on this item. I have plenty of these fire pits. (Actually I have none of them, as they are all drop-shipped from the manufacturer, but he has plenty of them and can make more if he runs out.)

If you click on the link to *Second Chance Offer*, it takes you to a page that lists all the losing bidders for your item.

If you look at the first two underbids in Figure 10.1, they were for $240 and $250, both of which are higher than my target of $219. The third bid, at $89, is too low, as are all the other bids. To make Second Chance Offers, I simply check the boxes next to the two highest bidders, and hit the *Continue* button at the bottom of the page. eBay will send the next two highest bidders automated e-mails making the offer. They will have three days to respond. The e-mail that goes out from eBay will have a PayPal button embedded in it. All the bidders have to do to accept is hit the PayPal button, and I will receive both a notice of acceptance and a payment deposited into my PayPal account.

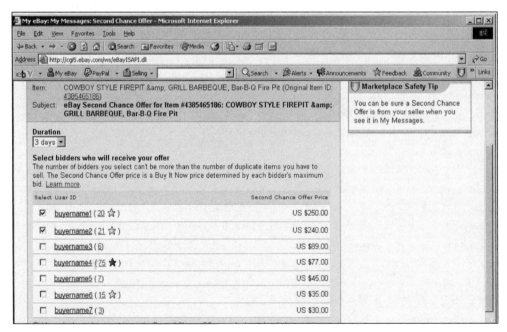

Figure 10.1   Second Chance Offer Bids

eBay will charge me a final value fee on each item sold, but I have sold a total of three items for one listing fee. This works out to $745 in sales from one auction.

THE BEST TIMES TO LIST AND END AUCTIONS

eBay offers five choices of auction duration: one, three, five, seven, and ten days. (Only Fixed Price listings and eBay store inventory have the thirty-day option.) How long should your auction last? This is an area where many PowerSellers disagree, and there isn't really a hard-and-fast rule.

One theory is that the shorter the auction the better, because people don't like to bid on auctions that have a long waiting period until they end. Auctions attract impulse buyers. These types of bidders will definitely seek out shorter auctions. This is especially true if you are selling common products that are always available on eBay, such as children's clothes, low-cost jewelry, leather jackets, digital cameras, MP3 players, designer brand-name goods, and the like.

If you are selling something of a collectible nature, as opposed to a readily available product, you will want to expose your auction to as many people as possible over the longest period. Collectors tend to be more careful and will shop diligently for specific items for their collections. For rare collectibles, then, I recommend the ten-day auction.

The more important decision is this: On what day should your auction end? Different types of people shop at different times. The most popular prime-time shows are on Monday, Tuesday, and Wednesday evenings, meaning fewer people may be shopping on eBay at those times. Young people are usually out Friday and Saturday nights. Older folks who stay home spend a lot of time on eBay during the day and on Saturday evening, because it's usually a lousy TV night. Table 10.3 spells out the best and worst days to end an auction.

The auction duration you select determines which day your auction will end. I personally prefer to launch my three-day and ten-day auctions on Thursday evenings, so they end on Sunday evening. Between 4:00 and 6:00 p.m. PT (7:00–9:00 ET) seems to work best for me, but you should experiment, based on the types of products you are selling. Remember: eBay time is Pacific Time, so you have to add three hours to calculate the time on the East Coast. Forty-four percent of the U.S. population live in the Eastern time zone, and sixty-nine percent live in the Eastern and Central time zones combined. So be careful not to allow your auctions to end too late in the evening in the Central and Eastern time zones.

Another factor to consider when choosing which day to end your auction is *where* your auction will appear.

When bidders perform a search or go to the listings page for a category, they are given several choices of how the auctions are sorted, including *Time: newly listed* and *Time: ending soonest.*

If you launch a three-day auction on a Friday, it will appear in a prominent location several times over the weekend, which is the time of highest bidding activity. On Friday it will show up near the top under *Time: newly listed* and on Sunday it will show up near the top in *Time: ending soonest.*

Having said all this, once you have settled on a product or category of products to sell, you'll want to run your own tests to determine the best time to list and end auctions for the products you are selling. Some products seem to sell at different times. I used to have a product that I sold to businesses. When I tested various ending times, the optimum was Monday and Tuesday between 11 a.m. and 1 p.m. (Pacific Time).

Table 10.3 **Best Days and Times to End Auctions**

DAY	RATING	COMMENT
Monday	Good	A lot of people surf eBay at work. After the weekend, they need their "eBay fix." Monday evenings are also very good.
Tuesday	Worst	Tuesday statistically receives the lowest number of bids on eBay.
Wednesday	Poor	According to studies, Wednesday is not quite as bad as Tuesday, although it is still not a great day to end an auction.
Thursday	Fair	Thursday is not a bad day to end an auction in the spring and summer, because people going away for the weekend may place bids on Thursday before they leave.
Friday	Fair	Ending your auction Friday before 6:00 p.m. may attract bids from students and young people who are not usually home on Friday and Saturday evenings.
Saturday	Good	Weekend days are usually more profitable than weekdays, probably because more people have time to shop.
Sunday	Excellent	Sunday evening is the period of highest bidding activity on eBay. If your auction ends at about 11:00 p.m. Eastern Time, you will maximize your bidding activity.

POWER MOVES

❏ Go to http://pages.ebay.com/help/sell/fees.html and become familiar with the complete eBay fee schedule. Bookmark this link and be sure to check it before listing an item. This will help you understand your potential costs when deciding on your pricing strategy.

❏ Do a completed listings search for the product you plan to sell. Select the *Price: highest first* as the sort order to display the Search Results. Look at the items that sold for the most money, and open the auctions to see on what days and at which times they ended.

CHAPTER 11

✦ BUILDING GREAT ✦ FEEDBACK

I HAVE HEARD SOME EBAY USERS remark that feedback isn't all that important, commenting that "No one reads that stuff." Nothing could be further from the truth. While eBay novices often overlook the feedback factor because they don't understand it, veteran buyers will almost always check your feedback before placing a bid. If they see comments like "Product not delivered," "This guy is a fraud," or "Terrible seller," they will never purchase your merchandise. Once you have hundreds of feedback posts, you can survive the occasional negative feedback comment. As a new seller, you need to have an outstanding feedback rating, brimming with positive comments, to quickly grow your eBay business. To attain that outstanding feedback rating, you'll need to provide impeccable customer service. In business circles, there's an old saying that, if you want to keep your customers happy and coming back, "You should not just service your customers, you should delight your customers."

Customer service encompasses each interaction with everyone from potential bidders to those who win your auctions or buy from your store. Always answer a bidder's and/or buyer's e-mail as quickly as possible. Whether the customer is praising your product or complaining, whether he is offering his input or asking a question, he deserves an answer—especially on eBay, where feedback really counts!

THE VALUE OF FEEDBACK

In the first chapter, we introduced you to the concept of feedback on eBay by comparing it to a shopping mall where, outside each store, customers could post comments about the store's products and customer service on a large board. And store personnel were not allowed to remove or change the comments—they were there for all to see before entering the store. Would you look at the messages before shopping at the store? Of course you would. Well, this is the role feedback plays on eBay. Everyone gets to see a review of your customer service and integrity *before* placing a bid on your item.

There is a second facet to feedback, called Detailed Seller Ratings (DSRs). These are one- to five-star ratings on four aspects of the transaction that are considered the most important to buyers. They are:

- ✳ Item as described
- ✳ Communication
- ✳ Shipping time
- ✳ Shipping and handling charges

These ratings are in addition to the feedback comment and are completely anonymous (so there's no DSR withdrawal process, as there is with feedback). Your feedback profile shows the average rating for each DSR item over the last twelve months. In your Seller Dashboard you can see your thirty-day average. This is important because if any of your thirty-day DSR averages falls below 4.1, you will be prevented from listing any more items until either the ratings buyers leave for your current auctions bring your score above 4.1, or thirty days have passed. This assumes that your twelve-month average is above 4.1. If it isn't, you'll have to wait until the lower ratings drop off (which could take up to twelve months), bringing your average back up. If you don't have an established track record, eBay will look at your twelve-month rather than your thirty-day average.

Also, DSRs are part of the algorithm eBay uses to determine your item's placement in the default search order, Best Match. This can seriously impact your business. If any of your DSRs drop below 4.3, you will be further demoted in Best Match until your ratings improve.

The point of mentioning all this is to show you how important feedback really is. So how do you get an excellent feedback rating? By delivering quality products quickly, efficiently, and honestly. If you are looking to make a quick buck or stage a "hit-and-run" action, eBay is not the place for you. You can build a hugely profitable and legitimate business on eBay without cheating or misleading anyone. I know—I have done it.

There will always be a few rogue customers who claim they never received their product, or you were too slow to deliver it, or they were unhappy with what they received. We all know the customer is not *always* right.

My recommendation for dealing with such problem buyers is simply to offer a thirty-day, no-questions-asked refund. Offering a bidder a refund can head off negative feedback posts.

Once you have a high feedback rating (over 100) you can tolerate the occasional negative feedback comment. But, until then, you should take the long view and remember that you are trying to build a long-term business that can generate thousands of dollars in income. Don't take issue with a $9.00 item that someone was unhappy with. Just refund the buyer's money and move on.

HOW TO BUILD FEEDBACK QUICKLY

Here are some tips to build your feedback rating quickly:

* Sell low-cost items, such as baseball cards, stamps, or inexpensive pieces of costume jewelry for $1 each. You won't make much money, but you can sell dozens, even hundreds, of items in a short time and quickly build your feedback numbers.

* When your auction ends, send the winning bidder a confirming e-mail. Offer to exchange positive feedback with each buyer who pays quickly, and provide buyers with a link they can easily click to leave feedback. This will help build your feedback rating, and your customers will appreciate it as well.

* Your e-mail signature to buyers should contain the current *Leave Feedback* link. As of this writing it is:

  http://cgi2.eBay.com/aw-cgi/eBayISAPI.dll?LeaveFeedbackShow

  (Note that eBay often changes its links. See eBay's site map for the most current link.)

* Here is an interesting statistic from eBay: Only 45 percent of buyers bother to leave feedback. Many sellers add a personal touch by including a handwritten thank-you note when they fulfill an order. Such notes should thank buyers for their business, encourage them to contact you with any questions or concerns, and remind them that you left positive feedback for them. I include the following preprinted note in all my packages:

  Thank you for your business. I have posted positive feedback for this transaction. If there is anything wrong with your order, please contact me immediately and I will do my very best to correct the problem or make it right.

  I include my e-mail address and phone number after the message, and then sign each note. These notes are printed on four-by-five-inch colored stock. I have them sitting next to my shipping station (see chapter 17), so that it is easy for me to grab one, sign it, fold it in half, and insert it into the box.

* Create a little giveaway of some kind. When someone buys an item over $50, I include an eBay pen. They cost me thirty cents each from the eBay shop. If this is too expensive, eBay also has little packets of mints that come in an eBay wrapper and only cost a few cents each. One woman I know who sells autographs and other paper memorabilia wrote a short article on how to spot fakes. She inserts a copy of the article in each shipment she sends out. Just use your imagination and you can probably come up with several ways to surprise and "delight" your customers.

✳ Customers sometimes forget to leave feedback after they receive the product, because it has been a week or so since your last e-mail and your message is buried in their e-mail files. To combat this "out of sight, out of mind" effect, calculate the average shipping time to your customers. If the customer hasn't posted feedback on the transaction by the time you figure that he's received the merchandise, send an e-mail that includes your *Leave Feedback* link. Your e-mail could say something like this:

> *By now you should have received your unique baseball batting glove.*
> *I hope you have had a chance to try it out. If you have any questions, or if there are any problems with your order, please e-mail me immediately.*
> *I enjoyed doing business with you and I have left positive feedback for this transaction.*
>
> *Best regards,*
> *Sammy Sosa*
>
> *P.S. If you would like to leave feedback about our eBay transaction, please go to:*
>
> *http://cgi2.eBay.com/aw-cgi/eBayISAPI.dll?LeaveFeedbackShow*

An e-mail like this reminds your customer to leave feedback. I have tested this type of e-mail, and it has increased my feedback response by at least 20 percent.

Another way to increase your positive feedback quickly is to be overly generous in posting your feedback. If the buyer didn't send the PayPal payment until seven days after the auction ended, so what? I still post a nice feedback notice. If someone cancels or doesn't follow through, I rarely bother leaving feedback, although I do file a nonpaying bidder request to recover my fees.

Ask yourself: How many times have I misplaced an e-mail or had an emergency to deal with and forgotten about everything else? Not all slow payers are nonpayers. Sometimes, people really do forget. Why make an enemy? Remember: You cannot leave negative feedback for buyers, but even if they don't pay, they are still able to leave neutral or negative feedback for you.

I remember the story of one poor lady who had a heart attack. Before this incident, her feedback rating was over 500, with a 100 percent positive rating. While she was recuperating from her heart attack, several winning bidders who hadn't heard from her left brutal negative feedback comments. A week or so later, her daughter sent all of them e-mails explaining the situation. Surprisingly, several of the buyers didn't believe her. They continued to send abusive e-mails and complaints to eBay. It took copies of her surgery report and a letter from her doctor to get the negative feedback comments removed.

Amazingly, giving out your telephone number can actually save you time. I've started listing my phone number in my e-mail signature. Sometimes a phone call can clear up an issue in much less time than it takes to send several e-mails back and forth. Also, the fact that you list your phone number enhances your credibility and reduces suspicion.

CUSTOMER SERVICE DOS AND DON'TS

Always respond quickly and clearly to questions from eBay bidders and buyers. If I have auctions running, I check my eBay messages at least three times a day, and always a few minutes before the auction closes, in case bidders have any last-minute questions. If you fail to answer e-mails quickly, you may receive negative comments, such as "Unresponsive seller" or "Ignored my repeated inquiries," in your feedback file. You will almost certainly also get a lower rating for the Communication DSR.

Keep your answers short, courteous, and to the point. Provide all relevant information and be friendly; however, don't get bogged down in long e-mail conversations or let the customer lead you on an irrelevant tangent. Your time is money.

All your business policies as they relate to shipping, payment, feedback, and so forth should be written in a clear, personable style, and specified at the end of each of your item descriptions. You want to convey your policies without listing a set of rules that turn people off. It is also helpful to explain why you have certain policies. For example, if you only ship via Priority Mail, you might want to say something like:

> We use Priority Mail for all shipments under five pounds. Priority Mail costs less than UPS and includes free boxes and shipping materials so we don't have to charge you for those or build in a hefty handling fee.

SHORTCUTS TO SUPERIOR SERVICE

When it comes to customer service, you need to balance time, efficiency, and courteousness to maximize your selling potential. One way to save time is to create a folder in your e-mail program, called Prewritten Messages, in which you store template messages for answering common questions like these:

* When was my item shipped?
* Did you receive my payment?
* How long does shipping take?

You'll create additional prewritten messages, customized to fit your particular product, as you continue to receive similar questions and comments from customers.

It is much easier to send out a prewritten e-mail than to write a specific answer to each inquiry. However, to prevent your e-mails from sounding like form letters, add a personal touch whenever possible. Use the person's name if you know it, or her eBay user ID if you don't. Always "sign" your name at the bottom.

BIZ BUILDER

If I am about to buy something, I always read the feedback details for a seller who has more than one negative comment. When someone leaves negative feedback for you, you get to make a response. I once read a negative comment from someone whose order was wrong and late. The seller's response was this: "I screwed up! It doesn't happen often, but this one was my fault." I was so impressed by the seller's honesty, that I didn't hesitate to buy from her.

FEEDBACK REMOVAL

Getting eBay to remove a negative feedback comment is extremely difficult. There are only certain circumstances in which eBay will do so, such as when a buyer includes personal details in the feedback comment (like your name or phone number), or eBay is issued with a court order to remove it. The full details on removing negative feedback are available at http://pages.ebay.com/help/policies/feedback-removal.html. There is one other option, called Feedback Revision. Let's say a buyer leaves negative feedback because an item didn't arrive. However, a couple of days later the package shows up and the mailing date shows that the seller actually did ship it on time, but it got delayed in the mail. The buyer may want to change the negative comment. The seller can initiate the Feedback Revision process. This allows the buyer to change the feedback rating (positive, negative, neutral), the comment itself, and also his DSR ratings (so, for example, this buyer could change the Shipping Time DSR from a 2 to a 5, since it wasn't the seller's fault that the package was delayed).

Here's the catch—there is a limit to the number of feedback revisions a seller can request. It is currently five revision requests per one thousand feedback comments received, per twelve months. So the Feedback Revision process does not take the place of creating a good eBay experience for your buyers; it only addresses occasional mistakes made by either the buyer or the seller.

If you have exceeded your maximum, or the buyer won't change his feedback, you should still leave a follow-up comment. Go to the eBay site map and click on *Reply to Feedback Received*. This will allow you to select the transaction and leave a comment explaining what happened. Remember the seller who responded that she had messed up? Mistakes do happen. So if this happens to you, acknowledging it and explaining how you fixed the problem will help instill confidence in other potential buyers.

BUYING VERSUS SELLING FEEDBACK

On your Feedback Profile, there are separate tabs for *Feedback as a Buyer* and *Feedback as a Seller*. This is valuable for the following reason: Suppose you're interested in bidding on an item, and you see that the seller has a feedback rating of 35. When you look more closely, however, you notice that most of the feedback comments are from *sellers,* for merchandise the seller *purchased*. His feedback for items he's *sold* may be quite low or even nonexistent. Therefore, you, as a buyer, may be wary of purchasing from this seller. I know this will hamper new sellers—but all of us were new at one time. Most PowerSellers worked very hard to build their rating over a long period.

You can also view the feedback a member has left for others, on the tab *Feedback Left for Others*. I like to see what kind of feedback sellers leave for other people. Someone who leaves a lot of negative feedback is less likely to get bids from me. Why take the risk?

In the end, building positive feedback is all about honesty, fair shipping costs, and customer service. If you are honest in your descriptions and provide good customer service, your feedback rating will climb rapidly.

POWER MOVES

❏ Go to the eBay site map and click on the links under the heading *Feedback*.

❏ Bookmark (add to Favorites) the links you will use most often, such as:

> *Follow Up to Feedback You Left for Others*
> *Leave Feedback for a Member*
> *Leave Feedback for a Transaction*
> *Reply to Feedback Received*

❏ For the auctions you launched in chapter 9, send winning bidders confirmation e-mails and encourage them to leave feedback. Make sure you leave positive feedback for them as well.

❏ Sell a series of inexpensive items for the purpose of quickly building your feedback rating. Include a personal note in each package, thanking the customer for his order and stating that you have left positive feedback for the transaction.

❏ Consider sending a follow-up e-mail to buyers who have not left feedback. Always include the *Leave Feedback* link in your e-mails to buyers.

❏ Set up a folder in your e-mail program for Prewritten Messages. Create template messages for answering common questions you receive.

CHAPTER 12

✦ WRITING YOUR SUCCESS PLAN ✦

IN THE INTRODUCTION, I asked you to evaluate your personal definition of success. This is an important concept. Now that you understand some of the basics involved in running an eBay business, it is a good idea to ask yourself the following questions: What are my goals? How much time do I want to devote to eBay? And how much money can I make, given the time and resources I have to commit to this business?

Most people launching a business write a plan and establish their goals before they start. However, before you attempted that, I wanted you to have a better understanding of how eBay works and what is involved in selecting a product to sell. Now that you understand the work and costs involved, you're ready to put together your business plan.

In the business world, almost every company has a business plan that its executives continually revise and update as the business develops. For selling on eBay, you don't need a full-blown business plan with financial statistics and detailed marketing strategies, but you do need to set some basic goals and map out a series of steps to help you reach those goals. As we conclude Week 1 of this three-week program, we will focus on the basics of setting some realistic objectives and writing a success plan to guide you through the next stages of developing your eBay business.

EVALUATING YOUR EARNING POTENTIAL

The first question you have to answer is how big you want to be, or, put another way, how much money you want to make. If you already know what you want to sell on eBay, this is a much easier question to answer—your anticipated revenue depends on the price point or the final value of what you will be selling. Let's do some simple math to demonstrate this point.

If you are selling a product with an average selling price (ASP) of $50, and the item costs you $30, you will make an average of $20 on each successful auction (less eBay and PayPal fees). So if your goal were to make $3,000 a month on eBay, you would have to close 150 auctions a month. Experienced sellers will successfully close (or convert) as many as 70 percent of all their auctions. So you would have to launch about 215 auctions a month—or just over 50 auctions a week—in order to close 150 auctions successfully. Alternatively, if you were selling a $100 item for an ASP of $160, you would make $60 an auction. Now you would only have to convert 50 auctions a month to make the same amount of money. For more on conversion, see the sidebar titled "Best Practices: Defining Metrics" on p.115.

If you focus on selling higher-value merchandise, you will make more money for the same amount of work. The key to moving "upmarket" is to thoroughly research a product to make sure there is a market for it, and that you can buy it at a price where you can make money selling it on eBay. Remember—you make money when you *buy*, not when you sell. In other words if you buy at a low enough cost, you always have room to make a profit.

So if you haven't yet researched and selected a product or products to sell on eBay, now is the time to complete these tasks. You first must determine what you are going to sell and what your average price points will be before you can start setting concrete goals and crafting a business plan.

SETTING GOALS

I know plenty of people who are successful in life and in business who do not create formal, written goals. But I know far more who *do*—and, on average, the ones with written goals tend to be much more successful than those without.

Written goals serve several purposes. Long-term goals give you a vision of where you want to be in the future; short-term goals provide the stepping-stones to get there.

To be useful, your goals should be both specific and achievable. A goal "to become a millionaire within three years" is both vague and difficult to achieve, unless you already have $500,000 in assets. A better goal would be "to achieve Gold PowerSeller status within one year and Platinum PowerSeller status within two years."

.... BEST PRACTICES ....

TYPES OF POWERSELLERS

PowerSellers are top eBay sellers who average consistently high volumes of sales from month to month, maintain a high percentage of positive feedback, and comply with eBay's policies. PowerSellers are divided into six tiers, based upon sellers' average monthly sales totals. Certain benefits and services vary with each tier. eBay automatically calculates sellers' eligibility each month; if you qualify, you will be notified of your status via e-mail.

The following are the sales criteria for each PowerSeller tier:

Bronze	Silver	Gold	Platinum	Titanium	Diamond
$1,000	$3,000	$10,000	$25,000	$150,000	$500,000

If you want to relate your goals to income, you could set up steps like these:

1. Earn $1,000 a month by (date)
2. Earn $3,000 a month by (date)
3. Earn $5,000 a month by (date)

Once you establish your primary business goals, you should set subgoals, or a list of tasks that have to be completed to get you there.

Your first set of tasks should be a list of all the things you have to do to set up and organize your business—we covered these in chapter 1. These include getting your state sales tax number, opening your business checking account, verifying your PayPal account, and so on. You should make a complete list of all these tasks and treat each one as an individual goal.

Next, you will want to set specific business goals. This will involve determining how many auctions you will run and how often. You should also set your goals for reaching certain metrics, such as conversions (see the sidebar below, titled "Best Practices: Defining *Metrics*"), sell-through rates, and average selling price.

.... BEST PRACTICES ....

DEFINING *METRICS*

Metrics is a term that means "measure." There is an old saying in business: "If you can't measure something, you can't control it." Some of the more important metrics in eBay selling are the following:

Conversion or Sell-Through Rate: This is the percentage of auctions you close versus the number you listed. If you listed one hundred auctions and successfully closed sixty-five with a sale, your sell-through rate would be 65 percent—or you might say you "converted" 65 percent of your auctions.

Average Selling Price (ASP): This is the average price of all the items you listed that sold (ASP does not include listings that did not sell).

Gross Merchandise Sales (GMS): GMS is the total dollar value of your sales for the month (or week, or year, and so on).

Gross Margin: This is the amount you made on your sales after taking into account the cost of the items you sold, your eBay listing and selling fees, and your PayPal fees.

There are many other, more detailed metrics that eBay sellers track on a daily, weekly, and monthly basis; however, they are all variations or extensions of the ones specified above.

The purpose of establishing goals is twofold: First, you want to set targets to achieve. Second, you want your progress in reaching these targets to be measurable.

Remember that goals can have a numerical value, such as "dollars earned," and/or an accomplishment value, such as "Completed Phase I of my product research." But all goals must have a time value (the date by which they are to be accomplished) to be meaningful.

Here are some points to help you set and achieve your goals:

* *Keep moving forward.* Never look back, except to learn from your mistakes.

* *Focus your energy.* Don't be distracted by other issues and businesses.

* *Hone your skills.* Practice and experiment for success.

* *Increase your knowledge.* Read everything you can find that relates to your business and your goals.

* *Manage your time and your energy.* Set aside some time for yourself, your family, and your friends. Otherwise, you're likely to burn out.

* *Surround yourself with positive people.* Don't listen to those who say you can't be successful.

* *Most of all, have fun!* If you enjoy what you're doing, you're more likely to work hard and be successful.

YOUR BUSINESS PLAN

Now that you have your goals specified, it's time to write your business plan—or, as I like to call it, your *success plan.* You have already done most of the work by establishing your goals. Your business plan is nothing more than a statement formalizing these goals in writing:

* What business you are in

* Where you want to go with this business

* What resources you will need to get there

* What will determine your success

You might be tempted to skip this step—or take mental notes rather than writing down the details. That would be a mistake. The act of writing this information down in an organized fashion will help clarify your thinking. If you are starting a business with your spouse, you should create this plan together and discuss each of the points. If you are married or living with someone and are doing this alone, you should still discuss your plan with your significant other to get his feedback and to make him part of your success plan.

My wife and I have been running a successful eBay business for over nine years, and I am good friends with several of the top PowerSellers on eBay. We know—and they know—that there are no shortcuts to success on eBay. If someone tells you she has the "instant secret to success on eBay," and that you can make $5,000 a month by working only a few minutes a day, she is trying to sell you something. Furthermore, she has probably never actually sold anything on eBay. Yes, you can make $5,000 a month on eBay (and even more), but you cannot accomplish this with just a few minutes of work a day. Now that you know what is involved in launching auctions, part of setting your goals is assessing the amount of time and resources you can devote to the business. If your business plan is realistic and you see progress week after week, you will be encouraged to keep pursuing your goals.

I am doing my best to reveal all the tips and tricks I have learned over the last nine years to help you succeed. However, none of these takes the place of planning, research, and hard work. Now that you understand the basics of selling on eBay and how the system works, take the time to set your goals, write a plan, and create a schedule for success. In Week 2, we are going to delve into the advanced systems and techniques that will save you time, reduce your costs, and help you launch professional-looking auctions to ensure that you build a long-term profitable business.

POWER MOVES

- [ ] In your eBay binder, write down short- and long-term goals for your business. Determine how much money you are looking to make and how much time you can realistically devote to achieving your goals on eBay.

- [ ] Review your research and estimate the average selling price of your product(s). Using the formula discussed in this chapter, calculate how many auctions a week you would need to launch to reach your monthly goals.

- [ ] If the number of auctions you need to launch to reach your goal will take more time than you can realistically devote to your business, reassess your product selection. Do additional research, if necessary, to come up with alternative products to sell.

- [ ] Either with your partner or alone, turn your goals into a formal business plan. Keep updating and revising this plan as your business grows and develops.

WEEK
2

PUTTING YOUR AUCTIONS TO WORK

By now you have organized your business, completed your product research and determined what you want to sell, and even taken steps to acquire the products. You have launched your first eBay auctions and worked through the steps of getting paid, communicating with customers, and delivering the product. You may even have earned a few feedback comments. Now it's time to start building and refining your skills, to make your fledgling business a success.

In Week 2, we're going to focus on specific ways to improve your auctions and grow your profits on eBay, including driving customers to your auctions by using strategic category selection, writing auction titles and descriptions that sell, improving the effectiveness of your auction photos, and using listing upgrades to promote your auctions across eBay. In addition, we'll discuss how to increase profits by selling internationally, and how to minimize your costs and maximize your buyers' confidence by choosing wisely from various shipping, payment, and insurance options. Finally, we'll explore how to monitor and revise your auctions so they are as successful as possible, and review the steps you need to get paid in full and in a timely fashion.

You have already encountered some of these choices and tasks as an eBay seller. We'll now discuss these topics in greater detail, and reveal how to set up processes and systems so you can run your business like a pro, saving you both time and money—and boosting your profits.

CHAPTER 13

✦ CATEGORY SELECTION ✦

CATEGORY SELECTION IS IMPORTANT for several reasons. While 80 percent or more of eBay buyers find items by *searching*, that still leaves about 20 percent who locate products by *browsing*. Browsers are usually looking for particular kinds of items, so they tend to browse by category, and they're generally impulse buyers (as opposed to searchers, who come to eBay looking to buy something specific). This impulsiveness can prompt unexpected sales or increased bidding activity, which, as we discussed in Week 1, can generate more interest from *all* potential bidders.

With eBay's Refine Search options, buyers who initially search for an item can then select from the list of categories to narrow down their search to a specific category or subcategory. For example, a buyer might search for a *3T jumper dress*, but get so many results that she then narrows them down to the Infant and Toddlers category within Clothing, Shoes & Accessories; then Girls; then 3T. If your item is miscategorized, neither this searching buyer nor a browsing buyer will see it.

Table 13.1 Main eBay Categories

Antiques	Crafts	Pottery & Glass
Art	Dolls & Bears	Real Estate
Baby	DVDs & Movies	Specialty Services
Books	eBay Motors	Sporting Goods
Business & Industrial	Electronics	Sports Memorabilia, Cards & Fan Shop
Cameras & Photo	Entertainment Memorabilia	
Cell Phones & PDAs		Stamps
Clothing, Shoes & Accessories	Gift Certificates	Tickets
	Health & Beauty	Toys & Hobbies
Coins & Paper Money	Home & Garden	Travel
Collectibles	Jewelry & Watches	Video Games
Computers & Networking	Music	Everything Else
	Musical Instruments	

In this chapter, we'll discuss how to drive more traffic to your auction by choosing the most strategic category for your item, as well as when to list in more than one category and how to take advantage of prefilled item information.

THE MANY CATEGORIES OF EBAY

To date, eBay has thirty-four main categories and more than twenty thousand subcategories. Table 13.1 spells out the main eBay categories.

eBay gives you some flexibility in choosing categories, but the item must somehow be related to the category you are selling in. Selecting the optimal category and subcategory (for simplicity's sake, going forward we'll refer to both collectively as *categories*) for your item is important because you want your item to be listed where other similar items can be found. Remember: You are trying to reach browsers, impulse buyers, and searchers who narrow down their categories, so you need to list your goods where all these folks are looking.

Before you list your item, do some research. Search for items on eBay that are similar to yours, and pay attention to which categories they are listed in. Try several different keyword searches and see if you find particularly active categories (those with more than five thousand auctions). Think creatively about your item. For example, maybe the hand-thrown pottery lamp you first thought belonged in Antiques/Decorative Arts is better suited for Home & Garden/Home Décor. (To see which category an item is listed in, just look at the top of the auction listing, as illustrated in Figure 13.1.) Look at the page-view counters and numbers of bids for similar items listed in different categories. Select categories where other sellers are conducting successful auctions.

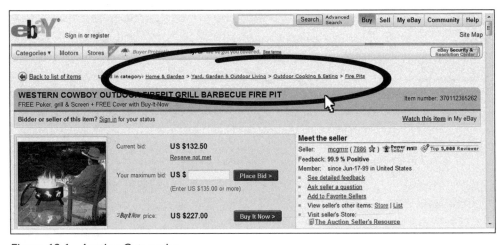

Figure 13.1 Auction Categories

eBay will suggest the most likely categories for your item when you enter the keywords in the category search at the beginning of the Sell Your Item form. It's entirely up to you if you want to use one of these categories or a different one that your research has suggested would be better.

Before listing your item in any category, follow these simple steps: First, browse through all of eBay's categories, and write down which ones you feel are relevant to your product. You should be able to find at least three to five possible fits. Next, write down the number of auctions currently under way in each of those categories (this information will appear next to the category name). If there are less than five thousand auctions under way when you check a category out, you may consider it *inactive*.

I consider categories with over 5,000 auctions to be *popular* and those with over 20,000 to be the *most popular*. Some categories have over 100,000 auctions going at any one time. Using this ranking system, rate the categories you have chosen for your product.

I recommend listing in the most active categories because they get the most traffic. If you put your product in an inactive section of eBay, you may get few or no bids, even if you feature it. Avoid categories with less than one thousand auctions, unless your product is highly specialized to that category. You should also note that if you're selling using a Fixed Price listing, the final value fee varies based on the category, so a lower-priced category is usually a better option (as long as it meets the active test).

LIST IN TWO CATEGORIES

eBay has another feature called List in Two Categories. Listing in a second category is a great way to reach more eyeballs and generate more bids for your item.

For example, an old tray table from China could fit in both Asian Antiques and Antique Furniture. By listing in both locations, you can attract browsers in each category.

Listing in two categories incurs an additional expense, and I only use it for items that I expect to sell for over $50. When you list in two categories, eBay doubles your insertion fee, as well as the fees for most listing upgrades (Bold, Highlight, and so on). Scheduled Listing and Homepage Featured fees are not doubled; similarly, final value fees are unaffected. eBay claims to have research proving that listing in two categories will, on average, increase final values by 17 percent. If you are selling an expensive item, this can be quite profitable. When you select that second category, be sure to select a highly active one with plenty of ongoing auctions. This will get you more bang for the extra buck you are spending.

PRE-FILLED ITEM INFORMATION

For certain categories, such as Books, CDs, DVDs, and Video Games, eBay offers a useful feature called Pre-Filled Item Information. When you list in those categories, the pre-filled information form comes up automatically. Simply enter the title, author, director, artist, ISBN, or UPC code into the form, and this handy tool will automatically fill in your listing with a title, item specifics, a stock photo, and a short description of the item you are selling. You may customize the item information further with additional item details or use a photo of your own.

This feature is a huge time-saver. I once had a large lot of books to sell on consignment for a friend. I was able to open an auction listing for one of the books, type in the ISBN, add a couple of lines about the original cost and the condition of the book, and launch the auction in less than ninety seconds. In fact, using the Pre-Filled Item Information, I was able to launch thirty auctions in about forty-five minutes.

When you use the pre-filled item tool, you must list in the category eBay selects for that item, but you can still select a second category. While this feature may not be a determining factor in selecting a category for your item, it's a potentially valuable tool that you should try to take advantage of as your business grows.

POWER MOVES

❏ Take some time to go through any categories relating to the products you plan to sell. Explore the various subcategory listings, including the number of auctions in each one.

❏ If you are going to sell books, music, or movies, go to the eBay *Help* tab at the top of any eBay page and type in *pre-filled information*. This will bring up a link to an excellent tutorial on how to use this feature.

CHAPTER 14

✦ WRITING AUCTION TITLES ✦ AND DESCRIPTIONS THAT SELL

THE TWO MOST IMPORTANT FACTORS in attracting bidders to your auctions and closing the sale are your *title* and your *item description*. The title is what potential bidders see when they perform a search or browse through the categories. The item description is your sales pitch—a description of what you are selling and why the person reading it should bid on it or buy it. In this chapter, we will look at what constitutes a good title, how to use keywords to win search results, and how to write a benefit-rich auction item description that closes the sale.

YOUR TITLE

The title is the single most important item in your listing. An arresting title has the power to "get the eyeballs" (eBay slang for getting people to view your item). Your title should immediately attract potential buyers to your listing—once you get someone to click on your title, your odds of getting a bid or making a sale go up by about 100 percent.

When a buyer performs a search or clicks on a category, she is presented with a page listing about fifty auction titles (the buyer can select up to two hundred per page). The potential buyer scans the list, looking for something that catches her attention. Making your title stand out in this list is critical to your success.

Viewed this way, a title is nothing more than a collection of words designed to stop your potential buyer's eyes from scanning the page, and instead linger long enough for him to eventually click on your listing. To accomplish this, the title must first contain a keyword that describes the item the buyer is looking for. It should also be compelling, right to the point, and state or imply a benefit to the buyer.

Keywords

The single most important criterion for titles is the use of relevant keywords. According to eBay, over 80 percent of bidders find items on eBay by using the search feature. Therefore, your title should be as precise as possible—yet also contain specific keywords that will make it come up in the greatest number of searches. Look at this title:

JERRY RICE SIGNED FOOTBALL JERSEY FROM 1982 SEASON—NR

This is an excellent title for several reasons. First, it exactly describes what is being offered. Second, it is rich in keywords. It would come up in a search for the following terms:

* *Jerry Rice*
* *Football*
* *Football jersey*
* *Jerry Rice signed*

eBay allows fifty-five characters (including spaces) in an auction title. This one uses fifty-four. (Note that, to remain under this character count, the seller has used the abbreviation *NR* for *no reserve.* See the sidebar on page 127 for a list of abbreviations frequently used in auction titles.) Here is another example of a keyword-rich title:

TRUE RELIGION DESIGNER BLUE JEANS, SIZE MEDIUM M 30
(Fifty-two characters)

A woman searching for designer blue jeans might type in several combinations of keywords such as: *blue jeans, designer blue jeans, True Religion* (a popular brand name), *blue jeans medium, jeans M, blue jeans 30, True Religion jeans M,* and the like. Any of those keyword combinations would bring up this auction in a search. This title also uses fifty-two characters.

Sometimes you need to describe the condition of an item:

STEINBECK SIGNED 1ST EDITION ~ OF MICE AND MEN, MINT

The word *mint* tells the buyer that this book is in perfect, like-new condition— something every book collector searches for.

Notice that I use all caps in my titles. Experience has shown that all-caps titles will generally stand out better in a list of auctions than will those with a combination of upper- and lowercase letters.

Because people are searching for products by keyword, it is extremely important for you to use correct spelling. If you are selling a Staffordshire plate and spell it *Stafordshire*, your auction will not come up when bidders use the eBay search feature to find items.

COMMON ABBREVIATIONS USED IN AUCTION TITLES

In order not to exceed eBay's strict character limit for titles, eBay sellers often use the following well-known abbreviations in their auction titles:

NR	No reserve
NIB	New in box
NWT	New with tags
FS	Free shipping

You can find more abbreviations in the glossary at the end of the book.

Hot Button Words

Years of research by direct marketers have proven that certain words have the power to make people act. If you have room in your title, after including all the relevant keywords, you should try to include *hot button words* in your title. These are words that motivate people and increase interest. Table 14.1 lists some of the best-performing hot button words, according to the Direct Marketing Association.

Table 14.1 Hot Button Words

RARE	NEW	LIGHTLY USED
SECRET	VINTAGE	BEST VALUE
TOP SELLER/SELLING	UNIQUE	UNBELIEVABLE
BEST SELLER/SELLING	SEXY	LOVE
FREE	SUPER DEAL	HARD-TO-FIND
UNUSUAL	AWESOME	BEST ____ ON EBAY
LOOK BETTER	GUARANTEED	RELIABLE

Be reasonable and accurate with your choice of words. Your credibility is on the line. If a title makes a buyer click on your auction and it's immediately obvious that the bidder is being misled, you have just written a check that you can't cash. Potential bidders will just hit the *Back* button on their browser and move on.

Remember that eBay gives you fifty-five characters to get your point across. Use every one of them as if it were a valuable piece of real estate.

ITEM DESCRIPTIONS

Once a person clicks on your auction, you have the opportunity to sell to him—and your description is your best sales pitch. The first goal of your item description is credibility. Your auction description must inspire trust, so forget about making irresponsible, wild claims. If your item descriptions are too far-fetched, overuse adjectives, or make unfounded claims, you will sow doubt in prospective bidders' minds. Although the item description is basically a sales letter, it is important to strike a balance between compelling copy and silly or outrageous claims.

One way to inspire trust is to accurately describe your product, including any shortcomings. If a product has a flaw, mention it. If the product is new, but the box is damaged, be sure to inform prospective buyers about this. If a product is perfect except for a small scratch, tell bidders and show them a photo of the scratch.

Just the Facts, Please

The first part of your description should be no more than an accurate portrayal of the product. Describe what you are offering before you start to sell it. You want to be very specific. Include model number, size, weight, color, and any attachments or accessories—any information that will help bidders understand exactly what they are about to bid on or buy. There should be no confusion about the product.

It is critical that this information be contained in the first paragraph of the description. If bidders have to scroll through the entire page to find out exactly what is included in the auction, you risk having them click away. If there are a lot of specifics, you might use a bullet list to make the information easier to scan.

Know Your Audience

Before you start writing your description, decide who you are writing to. If you are selling baby clothes to stay-at-home moms, your item description will be quite different than if you are selling software to computer users. Look at your niche market and try to picture your customers. What are their likes and dislikes? What are they looking for? How old are they and what sorts of jobs do they generally hold? What are their hobbies and interests? What makes them tick? Do they have plenty of disposable income? Are they seeking quality—or a bargain? The tone of your description should reflect all the facts and benefits you emphasize.

What's the Benefit?

Next I like to talk about the product's benefits. Words mean something. Use their power to convey the benefits readers will enjoy when they buy your item.

To do this, first list all your item's benefits on a sheet of paper. Then arrange them in order of priority (for your target customer), and place this list next to your computer. Now, start describing the first benefit on paper—and move down your list until you've exhausted every benefit of your product. Keep these sheets of paper in the binder by your computer for easy reference.

Be sure to write here about the product's *benefits*—not its *features*. For example, "This barbecue grill has two height settings" is a feature. Compare it to this statement: "This barbecue grill has two height settings, an upper setting to cook slowly so your food doesn't burn and a lower setting to sear your meat instantly for the best taste." The benefits here are *so your food doesn't burn* and *sear your meat instantly for the best taste.*

A successful sales pitch appeals to the base desires and self-interest of the customer. When composing a sales pitch, attention to psychology counts more than attention to writing style. What do people want? They want to be loved or liked. They want to be rich. They want to look better. They want to be successful. They want to feel that they have just scored an incredible bargain. They want to believe they are doing some good in the world. These are the factors that Madison Avenue advertisers consider when conceiving big-budget ad campaigns. However, you don't need all their talent and experience to write great item descriptions. You just have to keep in mind who you are selling to and what stimulates people to buy.

I once bought a wholesale lot of Tommy Hilfiger polo shirts from an overstock dealer. I thought I was getting a mixed lot of shirts. When they arrived, they were all large and extra-large, and all of them were black. I was really annoyed; however, I now owned the shirts and had to make the most of them. I reasoned that men who wore large and extra-large shirts were probably a little thick around the waist. So I wrote an item description that first described what I was selling. In the second paragraph I said:

> *I love these black polo shirts. They have the classic "Tommy" look—rich and elegant, and the black tends to hide my middle age paunch. When I wear my Tommy Hilfiger black polo shirt, my wife says I look thinner.*

Now, I wasn't lying. It is well known by fashion designers that black is slimming. In fact, my wife did say I looked good in the shirt. I got top dollar for the entire lot—several customers bought two or three shirts at a time. (I offered free shipping to anyone who bought two or more.)

Potential buyers want to know what your product will do for them, and do not need a lot of useless distraction. Again, your item description must appeal to the profile of the buyer, display your professionalism, and promote a feeling of trust in you as the seller.

All the romancing you can do with a product is based on the product's real or perceived benefits. If I can't come up with enough benefits, I will often do a Web search for the product to review the advertising that others have done. You don't want to plagiarize the consumer advertising copy, but you can certainly get ideas from it.

White Space and Boldface

I'm constantly frustrated on eBay by auction descriptions that appear in small type and go on and on in one long paragraph. See Figure 14.1 for an example. This is a screenshot from an actual auction. The description is fairly well written, but because it's all run together in one long paragraph, it is somewhat hard to read. Breaking the description into three paragraphs with white space separating them would dramatically improve this description's readability.

Description

This LUCY COLA CLUB SODA SIGN is GUARANTEED 100% ORIGINAL and very OLD. Circa 1940's. This is a **VERY RARE** and outstanding **Early soda fountain/country store sign**. Sign is in **Near Mint Condition**. This Sign was **NEVER USED** as seen by no holes were ever punched for mounting. This is a "tacker" sign which means the first time it was mounted the sign had to be "tacked" in placed by driving a tack and creating the holes. Sign is made of Painted Metal. This sign has outstanding Artwork with highly detailed graphics. The Colors are Excellent as from day one. This sign has light wear only due to its age but the sign still displays great in an outstanding way. Excellent size for easy display. Measures 27" X 10". Please add $17.75 Shipping and Insurance. Please read payment instructions Before you bid. Please do NOT ask me to end this auction early. I will ship within the USA Only. Thanks for your bids.

Figure 14.1   Sample Auction Description

People tend to scan a Web page looking for something that grabs their attention. Instead of one long paragraph, I recommend using a series of short paragraphs of three or four sentences each. Make lists, use bullets, and highlight important information with boldface type. (Just don't overdo it. If every other word is in bold or all caps, you lose the impact.)

By using short paragraphs and lists, you create *white space* in your auction. This makes it easier for people to scan the page to find the information they want.

The other major auction killer is *reverse* or *drop-out* type. This refers to featuring white or light-colored type against a dark background. It may look artistic, but it can be difficult to read. If you are selling anything to people over forty-five, this factor is very important. As people age, their eyes require more light and greater contrast to see well. An older person will have a difficult time reading yellow type on a black background.

Type size is another factor. If you are selling body jewelry to teens, they probably won't have difficulty reading eBay's small, default type size. But if you are selling products that older customers might want to buy, remember that many people over forty need bifocals, or reading glasses, to read. Therefore, a larger type size may be more effective. To increase the type size in your auctions, in the Sell Your Item form, select the larger type size in the HTML editor.

Increase Bids with a Call to Action

Salespeople have an old saying: "If you want to make the sale, you have to ask for the order." I have worked in sales and sales management, and I can tell you that that statement is 1,000 percent correct. I cannot tell you how many times I have seen a salesperson go through a perfect product presentation and then conclude with a weak statement, such as "Well, what do you think?" You don't want to take the time to write a terrific auction description, only to water it down with an ineffective final statement. Instead, ask for the sale: "Don't be knocked out by a sniper. Place your best bid now so you can enjoy a sizzling steak on your new barbecue this weekend."

I always end my auctions by asking for the bid. This is known as a *call to action*. Think of all the direct marketing pieces you've received in the mail over the years. Didn't all of them end with something like this: "Don't let this once-in-a-lifetime opportunity pass you by. Call now!" You need to end your auction with a similar punch.

THREE QUICK WAYS TO DISCOURAGE BIDDERS

There are three common errors that eBay sellers make, all of which discourage bidders:

1. They use short, incomplete descriptions.
2. They overindulge in large, colorful type or too many colors of type.
3. They write payment, shipping, and return policies that sound like jailhouse rules.

At least once or twice a day I will surf eBay and come across an auction that includes a statement like this: "If you don't pay right away I will report you to eBay and give you negative feedback." Who would want to do business with this kind of seller?

Last is the drill sergeant mentality. This refers to people who spell out their shipping, payment, and return policies in harsh language, often in all caps. Here is one I saw recently:

> *I SHIP ON TUESDAYS AND THURSDAYS SO GET YOUR PAYMENT IN BY THOSE DAYS OR WAIT UNTIL THE FOLLOWING WEEK. I ACCEPT PAYPAL. DO NOT SEND A CHECK. IF YOU DO I WILL THROW IT AWAY AND RELIST THE ITEM.*

It is important to spell out your payment, shipping, and return policies. However, the policies should be realistic, and they should be written in friendly language that *explains* rather than *dictates* your policies.

Here is another example from an actual auction. This seller had a feedback rating of just over 50 percent with twelve negative comments (no wonder):

> *I ship everything by Priority Mail on Monday and Friday. I charge the Priority Mail rate plus $2.00 to pay for box and packing material. I don't guarantee anything. If you want insurance the extra cost is $5.00. I know it doesn't cost that much to insure a package but I have to wait in line and fill out forms at the post office and keep the forms until a claim is made and that is a big pain but I will do it for $5.00.*

This seller is doing everything he can to tell me he doesn't want my business. If the tone of his e-mails to customers is anything like his policy statement, it is no wonder he has poor feedback. If someone pays on a Monday night, he won't ship until Friday and the parcel likely won't arrive until the following Tuesday or Wednesday. The whole point of paying for Priority Mail is to get something quickly.

By contrast, the following is an auction description we use to sell a line of expensive decorative fire pits. Others are selling similar items for much less, yet we tend to outsell our competition. Notice how we appeal to the prospective bidder's desire for quality and how we communicate the product's benefits. Also note the use of white space, the call to action, and the inclusion of shipping and payment details.

> *YOU ARE BIDDING ON THE WORLD'S BEST SOLID-STEEL, HAND FORGED, FIRE PIT AND GRILL*
>
> *Perfect for barbecues, gatherings, camping, or a quiet evening at home. Our fire pits are handcrafted from durable cold-rolled steel and **include a FREE BBQ grill, a poker for stirring coals, and a spark-arresting screen** to let the fire die down safely.*
>
> *Unique flame cutout Santa Fe–style designs provide ventilation and add to its unique charm. Creating the perfect complement to your backyard couldn't be easier. Natural rust patina finish, no assembly required. Made by hand. This is not a mass-produced product.*
>
> *These fire pits are normally only sold in high-end mail order catalogs and expensive gift shops out West. **The normal retail price is $399.** We are starting the bidding at $1. I have placed a reserve at my cost.*

Limited time offer: If you buy this fire pit from my eBay Store or at the Buy It Now price, I will give you a FREE $29-value custom cover.

You can click on the group photo to see the other designs available from our other auctions and eBay Store.

The fire pit is 31" x 31" x 17" and weighs 51 lbs. Just think how good steaks would taste cooked on this grill, grilled over some real mesquite wood.

It is not just a fire pit—it comes with a free removable grill top so you can cook steaks, burgers, hot dogs, and more on it.

THIS IS THE BEST FIRE PIT I HAVE EVER OWNED.

I have owned several fire pits of different designs and have always been disappointed. When I found this fire pit, I bought one for myself. The very first evening we had friends over, I sold two of them on the spot.

This is absolutely the best fire pit on the market—bar none. The top cover is a very fine mesh so large sparks don't fly out and burn your clothes. THE CUTOUTS IN THE SIDE PROVIDE PERFECT UPWARD VENTILATION. The smoke really goes UP. It doesn't blow around sideways, so you can sit close to it and get all the warmth without being bothered by smoke and sparks.

Also, if you live in an area where open fires are banned, you can still use this model, because it qualifies as a COVERED GRILL.

We also have this model and other designs in our eBay Store for immediate purchase. The other themes include Chinese, Grapevines, Bear & Moose, Santa Fe, Kokopelli Indian, Western Broncos (in photo w/cowboy) and Moon & Stars.

*Shipping and handling is $55. I am sorry but we **cannot ship to Alaska, Hawaii, or Canada.** Please Note: We do not stock these because of the size and weight. They are drop-shipped directly from the forge. Shipping can take as long as 5–7 days to the East Coast. Sorry but we cannot ship this item overseas. Insurance is $4.90 and is REQUIRED.*

Don't lose out to a sniper. Place your best bid now. Or, buy it from our Store and get a free $29 cover. I am going to go out on a limb and offer a money-back guarantee on the cost of the pit and the outbound shipping. Keep it for 30 days and use it for a few fires. If you are not completely satisfied, send it back (at your expense) and I will refund all of your money, including the $55 shipping cost. Your only risk is the *return shipping cost. I know you will love this grill and I don't really expect to get any back, but I will stand behind my guarantee if I do.*

This transaction is insured against fraud. Please note the buySAFE Seal on this page. This means that every auction is insured against fraud by buySAFE and by a $25,000 bond from the Liberty Mutual Insurance Company. Please click on the buySAFE Seal to get more information.

We have an excellent feedback rating and strive to keep it that way. Your complete satisfaction is our first priority. Please visit our About Me Page to learn more about our company and our feedback, and to see our other auctions.

Thank you for looking.

After reading all this, you may worry that writing successful auction descriptions is difficult or a lot of work. It's not, once you get the hang of it. Take your time crafting effective auction descriptions as you are getting started, and after a while you will find that it becomes second nature.

POWER MOVES

TITLES:

❏ Sit down with a notebook and a pen, and write out as many keywords as you can think of for your product.

❏ Now do a search on eBay for those keywords. Write down the titles that appeal to you. Open those auctions and look at the corresponding hit counters. Determine which titles appear to get the most hits.

❏ Using the above information as a guide, begin creating your own attention-grabbing titles.

DESCRIPTIONS:

❏ In your binder, list every benefit of your product. Now write a sentence about each benefit and how it relates to a buyer.

❏ Once you have done this, list your item for sale. In the description field, first include all the facts about the product that you are selling. Fill in the rest of the description with the benefit statements you created.

CHAPTER 15

✦ MASTERING AUCTION ✦ PHOTOGRAPHY

AS AN EBAY SELLER, you need to take sharp, attractive photographs. Photography is one of those skills that can take years to learn well. Fortunately, digital cameras—with all their automated features—have made this task much simpler. In this chapter, we will look at the equipment and software you will need to take digital photographs and upload them to your auctions. We'll also discuss powerful techniques for taking photographs that sell, and the most efficient ways to host and upload your pictures.

DIGITAL CAMERA SELECTION

Your first task is to select a good digital camera with all the features you will need. There are hundreds of digital cameras on the market, and new models are coming out every week. The trend today is toward higher and higher image quality. This is expressed in the number of pixels or megapixels a camera can resolve. In general, the higher this number (or the greater the resolution), the more expensive the camera.

Luckily, you do not need extremely high resolution for your auction photography. In fact, high-resolution photos are undesirable because they take a long time to download when someone opens an auction.

eBay recommends limiting photo file sizes to 300–600 KB. This is usually the 1024 × 768 setting on the camera, which is relatively low resolution. So this is one of the first features you should look for when buying a camera—make sure it has a low-resolution setting. (Most digital cameras include this feature, so it should be relatively easy to find one you like with this option.) If you are selling a product where detail is important, then you will want to shoot at a higher resolution, at least one or two megapixels, and crop or resize the photo with software such as Adobe Photoshop to get the file size down. Shooting at this higher resolution will preserve the detail when you crop or resize. You don't want to have too low a resolution setting because you can lose detail in supersize views. For items that are not well known (clothing, collectibles, etc.) details are important. Also, try to do all your editing at once. Multiple saves in jpeg format (the required format for eBay Picture Services) compress the quality, so the fewer intermediate saves the better.

Here are some of the features you will need in a camera used for auction photography:

* **TRIPOD:** Almost all cameras include a standard tripod screw mount at the bottom. It is very important to use a tripod when taking auction photographs to avoid the blurred images that occur when you hold a camera by hand.

* **MACRO SETTING:** *Macro* is the photographic term for the ability to focus very close to an object. Typically the macro feature will allow you to focus as close as three or four inches (8 or 10cm) from the subject. This is important for photographing small objects or showing details, such as the original manufacturer's price tag or a maker's mark on pottery or silver.

* **WHITE BALANCE ADJUSTMENT:** We will talk about white balance in detail shortly. Basically, this is how you adjust a camera to account for the different "color temperatures" of light. (The color reflected from an object will vary subtly, depending on the type of lighting.) Almost all cameras have an automatic white balance adjustment feature, but you want to make sure you get one that allows you to manually choose between daylight, fluorescent, halogen, and incandescent settings.

* **MANUAL FOCUS:** The ability to manually focus on an object or part of an object is very important, because oftentimes the autofocus feature will not provide the exact image quality you are looking for.

* **EXPOSURE ADJUSTMENT:** The light meter in a camera can be fooled by bright backgrounds. Since you'll often be shooting against a white background, especially when using a light tent (see page 138 for more about this), you need a camera that allows you to adjust the exposure. This is referred to as "exposure compensation" in most camera manuals.

* **OPTICAL ZOOM:** Digital cameras come with optical zoom and/or digital zoom. Digital zoom is restrictive and difficult to work with; therefore, make sure your camera has a basic optical zoom feature. You can tell if it does by pushing the *Zoom* button and seeing if the lens actually moves in and out. If not, the camera is using digital zoom.

* **APERTURE PRIORITY SETTING:** The ability to select a small lens opening (aperture) allows you to achieve what is called depth of field. This means that objects close to you and far away will both be in focus.

Nikon, Sony, and Canon all make fairly low-cost cameras that fit these criteria. Since models change so rapidly, I'm not going to recommend any specific one. Just make sure to look for the features I've specified.

TAKING PHOTOGRAPHS THAT SELL

A complete course on digital photography is a subject for another book. Instead, I have organized the most important information as a series of tips. If you want to learn more about digital photography, there are several books on the market that run the gamut from beginner to advanced. For a handy, basic book aimed at the auction photographer, check out *Online Auction Photo Secrets*, available through my Web site (www.skipmcgrath.com).

Use a Tripod

Unless you are shooting outdoors or using a flash, digital cameras tend to use a very slow shutter speed. With a slow shutter speed, typically under 1/125th of a second, most people cannot hold a camera steady enough to prevent blurring. Using a sturdy tripod will allow you to shoot all the way down to 1/30th of a second with good results. Make sure your tripod has an adjustable head that will rotate the camera both horizontally and vertically. A quality tripod can cost as much as $100, but I have found that most large photo stores often have good—even professional-quality—secondhand tripods for as little as $20–$30.

Focus Carefully and Correctly

I see out-of-focus pictures on eBay every day. One reason for this is autofocus malfunction. Most digital cameras project a laser or infrared beam onto the object being photographed and measure the reflection to determine the focus. Problems may occur when large objects allow the beam to spread out, or when something reflective on the object itself "fools" the autofocus feature.

The other issue is depth of field. Have you ever looked at a photograph where the subject is in focus and the background is all fuzzy? Depth of field is the focal distance, from near to far, in which a camera can focus. The aperture, or lens opening, on a camera adjusts to allow more or less light into the camera. When the lens opening is large, the camera has a very narrow range of focus. When the opening is small, the focal length is longer. This effect is magnified when you are shooting very close up, such as when you are photographing small objects.

The aperture can be set manually on most of the digital cameras listed earlier, and on many others. Lens openings are marked as a series of numbers that range from 3.5 to 16. The higher the number, the greater the depth of field you will have. This is critical when shooting up close with the macro function, because the macro function also limits the depth of field (for technical reasons I won't get into here). If I am shooting an object close up, I typically use an aperture of 8 or higher. With automatic digital cameras, when you set the aperture at a high number, the camera compensates for the reduction in light by slowing down the shutter speed. This is why you need a tripod. If you try to handhold a camera at a slow shutter speed, you will almost always get a blurry photo.

Finally, using your camera's Aperture Priority mode to narrow the lens opening can improve the performance of your autofocus, if you are using that feature, by improving your depth of field.

Use Soft Lighting

Sunlight or direct light from a bulb or a flash may create hot spots and reflections in your photos. If you are shooting outside, you should shoot in bright shade or on a cloudy day. If you have a north-facing window, this can often produce very nice, diffused light. If you are using lights, you can either purchase white plastic light covers to diffuse the light or use a light tent like the EZ Cube pictured in Figure 15.1.

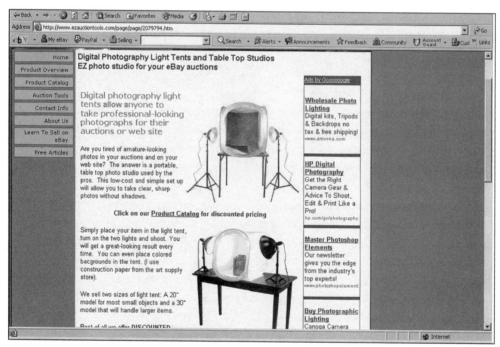

Figure 15.1   EZ Cube Light Tent

The EZ Cube is widely used by eBay sellers. It makes taking great photographs easy. You simply place an object inside the light tent, shine the lights, and shoot. This eliminates glare and reflection from shiny objects. Place colored paper or cloth in the background to create different effects. You can purchase EZ Cube light tents at a discount at www.EZAuctionTools.com. They start at around $75 and go up to just over $100 for the tents and $175 to $300 for the complete sets with lights.

Avoid Clutter

Try to photograph only the object you are shooting. Placing an object on a table with other stuff in the background will distract from your subject. If you use a system like the EZ Cube, this should be easy. However, you will sometimes have to photograph large objects that do not fit in the cube. In this case, be sure to clean up the background as much as possible. If you are shooting a computer, for example, remove everything from the desk it's on and hide the wires or any other distracting objects. If you are shooting a car, drive the car to a park where you can shoot it with grass and trees in the background, instead of in your garage or driveway.

If you are shooting apparel, you should invest in a dress form or mannequin. Place the mannequin against a wall draped with cloth to contrast the color and diffuse any shadows.

Avoid Underexposure

If you are shooting against a white or bright background, or shooting outside in bright light, your camera's automatic light meter may "read" the surrounding light instead of your object, underexposing the image. Most good digital cameras include an over/underexposure compensation adjustment feature. If you are shooting against a white background, such as in an EZ Cube light tent, try adjusting your camera's exposure setting to +1 or even +1.5. This will prevent the subject of your picture from appearing too dark, as your camera adjusts to the white background (a case of underexposure). One way you can tell whether you are underexposing your pictures is if white backgrounds appear gray in the photographs. If this happens, or if your objects are just too dark, then try adjusting the exposure compensation until the white looks truly white.

Use the Correct White Balance

Different types of light have different wavelengths. Without getting into a discussion of optical physics, this means that you have to adjust your camera for the type of light you are using. If your camera is set on *daylight* and you shoot with an ordinary household lightbulb, your photos will appear yellow. If you shoot with a fluorescent light, your photos will appear blue gray. You can purchase daylight bulbs—ordinary lightbulbs with the same wavelength as daylight—from almost any grocery or hardware store. They are even available in the modern compact-fluorescent bulbs that do not get hot like regular incandescent bulbs, and last a lot longer. All the digital cameras mentioned above have a white balance setting. If you are using halogen, indoor lightbulbs, or fluorescent lights, just set your camera for the type of light you are using.

Get Close

Getting close to your subject will produce a better photo. It is easier to focus accurately when you are close, and you'll capture more of the object without the distracting clutter.

The best way to learn to take good photos is to practice. Read your camera's instruction manual from cover to cover, and experiment with all the controls and functions until you are comfortable with them. Fortunately, with digital cameras you don't have to spend a fortune on film and developing to learn how best to use your camera.

BIZ BUILDER

When shooting a colorful item, try placing a piece of colored cloth or craft paper behind the object. Pick a color that matches one of the minor colors—not the main color. For example, if you were shooting a blue teapot with a gray or yellow trim, you would use a gray or yellow background paper. This is a trick used by professional photographers that will give your photo an image of greater depth and allow the main color to "pop" in the photograph.

MANAGING YOUR PHOTOS

Image management is the term used by eBay sellers for editing, storing, and uploading photos.

Editing Software

Most digital cameras come with photo editing software. I happen to like Nikon's the best. You can set it so whenever you plug your camera into the computer, the program automatically opens and you can import your photos with one click. If you own an Apple computer, you are lucky. All Macs come with iPhoto, which is one of the best all-around photo editing and management programs on the market. The Microsoft Office Suite comes with Microsoft Office Picture Manager. This is similar in features to iPhoto and is very easy to use. Since most PC users also have Office, this doesn't cost you anything extra.

There are also a number of software programs you can buy to perform these functions. There are some very advanced (and expensive) programs available, such as Adobe Photoshop; however, there are functional (and less expensive) programs available as well. If you go to www.shareware.com or www.tucows.com, you'll find a number of free image and photo management programs you can download (just type *photo editing* into the search box). One of the best is Serif Photo Plus. The download is free;

the company makes money selling the support and training tools, which cost far less than most expensive programs and are excellent.

Whichever program you use, you should be able to easily plug your camera into your computer, import the photos, give them file names so you can organize them, and then edit and crop the images. Most software programs allow you to adjust the brightness and contrast of your photographs. This is a real time-saver because you don't have to reshoot your product.

Storing and Uploading Your Images

Once you have your photos edited and named, you need to create a folder on your hard drive called *Auction Photos* (or something similar). Within this folder, you should create subfolders for the various product categories you are selling. Simply file your photos in the appropriate folders, so you can easily find them when you are ready to upload them to your auctions.

Once you have your photographs stored on your hard drive, you need to import them into your auctions. eBay offers two ways to manage your images. You can insert images one at a time from your computer's hard drive as you launch auctions. The first photo is free and each additional image costs $0.15. So, if you use four photos in an auction, you're spending $0.45 (on top of eBay's other fees), whether the item sells or not. This is obviously too expensive if you are running dozens of auctions a week. eBay also offers a subscription hosting program based on the amount of storage space you require (a function of the number and size of photos you host). The service starts at $9.95 a month for 50 MB, and increases to $14.95 a month for 250 MB and $19.95 a month for 1 GB. The basic plan (50 MB) will allow you to store over 500 average-size images. This service is also expensive, although eBay does give you free editing software when you subscribe to the service (you also get a discounted rate if you have a Premium eBay Store, and you get 1 GB free if you are an Anchor Store subscriber).

Another way to host your photos is with a Web site. If you already have a Web site, you can simply upload your photos to your site, labeling each one with a separate URL (Uniform Resource Locator, or the "address" of the photo), and then insert the URL of the specific photo into each auction. I don't recommend this option. Not only is it is time-consuming, but you also have to pay for the Web space and you need FTP (file transfer protocol) software to upload your photos.

Managing Photos with Auction Management Services

In chapter 23, we are going to cover auction management services. A good free one to start with is Auctiva.com. Other popular services are Vendio and InkFrog (www1.inkfrog.com). All these companies will host your images as part of their service. The money you'll save by forgoing eBay's hosting service will easily pay for all or most of an auction management service's monthly fee. In addition to photo hosting, you'll get numerous features so you can automate your auctions as well. In my opinion, this is the best option if you plan to launch fifteen or more auctions a week.

Here's how it works: You simply upload your images to the Web site of the auction management service, where they are subsequently stored (you can also organize them into folders). When choosing an image for your auction, simply double-click or check the appropriate photo. The auction management service inserts the URL of the particular image into your auction. When the auction launches, eBay looks for those images at the named URL, and they are displayed in your auction every time someone clicks on it. Make sure you select a Gallery image so the URL is fed constantly to eBay. This means the image is always visible on the Search Results and Category pages.

Once you start using an auction management service, you will appreciate the speed—and therefore the time-saving aspects—of hosting your photos this way. You will also enjoy the additional benefits, such as templates, automated customer e-mails, shipping calculators, and inventory management tools, that come with the service— usually for what you would be paying eBay to host photos individually.

POWER MOVES

❏ After selecting the camera you are going to use for your auction photography, spend some time familiarizing yourself with the instruction manual. Pay special attention to the size settings, white balance, macro (close-up) feature, manual focus, and aperture priority settings.

❏ Once you understand how all the features work, take some practice shots. Upload them to your computer and use whatever imaging software you have to crop, rotate, and resize the photos.

❏ Don't forget to use a tripod. This is very important.

❏ Compare the costs and benefits of importing your photographs into your auctions using:

> eBay's Picture Services (Basic or Enhanced) to individually upload images

> eBay's subscription hosting program, called Picture Manager

> A third-party auction management service

CHAPTER 16

✦ PROMOTING YOUR AUCTIONS ✦

EBAY OFFERS SEVERAL OPTIONAL features to help you drive potential buyers to your auctions. While a few of them are free, most come with a fee. The key to using these features effectively is to make sure they are appropriate to the type and value of the auction you are running, and that the cost provides a good return on investment (ROI).

Now that you have enhanced your listings with photographs, descriptions, and titles that sell, the next step is to attract more buyers to your listings. In this chapter we will explore how to take advantage of various free promotional tools and evaluate the performance and ROI of those that are fee-based.

FREE PROMOTIONAL TOOLS

Obviously, free tools provide the best ROI. A free opportunity worth exploring is promoting your auction on eBay's homepage. eBay's homepage is the third most visited page on the Internet, receiving over 5 million hits a day. eBay creates several boxes on the homepage dedicated to promoting your auctions. If you look at Figure 16.1, a screenshot of the eBay homepage, you will see a seasonal promotional box, called Hot for Holiday. This box lists gift items below a certain price (in this case 30 percent off retail). You can't see it here, but all of the items in this promotion also offer free shipping.

Figure 16.1   eBay Homepage Insider Deals Winter Holiday Promotion

Keep an eye on the homepage. If you have inventory that matches (that is not already listed), list it as soon as possible following the promotion terms (in this case they are item- and price-specific, with free shipping) so that you can take advantage of the free advertising.

In the summer season, eBay often runs a $1 no-reserve promotion for summer-related items. When the promotion begins, eBay's search engine will seek out auctions in the listed categories that start at $1. When someone clicks on the box on the eBay home-page, your auctions will come up. This is a powerful promotion. Every summer my wife and I sell barbecue grills. My grill auctions normally receive about four hundred hits each over a seven-day period. During one week, when my auctions were linked to the eBay home-page, I averaged over fifteen hundred hits per auction, and my bids and final values rose significantly. One barbecue that usually goes for between $225 and $240 sold for $292!

Other free promotions offered by eBay include free listing days, where you may list as many auctions as you like with no listing fees. You can learn about these and other opportunities on the General Announcements page, accessible from the bottom of any eBay page. All announcements from the past two weeks are posted in chrono-logical order, with the most recent ones at the top. You should check this list first thing every morning, since free listings and listing discounts are always offered on very short notice—usually one day or less.

In addition to free listing days, eBay occasionally offers free Bold and Highlight features, and one-penny or free listing days. And, as we discussed in chapter 14, it costs nothing to create keyword-rich titles for your auctions. Remember: Over 80 percent of eBay bidders find items by searching. The more searchable keywords your titles contain, the more often your auctions will be viewed.

EBAY PAID PROMOTIONS

eBay offers you various listing upgrades, each for an additional fee. Let's take a look at each one. Fixed Price listings that run for the same length as auctions (three, five, seven, or ten days) have the same listing upgrade fees as auctions (in most cases). However, listing upgrade fees for thirty-day and Good 'Til Canceled Fixed Price listings are more expensive. The first number in the parentheses below is the fee for auction-style listings and Fixed Price listings running for three, five, seven, or ten days. The second number is the price for thirty-day Fixed Price listings.

Subtitle (Fee: $0.50, $1.50)

A subtitle is just that, a second title that appears in slightly smaller print just below your auction title on the eBay Search Results page. A subtitle can provide descriptive information about your item that buyers will see when browsing through categories or viewing Search Results. (Words included in the subtitle do not come up when buyers perform a basic search.) Subtitles are limited to sixty-five characters—ten more than the auction title. Because of the cost ($0.50), it's only advisable to use a subtitle for items whose profit margin you expect to easily cover the added expense. For example, if you were selling a product with a projected profit margin of less than $5.00, the subtitle would represent 10 percent or more of your profits. If you anticipate that the cost of the subtitle will come to more than 10 percent of your profit margin, the feature may not be worth its cost.

A subtitle allows you to spotlight features or benefits that may not fit in the title field, but would be of interest to potential buyers viewing a list of items. It may contain additional information about what you are selling, such as accessories included, outstanding benefits, special offers, and so on. I find that subtitles make your listing stand out somewhat from the other listings around it. In fact, according to eBay, listings using a subtitle are 18 percent more likely to sell. Here is an example of how I use a subtitle:

COWBOY STYLE, SOLID STEEL FIRE PIT & BARBECUE—NR
Free poker, grill & spark arrestor. Free Shipping with Buy It Now

Bold (Fee: $2.00, $4.00)

This feature presents your auction title in boldface type, making it stand out from other listings. This is one of my favorite options because it's a proven producer. eBay's own research has shown this feature to increase final values by an average of 21 percent. At a cost of $2, as long as you are listing an item that will sell for over $25 this is the single best promotional tool in terms of ROI. I use the Bold option in almost all my auctions.

Highlight (Fee: $5.00, $10.00)

Highlight is similar to Bold, in that it makes your auctions stand out. When you select this option, it places your auction title within a colored highlight band. Highlight costs $5. However, if you use Highlight without Bold, it can be somewhat difficult for the bidder to read your title. So, in effect, this option costs $7 when you add the Bold feature.

I am not a big fan of Highlight. eBay hasn't announced any research statistics on this feature, which suggests that it probably doesn't work that well. At $5, I would tend not to use it unless I were selling an item that I expected to reach at least $100 and that had a high conversion rate.

Border (Fee: $4.00, $8.00)

Border is like Highlight in that it makes your listing stand out. It places a colored border around your entire title and thumbnail picture. I usually see Border used in conjunction with Highlight, although it can be used without. At $4.00, it is quite pricey, so I wouldn't use it for a low-priced item.

Gallery Plus (Fee: $0.35, $1.00)

The small thumbnail photo next to your auction title on the Search Results and Browse pages is your Gallery photo, and this is free. For an extra $0.35 you can get an *Enlarge* tag below the thumbnail, which shows buyers that they can enlarge your photograph to 400 × 400 pixels (the thumbnail is ordinarily 96 pixels) by placing the mouse pointer over the image. This is not really a necessary option unless the thumbnail doesn't adequately show off the features of the item you're selling. For example, if you're selling a set of items together, the Gallery Plus feature may increase the chances of the buyer clicking through to your auction.

Featured Plus (Fee: $9.95–$19.95, $14.95–$39.95)

Whenever an eBay user performs a search or browses through a category, the first thing he sees is a list of items featured in that category. This is the function of the Featured Plus tool. This is a high-performing option; unfortunately, it's also a bit pricey. Your item displays in the Featured section of the Search Results page it naturally falls on. So if the buyer is using the *Time: ending soonest* sort order, your item will likely appear on the first page of the Search Results only during the last day, or even hours, of the auction (depending on how many other items matched the search term).

The fee is a scale based on the starting price of your listing, as seen in Table 16.1.

Table 16.1 Featured Plus Fees

Auction Starting Price	Fee
$0.01–$24.99	$9.95
$25.00–$199.99	$14.95
Over $200.00	$19.95

For Fixed Price listings, the fee is $14.95 for three-, five-, seven-, or ten-day listings, and $39.95 for thirty-day listings.

I only use this tool for high-priced items, to make sure they get the visibility they need. The performance of this tool is impressive—eBay reports that Featured Plus items are 28 percent more likely to sell and have an average 12 percent higher final value.

Homepage Featured (Fee: $59.95, $179.95)

The Homepage Featured auction is eBay's most expensive promotional tool, costing $59.95 for auctions and $179.95 for Fixed Price listings. Homepage Featured listings may rotate onto the eBay homepage; however, eBay does not guarantee when or if this will happen, and the box for Homepage Featured items is near the bottom of the page, far less visible to buyers arriving at the homepage. While Homepage Featured is a bit of a crapshoot, it does work most of the time.

I once had an auction ending on a Thursday night for a pair of antique silver candlesticks. The listing rotated onto the homepage about one hour before the auction ended. My auction received over five hundred hits in that last hour, and the candlesticks sold for almost double what I was expecting.

Featured First (Fee: $24.95, $74.95)

Like Homepage Featured, Featured First gives you the chance of being rotated into a prominent featured position, in this case into the Featured section on the first page of Search Results. There is no guarantee this will happen, but if it does, you'll likely get earlier bids and more watchers for your auction. I think Featured First is probably a better deal than Homepage Featured because it's cheaper, and it gets you in front of people specifically looking for your item.

For multiple-quantity items, this can be a great way to make that first sale. You get better promotion in the Best Match sort order if you already have a sale, so this can boost your promotion twofold. You also get free Gallery Plus included in the fee for Featured First.

If you have a Fixed Price listing, you can add Featured First for just seven days if you prefer (and pay the lower price) or have it run for the full thirty-day duration.

Featured First is only available to sellers who are at Standard or Elevated promotion in Best Match (you can find this by looking at your Seller Dashboard in My eBay).

Pro Pack (Fee: $29.95–$39.95, $34.95–$99.95)

Pro Pack is a combination of other features for a discounted price. It includes Bold, Border, Highlight, Featured First, and Featured Plus.

Because so many of these features now have scaled fees, you need to compare the cost of the individual features you were going to buy against the additional cost for the Pro Pack. For example, if you're selling an item at auction with a starting price of $24.99, and planned to use Featured First anyway, the Pro Pack may be a better option, since it's only $5.00 more and you get a lot more features. Still, keep an eye on your fees and projected profit. Don't let your fees overtake your profits.

Pro Pack is only available to sellers who have a feedback score of 10 or more.

Value Pack (Fee: $0.65, $2.00)

Like Pro Pack, Value Pack is a combination of other features. It includes Gallery Plus, Listing Designer, and Subtitle. We mentioned Listing Designer in Week 1. It costs $0.10 for auctions and $0.30 for thirty-day Fixed Price listings. If you were to buy all three features separately, your total would be $0.95 for auctions and $2.80 for thirty-day Fixed Price listings. So, if you're planning to use all of them anyway, this is a better deal, but if you're not planning to use them all, you could end up paying more than you planned.

Ten-Day Duration (Fee: $0.40)

I always use this option if I am paying for any of the other features (except just Bold), because I want to extend the life of the auction to amortize the cost of the other upgrades, such as Homepage Featured or Featured Plus, over a longer period.

International Site Visibility (Fee: $0.10–$0.40, $0.25–$2.00)

If you are specifically marketing to an international audience, paying for International Site Visibility is probably worth the cost. This will place your auction in the main Search Results for searches on international eBay sites (such as eBay.ca, eBay.co.uk, eBay.au, etc.). The fees are tiered, based on the starting price, as seen in Table 16.2.

Table 16.2 International Site Visibility Fees

Starting Price	Auction Fee	30-Day Fixed Price Listing Fee
$0.01–$9.99	$0.10	$0.25
$10.00–$49.99	$0.20	$0.50
$50.00 and up	$0.40	$1.00

This feature replaces the need to list the item on a particular international eBay Web site as well as on eBay.com, which would cost far more, and allows you to promote a one-time (unique) item to both international and domestic buyers.

Despite what eBay says about the performance of its various promotional tools, you should test each one yourself on your own auctions. eBay's numbers are averages over all types of products in all price ranges. You need to see what works for you and your product(s).

Set up a spreadsheet that lists your auction items and which, if any, promotional features you used. Now, create columns for hits, bids, final values, total fees, and net profits. Try running auctions with various combinations of options in order to gather a variety of data. Be sure to use similar ending times. If you compare an auction ending on Sunday evening with one ending on Friday evening, your results will be skewed due to the lower bidding activity on a Friday evening and not necessarily because of the optional feature you select.

Once you have a couple of weeks' worth of data, you will be able to determine the optimal combination for your particular product(s). Keep this spreadsheet in your reference binder so that you may access it when you are considering using these features.

There is a handy free eBay fee calculator by eBayCalc available at http://ecal.altervista.org/en/fee_calculator. You simply type in your price, optional feature fees, and shipping amounts and it precalculates your eBay and PayPal fees.

POWER MOVES

❏ Visit the eBay fees page at http://pages.ebay.com/help/sell/fees.html. Expand the listing to show all the fees and print out a copy. Having this information at the ready when you are deciding on which promotional items to use will save you time and help you make better decisions. eBay changes its fees and often offers special fee promotions, so you should bookmark the eBay fees page for easy reference.

❏ Create a spreadsheet for performance testing. After every auction, record the options used, the number of hits and bids the auction received, and the final outcome—no sale or the final value. Use this information to assess the performance of your auctions with and without various upgrade combinations.

✦ SHIPPING, HANDLING, AND INSURANCE ✦

POOR SHIPPING PRACTICES are a leading cause of negative feedback on eBay, and are specifically addressed by two of the Detailed Seller Ratings. eBay buyers have come to expect that they will receive their purchases intact and professionally packaged. What you charge buyers for shipping is also important, because that influences their expectations and feedback. Therefore, your challenge as a seller is to provide quality packaging and shipping at a low enough cost that it will be attractive to buyers.

In this chapter, we'll discuss the advantages of the various shipping carriers; ways to save on shipping costs, supplies, and insurance; and how to automate the process and set up a convenient and efficient shipping station.

SHIPPING WITH THE U.S. POSTAL SERVICE (USPS)

More and more eBay sellers are using Priority Mail to ship their items. For items that weigh less than six pounds (3kg), Priority Mail is competitive with UPS. (For heavier items, sellers don't seem to mind the extra charge of UPS, because they get their items much faster.)

USPS provides free boxes, envelopes, and labels for Priority Mail. When you add on the cost of shipping materials, Priority Mail is not that much more expensive than regular first-class mail—and it's a lot cheaper than UPS for small packages, where you have to provide your own boxes. Even purchased in large quantities, twelve-by-twelve-by-twelve-inch (30 x 30 x 30cm) boxes can cost as much as $0.90 each. When you buy them in small quantities, they can cost as much as $1.50 each.

Priority Mail offers both a simple flat-rate option, as well as the by-weight, zoned system. Flat-rate packaging includes envelopes and boxes of various sizes. For the Priority Mail envelope, the flat rate is the cheapest option; however, for boxes the by-weight Priority Mail price may be lower than the flat rate, depending on the weight and destination of your parcel. So it pays to do your research and see which is cheaper. Certainly, flat-rate boxes and envelopes are the most convenient for sellers because there is no weighing and measuring. To find a shipping rate, go to www.usps.com and type in your package's weight and the zip code you're shipping it to. You can order free shipping supplies online at http://shop.usps.com. There is also a special link for eBay sellers where you can order Priority Mail boxes with the eBay logo imprinted on them: http://ebaysupplies.usps.com.

DELIVERY CONFIRMATION

The USPS offers a service called Delivery Confirmation, which provides proof that the item has arrived at its destination. It does not provide tracking for your item (so you can't see where the package is while it's still in the postal system). The fees vary by service. If you purchase your postage online, Delivery Confirmation is free for Priority Mail and $0.18 for first-class or parcel post service. If you purchase Delivery Confirmation at the Post Office counter, it costs $0.65 for Priority Mail and $0.75 for first-class or parcel post service. You can enter the Delivery Confirmation number in the Track & Confirm box on the USPS Web site to verify that an item has or has not been delivered.

Private carriers, such as UPS and FedEx, provide Delivery Confirmation as well as in-transit tracking automatically as part of their standard service. Additionally, these services give you the option of requiring Signature Delivery Confirmation—which can be useful if you need to prove that a package was received. The USPS charges extra for Signature Confirmation.

ENDICIA

If you are using the U.S. Postal Service for most of your shipping, I strongly recommend signing up with Endicia, Inc. (www.endicia.com). Endicia is an online postal solution. Once you have an account with the company, you can download software (both Mac- and PC-compatible) that allows you to calculate postage and print out a label with Delivery Confirmation. There are two advantages to using this system: First, you get free, or significantly discounted, Delivery Confirmation; and second, you can drop your packages off at the back door of the Post Office without having to stand in line and purchase postage and delivery confirmations individually.

Of all the online postal solutions, Endicia offers the most features and is the easiest to use. In addition, it offers more options than Stamps.com and other similar services. One of Endicia's greatest features is Stealth Postage. With this tool, you can print a postage label that does not show the actual cost of the postage. It has a bar code that Post Office computers can recognize, but there is no postage amount printed on the label. So if your postage is $3.90 and you charge $4.90 for shipping and handling, your buyer will not be able to see this disparity when the package arrives. When you use Endicia, you can also purchase insurance from a private insurance company that costs less than that offered by the U.S. Postal Service. (See the next section for a detailed discussion of insurance.)

You can also print and pay for shipping through PayPal. This can be a time-saver because it automatically imports your buyer's address for you (so there's less chance of making a clerical error in the address label). Plus, you can use stealth postage (like Endicia) so your buyer doesn't see the postage amount. The downside to using PayPal is that your buyer gets an automatic e-mail when you print the postage for her item. Many buyers misinterpret this to mean that their item has been shipped. So don't print postage on Saturday if you're not going to ship the item until Monday.

Whether you use Endicia or PayPal, you will receive the lower "electronic" postage rates. This can add up significantly.

INSURANCE

Insurance can be a great moneymaker for eBay sellers. The truth about insurance is that very few packages are ever lost. We have been selling on eBay for nine years. In that time, we have only lost two packages out of the thousands we have shipped—and one of them eventually turned up. There are, however, three benefits to insuring all your shipments. First, you can make some extra money by providing insurance. Second, it gives buyers peace of mind. Finally, if customers know their items are insured, they are less likely to complain about inflated shipping charges.

I recommend the services of Ship Insurance (www.shipinsurance.com). Ship Insurance is a private discount insurer. Its rates are up to 90 percent lower than those of the Post Office or private carriers, such as UPS or FedEx. Unlike the Post Office, you can claim losses much sooner and get paid in about five days instead of thirty to forty-five days. One advantage of using both Endicia and Ship Insurance is that their systems are integrated. The Endicia Web site allows you to apply Ship Insurance amounts; in addition, you can get a printout at the end of the month for your Ship Insurance billing. An additional advantage of Ship Insurance is that it gives you a little card that says the package was insured. You place this card inside the box and the customer can see that you really did provide insurance when she opens the package. Also, the card has information on it advising the customer about how to make a claim if the item was damaged upon arrival.

BIZ BUILDER

If you will be shipping in large volume—one hundred packages a month or more—consider calling Ship Insurance and asking for a customized quote. The company's toll-free number is 866-852-9956.

Here is an example of how you can make a little extra money each year by using a discount insurance company. Consider the following costs:

USPS Priority Mail cost:	$5.90	What you charge for S&H	$6.90
Insurance cost ($100 item)	$0.45	What you charge for insurance	$1.05
Your actual cost	$6.35	Total charged to customer	$7.95
		Your profit	$1.60

It is not unreasonable to charge $7.95 for shipping and handling. The key to getting this across to the buyer is to have a statement in your auction *and* in your end-of-auction e-mail that reads something like this:

> *Please note that our shipping and handling charge is designed to cover the cost of shipping the item, insurance on the value of the item and the shipping charge, and our cost for materials to properly package your item so it arrives safely.*

If you ship two hundred packages a month and make an average of $1.60 on each one, that is $320.00 extra income per month, or $3,840.00 per year. Those monthly savings could cover a car payment for many people. If you are selling more expensive items, you can charge and make even more money on insurance. On a $300.00 item, I charge $3.75 for insurance. Since UPS insures the first $100.00 for free and Ship Insurance charges $0.55 per hundred for the next two hundred (this is a UPS-specific rate), I make $2.65 ($3.75–$1.10) on each transaction.

PRIVATE CARRIERS

If you are going to be a high-volume seller of items weighing more than five pounds (2kg), then you should open an account with a private carrier, such as UPS or FedEx. My current favorite service is UPS Ground. UPS offers a discount for eBay sellers that lowers their rates by over 30 percent, plus you can get their rates and select services in the *Shipping Wizard* in the Sell Your Item form. However, I prefer DHL for overseas shipments, especially to Europe. DHL is the largest carrier in Europe and its rates and service are excellent. (We'll discuss shipping overseas in the next chapter.)

To receive available discounts, first go online to the carrier's Web site and open an account. Once you have an account, you will be given information on how to contact an account representative. Contact your rep by e-mail or phone, and give her an estimate of your shipping volume. The representative will usually get back to you within a few days with a discount quote. Make sure you let her know that you are also getting quotes from her competition. For UPS, if you are printing your postage through PayPal, you will automatically get the reduced rate without having to open an account.

SHIPPING POLICY

Whether you use eBay's Sell Your Item form or a private auction management service, there is a place for you to spell out your shipping policy. This is an eBay requirement—you must specify your shipping charges and handling time (between receiving cleared payment and actually shipping the item).

Buyers sometimes become confused when looking at and bidding on multiple auctions. If there is a misunderstanding during the payment process, and you have specified a shipping policy in your auction, you can simply refer them back to the auction or copy and paste the specified shipping policy into an e-mail. Showing a buyer proof that he was informed of applicable costs usually circumvents any problem.

If you charge a handling fee in addition to shipping, this is the place to mention it. Remember: Don't just say, "We charge a handling fee on all sales." Instead, explain the reason for the extra cost: "I pack all our merchandise professionally in new packing materials. I add $1.25 to the actual shipping charge to cover the cost of shipping materials." At this point you should also explain your insurance policy—whether insurance is optional or required, and how much you charge per $100.00 of value.

SHIPPING STATION

To pack and ship items efficiently, set up a clean, organized shipping area in your home or office, with all your supplies nearby. This station should include boxes and packing supplies, a tape gun, a label printer, and a postage scale. Remember that your time is valuable. Having a dedicated and orderly shipping area can save you hours each week.

BIZ BUILDER

Experienced PowerSellers who manage large volumes of shipments often purchase cheap, secondhand computers for their shipping stations. To save time, you can connect such a computer to your postage scale and label printer. Also, because packaging items is so time-consuming, a lot of sellers hire neighborhood high school students to come over once a day and pack and ship their items. If the student has a car, she can even drop packages off at the Post Office for you.

HOW TO PACK GOODS

How you package your items is a major factor in your customers' satisfaction. Poorly packaged goods can lead to all sorts of headaches, from additional costs incurred to refund a customer's money or replace the original shipment, to negative feedback. Remember: Unpacking the item is the last impression your buyer has of you before leaving feedback.

Here are some packaging tips: For DVDs or CDs—whether they're movies, music, or software—use CD mailers. These are cardboard packages of just the right size for sending such items.

Tyvek mailers are ideal for shipping clothing and other soft goods. Wrap the clothing in blank newsprint or tissue paper, and then place the merchandise in these water-resistant, tear-proof mailers. Because Tyvek is so lightweight, shipping in Tyvek mailers is cheaper than shipping in boxes.

Postcards, photographs, stamps, and sports cards are also simple to mail. You can place the item between two flat, corrugated shipping blanks (sold at office supply stores) and then slide it into a bubble mailer, or you can purchase StayFlat Mailers. These mailers are difficult to bend and often come with self-adhesive strips on the flap.

For glass and other fragile items, I strongly recommend double-boxing. This is your best protection against breakage. Here is the proper way to double-box: First, wrap your item in bubble wrap and then place it in a box, leaving approximately two inches (5cm) of space on all sides of your piece. Fill this void with packing peanuts, balled up blank newsprint, or craft paper. You should then place this smaller box inside a slightly larger one and again fill the extra space with Styrofoam peanuts or bubble wrap.

Packing and shipping with care will make a big difference in your success as an eBay seller. When your box arrives at the buyer's house or office, his first impression is based on the condition of the package. If you send his treasure in an old shoebox stuffed with yesterday's newspaper, that impression will be less than flattering. He may not leave you negative feedback, but he won't be inclined to leave you positive feedback, either. And he probably won't become a repeat customer.

SHIPPING MATERIALS

Shipping materials, such as boxes, tape, bubble wrap, Styrofoam peanuts, and so on, can be very expensive. It turns out that one of the best places to shop for these materials is right on eBay itself. A number of dealers sell these materials at very competitive prices. Although shipping supplies are typically not heavy (with the exception of large shipments of cardboard boxes), they are bulky. Oftentimes, the shipping cost will have a large impact on your total cost.

The trick here is to shop locally. Look for eBay sellers that are located close by. I am in Seattle. I once bought a large quantity of padded envelopes from a seller in Georgia and didn't bother to check out the shipping cost. By the time I received them, they ended up being more expensive than if I had just purchased them at my local office supply store at the regular retail price.

I now purchase shipping supplies exclusively from sellers located on the West Coast.

Your local gift shop is a treasure trove of free shipping and packing materials. These merchants receive daily shipments of fragile items requiring large amounts of bubble wrap, Styrofoam peanuts, and sturdy boxes.

Local laws may require these shops to recycle packing materials, rather than throw them away. This can be expensive. Believe me—store owners are usually happy to give these things away. Other stores that receive large quantities of shipping and packing materials include kitchen stores, electronics stores (such as RadioShack), and small neighborhood hardware stores.

You should add a small amount to your shipping cost for packaging and handling, but this fee should not be excessive. Bidders get upset when they are charged $5.00 for shipping and they receive a package showing that the postage cost a mere $1.25. While it's acceptable to cover the cost of the box and the shipping material, the costs you pass on to the customer should be reasonable.

If something requires special packaging, such as an odd-size box or large amounts of packing material, explain these circumstances in the auction description.

POWER MOVES

❏ Set up a shipping station with tape, a tape gun, a scale, and any additional supplies you will need.

❏ If you decide to use Priority Mail, go online and order your supplies.

❏ Visit the Web sites for USPS, UPS, and FedEx Ground and compare the rates for the size and weight of the product you are shipping.

❏ If you decide to use a private courier service, visit the service's Web site or call Customer Service and open an account. If you will be shipping large quantities of packages each month, consider calling the company to get a discounted rate.

❏ Print postage online to receive reduced prices on postage and additional services.

CHAPTER 18

✦ BOOSTING YOUR PROFITS ✦ BY SELLING INTERNATIONALLY

THE ADVANTAGES OF SELLING internationally depend on the type of product you are selling and how easy or difficult it is to ship. Not all products appeal to international buyers and some products are illegal or just too difficult to ship. For example, you cannot export tobacco, alcohol, or certain electronic devices containing encryption algorithms. In general, you only want to ship products overseas that cost more than $50—otherwise, the shipping cost is too high, relative to the cost of the item.

Despite the challenges, opening your auctions to international buyers can greatly increase your profits: eBay operates in twenty-seven countries across the globe. In addition, people from dozens of other countries surf the U.S. eBay site. The first year I started selling internationally, overseas orders accounted for more than 19 percent of my business; today that percentage is even higher.

In this chapter, we'll discuss how to maximize your profits by selling internationally, and how to reduce costs so that your margins more than compensate for the additional efforts and expense of selling overseas.

POWERFUL PROFITS

The main advantage of selling internationally is profit. International buyers, especially those from Europe and Japan, tend to pay more than American buyers do for the same products. And they don't seem to mind the high cost of shipping. The best items to sell internationally are those with high dollar values relative to their weight. These include collectibles like ephemera, coins and stamps, and jewelry, as well as small electronics, such as PDAs, MP3 players, automotive accessories, and other lightweight, high-value items.

There is one potential drawback to selling internationally. Since shipments take longer and can often be delayed in customs, your buyers may occasionally leave you a low DSR score on shipping time. I know it isn't your fault—but unhappy customers will still take it out on you. For this reason, I usually recommend that new eBay sellers hold off on selling internationally until their feedback and DSR scores are high enough so that the occasional poor star rating does not hurt that much.

FIND YOUR MARKET

There are three major issues to consider when you sell internationally. The first is your product—does it appeal to international buyers? The only way to find out is to list your products in overseas markets. You do this by checking the *International Shipping* option in the Sell Your Item form and then specifying *Ship-to Locations* (see Figure 18.1). Simply check off each country to which you will agree to ship.

Figure 18.1   International Ship-to Locations

Provided you've set up your Buyer Requirements to block bidders in countries to which you don't ship, if someone tries to bid from a country that you have not selected, her bid will be automatically blocked by eBay. By listing internationally, you will be able to discern which parts of the world are viable markets for your product.

SHIPPING

The second consideration is shipping. Can you ship the product for a reasonable amount, relative to its cost? As a rule of thumb, if the shipping cost would exceed 20 percent of the estimated final value, I would probably not offer the item internationally.

Calculated Shipping

When we discussed shipping previously, I stated that I prefer to use fixed shipping rates. The rates to overseas countries are so varied, however, that this is often impractical. Therefore, you'll most likely find yourself offering Calculated Shipping when selling internationally. When you select this option, a shipping calculator will appear in your auction description. Overseas buyers can enter their country information, and the calculator will estimate shipping costs so they can see applicable rates before deciding to bid.

Your alternative is to use Priority Mail International Flat-rate Boxes. These are the same as the flat-rate boxes you use for domestic shipping. Each country has a flat-rate price, but the weight is restricted to twenty pounds (9kg) for international flat-rate shipments (otherwise you will need to pay the by-weight rate). You can see the international flat rates at http://www.usps.com/prices/priority-mail-international-prices.htm.

International Shipping and Customs

There are essentially two ways to ship internationally:

✳ **USPS PRIORITY MAIL INTERNATIONAL.** Shipping via the U.S. Post Office's Priority Mail International service has two distinct advantages—the costs are relatively low and you do not need a customs broker. On the downside, there's no signature required, making it difficult to prove delivery. In addition, the service may be quite slow. Local post offices in foreign countries can hold up items for weeks, awaiting customs clearance, before notifying the recipients that their shipment has arrived.

The good news is that PayPal offers its antifraud program (Seller Protection Program) on international parcels under $250 even if you don't have Delivery Confirmation (which the USPS doesn't offer for Priority Mail International). If you do need to file a claim, you will need proof of delivery and the customs form. If the item's cost is over $250, you will need to ship via USPS Express Mail International (because this provides tracking and proof of delivery) or via a courier service (UPS FedEx).

One disadvantage of shipping overseas via USPS is that it's hard to collect on an insurance claim. It can take up to twice as long for the U.S.

Postal Service to investigate and pay an insurance claim for an overseas shipment than it does for a domestic shipment. However, Ship Insurance, the insurance company we mentioned in the previous chapter, does a good job when it comes to international insurance. Ship Insurance is cheaper than USPS and it pays claims sooner.

* **INTERNATIONAL CARRIERS, SUCH AS UPS, DHL, AND FEDEX.** The advantages of shipping with private international carriers are threefold: reliability, the ability to insure the shipment (and collect on claims), and positive Delivery Confirmation. The primary disadvantage is the cost—these carriers are more expensive than USPS and, in most countries, your shipment must go through a customs broker. This incurs brokerage charges that start at $25 and can run as high as 1.5 percent of the value of the shipment, or as high as $250. The $25 minimum brokerage fee makes it impractical to ship items overseas that cost less than $100.

.... BEST PRACTICES ....

A WORD OF ADVICE ON INTERNATIONAL SHIPPING

Whenever you ship overseas, you have to fill out a customs form that states the contents and the value of the item you are shipping. Buyers may ask you to mark the item as a gift or place a low value on the customs form, so that they incur a lower duty. *Do not do this!* First of all, you would be breaking the law if you were using the U.S. Postal Service. Second, if the item were lost or damaged, you could only claim the value stated on the form. Finally, eBay's policies state that you must obey the laws of *both* countries—the one you are selling from and the one you are shipping to. If you violate this policy, eBay will suspend you or, in repeated cases, cancel your account.

When shipping internationally, I always place an invoice in the box, specifying the item description and the price the buyer paid. This prevents the customs official from having to guess at the item's value.

So, what *is* the best way to ship? Whenever I sell an item under $100 overseas, I go with the USPS. Yes, every once in a while a package goes astray and I lose money on the order. However, this does not happen often, and the extra cost is easily offset by the increased profits I earn from overseas buyers who *do* receive their merchandise.

When I sell an item worth over $100, I usually use UPS Calculated Shipping. In this scenario, I include a note in my auction that the buyer may have to pay a customs brokerage fee in addition to the shipping cost. I like to specify as many of the fees as possible in the item description. Be sure to be clear about the shipping method you'll be using, any risks associated with the item, the estimated delivery time, and if the buyer should expect any additional fees. eBay suggests that you advise potential buyers to research customs fees before placing a bid. As I mentioned previously, unhappy buyers tend to leave negative feedback, so once I figure out how I am going to ship and what the costs will be, I always write a detailed e-mail to the buyer explaining everything, including the fact that customs can sometimes delay a product and that shipments to his country could incur a customs broker fee. Stating all this information upfront can often prevent an unhappy customer from taking his frustrations out on you in the form of a poor feedback comment or DSR score.

PAYMENT

The third and final point to consider when it comes to selling internationally is getting paid. Fortunately, PayPal is set up to collect funds from forty-five countries (see the PayPal site for a complete list), as well as in several currencies, including the yen, the euro, and the British pound. eBay automatically converts the cost of a product to the user's default currency. So, if a British bidder is viewing an item listed on the U.S. site, she will see the cost in U.S. dollars *and* British pounds. To see what your product will cost in other currencies, visit eBay's currency converter at http://pages.ebay.com/services/buyandsell/currencyconverter.html.

If an overseas buyer pays via PayPal, you don't have to worry about the conversion rate. The buyer will pay PayPal in his home currency, and PayPal will pay you in U.S. dollars (or the currency of your country). I would also not accept payment via a credit card directly to your own merchant credit card account for any large overseas transaction, unless the buyer had an exceptionally high feedback rating (with excellent comments), and had been active on eBay for at least a year. Credit card fraud is much worse overseas than in the United States and Canada. The problem arises when someone pays with a credit card that clears, and then the credit card company discovers the card is invalid several weeks later—after you have shipped the product. In this case you are out the money, whereas with PayPal, you are still eligible for the Seller Protection Policy. This program protects you from fraudulent credit card transactions processed through PayPal. (You can learn more about this program at www.paypal.com.)

POWER MOVES

I would not suggest that you start shipping overseas until you have mastered domestic selling and shipping. But once you have successfully launched enough auctions that you know all the ins and outs of eBay selling, you should evaluate whether there is an international market for your product. You can do this in two ways:

❏ Search Completed Auctions on eBay. Look for successful auctions where the items sold at very high prices. Often these winning bidders are international buyers. Use this information to determine if there is an international market for your item. Also, evaluate the shipping policies specified by the sellers.

❏ Go onto overseas eBay sites, such as eBay.co.uk (the United Kingdom eBay site) or eBay.com.au (eBay's site in Australia). Unless you speak German, French, or Chinese, I would limit yourself to the English-speaking sites. Search Completed Listings for the product you are selling and see if there is a market for it in these countries.

CHAPTER 19

✦ MONITORING AND REVISING ✦ YOUR AUCTIONS FOR SUCCESS

PROFESSIONAL EBAY SELLERS stay on top of their auctions on a daily basis. They not only want to know how their auctions are doing, they often revise ongoing auctions if those are not performing well. Fortunately, eBay makes monitoring and updating auctions easy for sellers. This chapter will take you through the various tools eBay provides to help you monitor, manage, and revise your ongoing auctions.

THE MY EBAY DASHBOARD

eBay provides a convenient tool for monitoring your auction activity, called My eBay (see Figure 19.1).

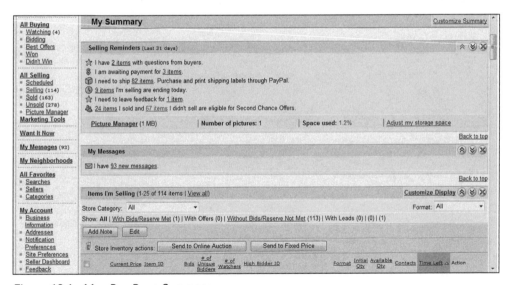

Figure 19.1 My eBay Page Summary

You can access My eBay from the top of any eBay page by hitting the *My eBay* button. The first thing you will see is *My Summary*. This includes *My Messages*—clicking on this link will bring up any questions from buyers about your auctions.

Next you will see a list of symbols followed by notes:

* **UNANSWERED QUESTIONS (STAR):** Number of questions from buyers you have left to answer

* **PAYMENT REMINDER (DOLLAR SIGN):** Number of items awaiting payment

* **SHIPMENT REMINDER (PACKAGE):** Number of items you have left to ship

* **FEEDBACK REMINDER (STAR):** Number of people for whom you need to leave feedback

* **SECOND CHANCE OFFER (TWO PEOPLE):** Number of closed auctions eligible for Second Chance Offers

After each of these symbols is a link. For example, if you click on the link after the dollar sign, you will arrive at a page listing all your auctions that are awaiting payment. Each listing includes a box you can click to send the seller an invoice (see Figure 19.2).

Figure 19.2   Menu Options for Sold Items

If you scroll farther down your My eBay page, you will come across a list of all the items you are currently selling (see Figure 19.3). Each item is listed by its auction title. Below each title you will find the following information:

* Current price

* Number of bids

* High bidder ID

* Number of watchers

* Number of questions

* Time left in the auction

* Actions (Here you'll find a series of boxes with applicable actions you can take)

This gives you a great snapshot of all your ongoing auctions. If you want further data, such as the number of hits your listing has received, you can simply click on that auction and look at your hit counter. If you see an auction without any bids halfway through the week and your hit counter shows few or no hits, you may have a problem with your auction title. You can revise your title in midauction, as long as you have no bids and there are more than twelve hours remaining until the auction ends. We will show you how to do this later in this chapter.

☐ Patina EVENING SKY MOON STARS FIREPIT BARBECUE GRILL											Sell Similar ▼
BuyItNow $46.00 $227.00	200275518154	7	2	2	Buyer1 (14 ☆)		🔎	1	1	--	1d 06h 10m
☐ PATINA COWBOY OUTDOOR WOOD PATIO FIREPIT GRILL Fire Pit											Sell Similar ▼
BuyItNow $99.00 $227.00	200275520178	0	--	1	--		🔎	1	1	--	1d 06h 16m
☐ NORTHERN IRELAND Starbucks Country Mug, New NR											Sell Similar ▼
BuyItNow $19.00 $39.00	200275526666	0	--	3	--		🔎	1	1	--	1d 06h 34m
☐ LONE STAR TEXAS OUTDOOR FIRE PIT PATIO FIREPIT GRILL											Sell Similar ▼
$170.00	370111278108	6	3	5	Buyername2 (2)		🔎	1	1	--	1d 07h 22m
☐ 30 Inch EZCUBE LIGHT TENT ONLY WITHOUT LIGHTS											Sell Similar ▼
BuyItNow $97.00 $109.00	200275871514	0	--	0	--		🔎	1	1	--	2d 03h 38m
☐ 30 Inch EZ Cube Product Portrait Studio set w/lights											Sell Similar ▼
BuyItNow $259.00 $259.00	200275892546	0	--	1	--		🔎	1	1	--	2d 04h 47m
☐ WESTERN COWBOY OUTDOOR FIREPIT GRILL BARBECUE FIRE PIT											Sell Similar ▼
BuyItNow $31.00 $227.00	200275908352	4	2	5	Buyer3 (18 ☆)		🔎	1	1	--	2d 05h 43m
☐ OUTDOOR WOOD BURNING MOOSE & TREES FIRE PIT, FIREPIT (Reserve Not Met)											Sell Similar ▼
BuyItNow $60.00 $227.00	370113565379	12	2	2	Buyername4 (1)		🔎	1	1	--	2d 06h 22m

Figure 19.3 Items I'm Selling

On the left-hand side of every My eBay page are your main navigation links (see Figure 19.1). These include:

* **ALL BUYING**: Clicking on this page will show you a complete list of all the items you are currently bidding on, the amount of your bids, the number of bids the item has received, and a link to contact the seller.

* **ALL SELLING**: This lists all your items currently for sale, whether at auction, listed with Buy It Now, or available in your eBay store.

* **MY MESSAGES**: This is a link to all questions and messages from current and potential buyers.

* **ALL FAVORITES**: This is where you can store your favorite searches and links to your favorite sellers, as well as categories that you are watching.

* **MY ACCOUNT**: Here you can access your current account, past invoices, and preferences for both your eBay and PayPal accounts.

Also useful is the *Related Links* navigation box located below the *My Account* links. Here you can link to your PayPal account, eBay Stores, Buying and Selling Resources, and more. From your My eBay page you may also link to the *Dispute Console*, where you can initiate and manage any disputes with sellers or report an unpaid item.

BIZ BUILDER

Every time I discover a competitor, I add him to My Favorite Sellers. When I am about to launch a new auction, I go to My Favorite Sellers and see what my competitors are selling the item for, if they have any clever new titles, how many hits their auctions are getting, and so on. If someone has just launched an auction with a starting price of $19.99, I might start mine, offering a similar item, at $18.99 to attract more hits when our auctions run together.

I also look to see when my competitors' auctions are ending. If a leading competitor ends her auctions at 6:00 p.m. PT on a Monday, I will end mine ten minutes earlier to appear above her in *Best Match* and *Time ending: soonest* Search Results.

When you monitor your auctions, you may notice some with numerous watchers and few (or even no) bids. Watchers are usually people who like to *snipe*—a term that refers to bidding at the last second, or using special software programs to do this for them. Oftentimes, an auction will run all week with few or no bids, and then receive heavy bidding activity in the last few minutes. So don't despair if you look at your auctions days before they end and they do not seem to be getting bids—this is perfectly normal. Nevertheless, if you don't have any watchers, you might want to open the auction to see if it is getting any hits. If not, you might consider revising your auction—especially the title or the opening price. (See below for details on how to do this.)

SALES REPORTS

From your My eBay page, you can also link to *My Subscriptions*. Subscriptions are special tools and reports for which eBay generally charges additional fees. One such tool offered by eBay is a monthly sales report (see Figure 19.4). This particular report is free, but others incur charges.

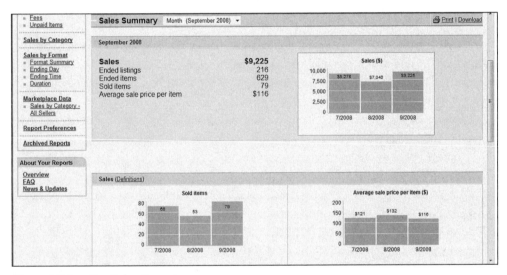

Figure 19.4   eBay Sales Report

eBay sales reports present a very detailed look at your sales. We spoke earlier about business metrics—how you measure your performance on eBay. You can determine most of your critical business metrics right from this report.

REVISING AN ONGOING AUCTION

Once an auction has been launched, you can revise almost any part of it, provided the item has not yet received any bids. If it *has* received bids, you can add comments and images to the auction, but you cannot remove anything listed in it.

The information that you can revise also depends on the time left before the auction ends. In most cases, you cannot change the listing format; that is, you cannot switch from an auction-style listing to an eBay store listing. You also cannot change your listing from standard auction format to fixed price, or vice versa.

If your listing has not received any bids and has at least twelve hours left to run, you may:

* Revise any information in the title or description

* Add or remove the following optional features: Buy It Now, eBay Picture Services, reserve price, ten-day listing

* Add optional features to increase your item's visibility (for example, Bold, Highlight, or Border)

* Add or change a Gallery photo

If your item *has* received bids, you cannot change copy, images, or words in the description; however, you can add special features such as Bold, Gallery, or Highlight, and you can add an additional image (although you cannot change or remove any of the existing images).

When you click on the link to revise your item, a new page will come up, as illustrated in Figure 19.5.

Simply make whatever changes you deem necessary in each section.

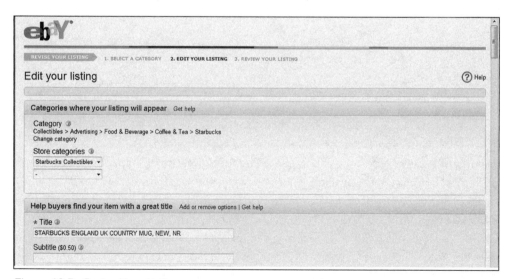

Figure 19.5   Revise Your Listing

ENDING AN AUCTION EARLY

If you inadvertently launch an auction for something you don't have, or if you find a critical mistake in your description, and your item already has bids, you can still end your auction early.

If the auction has no bids, go to the eBay site map and select *End Your Listing* under the heading *Selling Activities*. If your auction has bids, select *Cancel Bids on Your Listing*. Remember that if you wish to end a listing early, you must first cancel any bids that have already been placed.

If you end a listing, correct it, and submit a new listing within twenty-four hours, make sure to e-mail eBay's billing department. Explain to the billing representatives that you made a mistake and ended your listing, and then ask for a refund of your listing fee. If you include the item number of the new listing, eBay will usually give you a refund (essentially applying the listing fee of the canceled auction to the new one). You can find a link to e-mail eBay's billing department about billing issues in the My Account section on your My eBay page.

POWER MOVES

❏ Familiarize yourself with the layout on your My eBay Page, and all the links and tools available to you there.

❏ Click on the *Sales Reports* link through the *My Subscriptions* link on your My eBay page to read and understand what kind of information this tool provides. Once you start selling on a regular basis, I recommend that you subscribe to this service.

CHAPTER 20

✦ GETTING PAID ✦

GETTING PAID IS WHAT IT'S all about on eBay. In the early days of eBay, there was no PayPal and very few eBay sellers were set up to take credit cards. I can still remember receiving checks, money orders, and envelopes stuffed with cash from customers. One buyer even sent me a box filled with rolls of dimes and quarters to pay for a rare naval history book I had sold him!

As we wrap up Week 2, we'll conclude by exploring the various payment methods available to you as an eBay seller and how to use them. In addition, we will show you how to deal with nonpaying bidders and expose some of the more common frauds and scams that unfortunately plague eBay from time to time—and reveal how you can avoid them.

These days, all payments on eBay must be "paperless" (i.e., electronic). So checks, money orders, cash, and so forth are no longer allowed. In fact, eBay restricts you to a very limited number of services you can use. These include PayPal (which eBay owns), ProPay, and accepting credit cards through your own merchant credit card account. eBay has stated that they will also be adding other services as time goes on, so you should check the eBay Announcements Board for the latest information.

PAYPAL

Today the vast majority of eBay buyers pay with PayPal. It's easy to integrate PayPal into your auctions just by selecting an option in your PayPal account. If you opt to place a *PayPal* button in your auctions, when your auction ends, a *Pay Now* button will appear on the closed auction page for the winning buyer. If it is a Buy It Now listing, the buyer is sent directly to the Buy It Now Confirmation page, which includes the same *Pay Now* button (shown in Figure 20.1).

The buyer will also receive an automatic e-mail with a *Pay Now* button in it. When the buyer clicks the *Pay Now* button (either from the closed auction page or the end-of-auction e-mail), he is taken to the eBay Checkout page, shown in Figure 20.2. On this page he can select the shipping service he wants from the list you offered, and choose to add insurance if you offered it. Here he also chooses his payment method: PayPal or another method you've set up in your auction. If he selects PayPal, he will proceed to the PayPal Checkout page, shown in Figure 20.3.

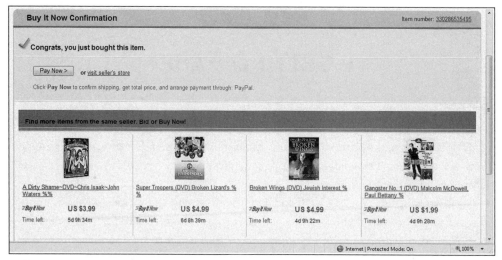

Figure 20.1   Buy It Now Confirmation Page

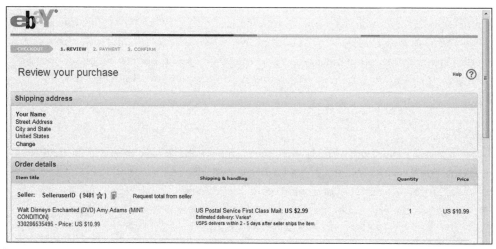

Figure 20.2   eBay Checkout Page

Once the buyer logs in and pays, you will receive an e-mail from PayPal, usually within minutes, notifying you that the auction ended and the buyer has paid with PayPal. It will also provide the buyer's shipping information. If you open your PayPal account, you will see that the money has been deposited.

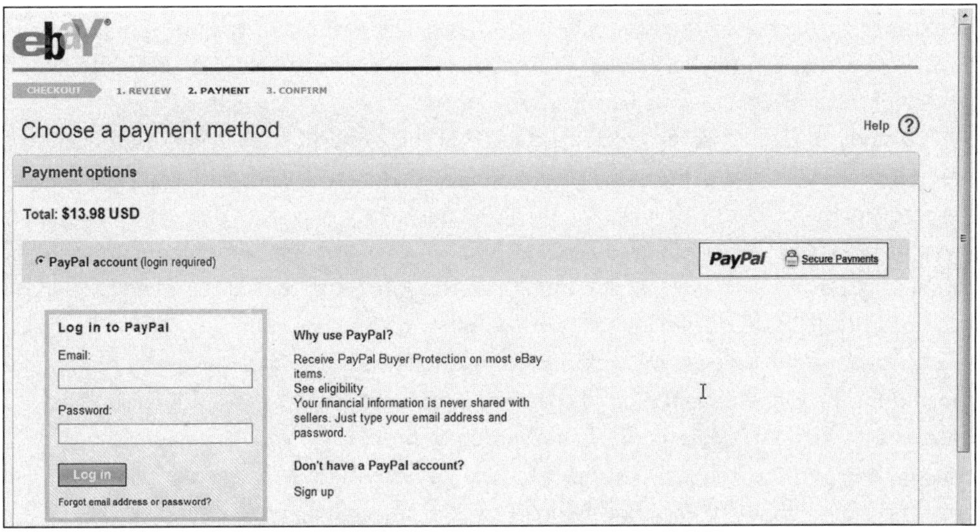

Figure 20.3   PayPal Checkout Page

A buyer does not have to have a PayPal account to use PayPal, because PayPal will also process credit card transactions. If someone selects PayPal and does not have an account, he will be brought to a page where he can enter his credit card and shipping information. PayPal then processes the credit card transaction for you and you get paid right away, just as with any other PayPal transaction.

You're probably familiar with the popular AOL voice prompt, "You've got mail." Well, if you have Microsoft Outlook, you can set up the program to always give you a voice or sound alert whenever an e-mail from PayPal arrives. One of my friends has his computer set up to sound "Cha-Ching" every time an e-mail from PayPal arrives.

All kidding aside, it is a good idea to set up an alert like this. If you are near the computer, you can log on instantly and send the buyer an e-mail confirming that you received her payment and that her shipment is on the way. People are amazed when they buy something on eBay and receive a shipping notice minutes later. (This is a great way to boost your feedback rating.) In chapter 23 I will show you how to automate this process so buyers receive their confirmation e-mails instantly.

ProPay is similar to PayPal and carries comparable fees. However, ProPay doesn't offer as many features and, in addition to transaction fees, ProPay charges both an annual and a monthly maintenance fee. In addition, it is only available to PowerSellers, so you cannot even join ProPay until you reach PowerSeller status. In all honesty, I think eBay allows ProPay simply because they have to offer a PayPal alternative, and they don't want to allow a competitor with better fees. The vast majority of buyers have PayPal accounts, and PayPal's Seller Protection Policy is pretty comprehensive, so, in general, I think that is the way to go. So my advice is just to stick with PayPal.

Although there is some credit card fraud in the United States, it's much more prevalent overseas. If you receive a credit card payment via PayPal, and it turns out that the card the buyer used was invalid, PayPal will debit your account. The same holds true if you have a merchant credit card account. With PayPal, you are also vulnerable to buyer disputes. A buyer can claim that she didn't receive your item, or that it arrived broken or was not as described. If she files a dispute with her credit card company or with PayPal, you will receive a chargeback until the dispute is resolved. Usually a thirty-day period is allowed for the dispute resolution; if the issue is not resolved by then, the chargeback becomes permanent. Unfortunately, the burden of proof is on you. You need to prove that you shipped the item, or that the item was as described in the auction, or—if it arrived broken—that you will take the item back or file an insurance claim.

Lest you worry too much about this, let me reassure you that these kinds of problems are rare on eBay. Out of the millions of transactions that take place every day, only a tiny fraction result in disputes. During nine years of selling, I can count the number of disputed transactions I have had on one hand.

NONPAYING BIDDERS

Nonpaying bidders are another story—and much more of a problem than disputed transactions or fraud. Depending on the category of merchandise you sell, nonpaying bidders—or NPBs, as they are referred to by experienced eBayers—are fairly common. Sellers of low-cost merchandise, such as videos, CDs, DVDs, inexpensive jewelry, and the like, can often see NPB rates as high as 6–10 percent. For some reason, sellers of higher-priced merchandise experience lower NPB rates—usually closer to 1–2 percent. However, the eBay fees on higher-priced items are also much higher, so the dollar amounts at stake are often the same.

When a bidder doesn't pay, you can file an Unpaid Item Report with eBay through the Resolution Center. This will sometimes result in a payment; if not, eBay will credit your final value fees. The problem is that, in either case, the nonpaying bidder can and sometimes does leave you negative feedback. If the buyer refuses to participate in the process, eBay will neutralize any feedback he leaves. But if he does participate and pay up, he can still leave negative feedback. There is nothing you can do about it, even if you did nothing wrong.

First let's review how the process works. Then I will show you a shortcut that can save you time and aggravation, and almost eliminate the negative feedback risk.

THE SAVVY CAT AND THE FIRE PIT

Sometimes NPBs can come up with laugh-out-loud excuses. One day a bidder hit the *Buy It Now* button for one of my expensive ($250+) fire pits. Payment did not come through, so I sent her an invoice. Later that day, I received an e-mail back from the buyer, claiming that she had been looking at the auction when her phone rang. While she was on the phone, her cat had walked across the keyboard and somehow "bought" my fire pit. Now, that is pretty funny when you consider that you must position your cursor directly over the *Buy It Now* button to activate it—and that once you activate the button, you are then taken to a *second* page with yet another button to confirm your purchase. I sent her a reply e-mail, congratulating her on having such a smart cat, and asking if the cat would mind participating in the dispute resolution process so I could get my fees refunded. She fessed up and admitted that she needed to back out of the auction because her husband had gotten mad at her when he found out that she had purchased the pricey fire pit.

Seller Files an Unpaid Item Dispute

Sellers can report an unpaid item up to forty-five days after the transaction date (the date when the buyer commits to buying the item and the seller commits to selling it). Usually the seller must wait seven days after a listing closes to file an Unpaid Item Dispute. However, in the following exceptional cases, the seller can file a dispute immediately:

* At the time of the filing, the buyer is no longer a registered user of eBay.

* The buyer is from a country to which the seller has indicated that she will not ship, as specified in the Shipping and Payment Details section of the listing.

In these two cases, the buyer will receive an unpaid item strike and the seller will receive a final value fee credit without any additional steps.

eBay Contacts the Buyer

Once the seller files an Unpaid Item Dispute, eBay sends the buyer an e-mail notification and displays a pop-up message if the buyer signs in to eBay within fourteen days of the filing. The e-mail and pop-up message will provide one of the following:

A FRIENDLY REMINDER TO PAY

The e-mail and pop-up message will remind the buyer that payment has not yet been received, and will provide simple instructions on how to respond or how to pay for the item. If the buyer does not respond to the e-mail or pop-up message within seven days, the seller may file for a final value fee credit. The seller also becomes eligible for a free Relist Credit. (*Note:* eBay does not refund the insertion fee; you must relist the item using the *Relist This Item* button on your My eBay page and pay the second insertion fee. If the item sells again, eBay will credit your account for one insertion fee.)

When buyers receive the e-mail or pop-up message, they are presented with several options for communicating with the seller:

* *I want to pay now:* For listings where PayPal is available, the buyer can simply pay via PayPal to close the dispute.

* *I already paid:* If payment has already been made, the buyer may provide details of the payment to the seller for review. The seller can then choose the appropriate option to close the dispute.

* *Communicate with the seller:* The buyer and seller can attempt to resolve the problem by communicating directly through the eBay Web site. The seller can close the dispute at any time by choosing the appropriate closure option.

CANCEL TRANSACTION INDICATION

Another way to end a disputed auction is by using the Cancel Transaction option. Both buyer and seller agree to end the auction. (It's sort of like having a marriage annulled.) The seller indicates through the Resolution Center that a mutual agreement has been reached with the buyer to cancel the transaction. When this occurs, eBay will ask the buyer through an e-mail to confirm this cancellation. One of three scenarios will then play out:

* The buyer confirms the seller's claim that the transaction was canceled by mutual agreement. The buyer does not receive an unpaid item strike and the seller receives a final value fee credit.

* The buyer disputes the seller's claim that the sale was canceled by mutual agreement. The buyer does not receive an unpaid item strike and the seller does not receive a final value fee credit. The dispute is closed immediately after the buyer responds, and the seller cannot refile an Unpaid Item Dispute for that transaction.

* The buyer does not respond to the e-mail or pop-up message within seven days, and the seller is then able to close the dispute. The seller receives a final value fee credit and the buyer receives an unpaid item strike.

Closing the Dispute

The seller can close the dispute after the buyer has responded at least once, or if the buyer does not respond within seven days. There are several ways for the seller to close the dispute, each of which involves going through eBay's Resolution Center:

* ✳ *We've completed the transaction and we're both satisfied.* With this option, the seller does not receive a final value fee credit and the buyer does not receive an unpaid item strike.

* ✳ *We've agreed not to complete the transaction.* As specified above, with this option, the buyer does not receive an unpaid item strike, the seller receives a final value fee credit, and the item is eligible for a Relist Credit.

* ✳ *I no longer wish to communicate with or wait for the buyer.* With this option, the buyer receives an unpaid item strike, the seller receives a final value fee credit, and the item is eligible for a Relist Credit.

A dispute can only be open for sixty days after the transaction date. If the seller has not closed the dispute within sixty days, it will be closed automatically. When this automatic closure takes place, the seller does not receive a final value fee credit and the buyer does not receive an unpaid item strike.

Streamlining the Process

Normally, eBay requires you to wait seven days before filing an Unpaid Item Dispute and then a total of thirty days before you can cancel the auction and get a refund of your selling fees. If you look closely at the Report an Unpaid Item Dispute form at the Resolution Center, there are several options to choose from as the reason for your claim. One of these options states, "We have both agreed not to complete the transaction."

Now here is the trick to making this work. Place the following text at the end of each auction description:

> *By bidding on this auction, you agree that if you have not paid for the item or contacted the seller to arrange payment within seven days from the end of this auction, then this auction is canceled by mutual agreement and neither party has any recourse against the other.*

What does this mean? Well, if the seller doesn't answer his e-mails, or claims he didn't bid on the auction or that it was some kind of mistake, you can file an Unpaid Item Dispute and state that the auction was canceled by mutual agreement. So it will be as though the auction never happened.

As noted, eBay will send an e-mail to the bidder, asking her to confirm the mutual agreement. In most cases the bidder will do this, since she probably does not want to pay for the item. If she does, eBay will immediately credit the final value fee (but not the listing or feature fees) to your account, and neither you nor the bidder can leave feedback. However, at this point you can relist the item, and if it sells the second time, eBay will refund one listing fee (called the *Relist Credit;* see page 178) so you don't lose those listing fees. Only PowerSellers are eligible to have their listing upgrade and feature fees refunded as well.

If the buyer does not respond to the e-mail from eBay, eBay will refund your final value fee and you can relist the item for free. If, however, the buyer disputes the mutual agreement claim, you lose. eBay will end the dispute and will not refund your fees. This happens very rarely, however, so I have always found it worth the risk, unless it was a very large transaction involving a hefty fee.

FRAUD WATCH

As previously noted, fraud is relatively rare on eBay, but it does exist and there are several scams you should watch out for. Most fraud is actually perpetrated by sellers, not buyers. However, there are certain schemes aimed at buyers that you, as a seller, should still be aware of.

Stolen or Phony Credit Cards

As mentioned above, sometimes people attempt to buy items with bogus credit cards. To protect yourself, consider only accepting credit cards from verified users and shipping to verified addresses. While you are already protected by PayPal's Seller Protection Policy as long as you ship to the address provided, this extra level of security means that you're less likely to be shipping to someone other than the account holder. (You can read about Seller Protection on eBay by clicking on the eBay *Help* tab and typing *seller protection* into the search box. You can also find this information at PayPal.) Whenever a buyer asks me to ship to a different address than the one specified on her credit card or eBay account, I check out her feedback and how long she's been on eBay. Also, I never accept credit cards from buyers in Eastern Europe (especially the Balkans), Russia, the Middle East (with the exception of Israel), any country in Africa except South Africa (and even there I am careful), and most of the developing countries in Asia and Central and South America. All these locations are hotbeds of Internet and credit card fraud.

eBay specifically restricts payments to electronic methods to prevent cashier's check fraud, money order fraud, and the like. So if you have a buyer (particularly a foreign buyer) who insists on paying with one of these methods, cancel the transaction. Anything you might lose in eBay fees is tiny in comparison to what you would lose in the case of a fraudulent buyer. Remember: As payment methods, Western Union and MoneyGram are specifically prohibited, too. Both companies actually have letters on eBay's Web site that inform their customers that their services are not appropriate for eBay transactions.

Account Takeover (a.k.a. Spoofing or Phishing)

This is still one of the most prevalent and insidious frauds on eBay (and the rest of the Internet) today. You receive an official-looking e-mail from eBay (or PayPal), stating that there is some kind of problem with your account, that the credit card you have on file needs updating, or that your account has been compromised. The e-mail often threatens to suspend your account if you do not take immediate action. The e-mail contains a link you are requested to click to access your information so you can update it.

When you click on the link, you are taken to a page on "eBay" (or "PayPal") that asks you to enter your user ID and password, followed by your name, address, and credit card information—including the three-digit security code on the back. Well, this is kind of a pain, you think, but what the heck? The problem is that you are not on eBay or PayPal. You have been led to a spoof site hosted on a server in Guatemala or Slovenia that looks just like eBay, but it's not. The thieves now have your eBay and/or PayPal password and all your credit card information, and are about to empty any money in your PayPal account and go on a shopping spree. The first time you realize anything is wrong is when you get your credit card statement, perhaps weeks later, and learn that *you* have purchased a top-of-the-line Rolex watch at the duty-free shop in Santo Domingo or Kuala Lumpur.

It's fairly easy to protect yourself from this type of scam. eBay and PayPal will never send you an e-mail directing you to click on an embedded link to enter either of their sites for account-specific information. Any legitimate account e-mail from eBay or PayPal will instruct you to go to the main Web site and log on in the normal way. Never click on any link in an e-mail directing you to a site where you are asked to enter security or credit card information.

Another scam involves My Messages. You receive an e-mail in your inbox with a question from a buyer. You click on the link, which should take you to *My Messages* to reply. Only, the page you are taken to is not eBay. Like the scam described above, you are redirected to a spoof site that appears to be eBay and are asked to log in to your account. In this scam, however, your login information is used for a different type of fraud. This time the scammer takes advantage of your good feedback record and lists a number of high-ticket items. Buyers send the payment, and never receive the items. This is called Account Takeover and is a big concern. It's also a reason why you must never have the same eBay and PayPal passwords. If you do get caught up in one of these scams, at least your PayPal account will not be compromised as well. Usually in account takeover situations, the scammer changes your password so you cannot get into your account to cancel the listings. If this happens to you, go to eBay's homepage and click on *Live Help*. This will connect you with an eBay representative who can help you.

One easy way of preventing this from ever happening is to install the eBay toolbar and set up the Account Guard feature. With this feature installed, a window pops up any time you type your eBay or PayPal password into a Web site that is not an official eBay or PayPal site. There are certain tricks to noticing when an e-mail is not from eBay (for example, official correspondence will have both your user ID and real name at the top), but having the Account Guard feature is always a good backup.

Phony Escrow Web Sites

Typically buyers are the victims of this fraud. I've included it here because, if you sell high-priced items, your bidders could be at risk.

Fake escrow Web sites may be one of the most successful Internet scams of all time. They prey on big-ticket auction winners and rely on the consumer's trust of escrow Web sites—once considered the safest way to make an exchange when an online auction involves an item of higher-than-average value. Victims of phony escrow sites can lose tens of thousands of dollars at a time; total losses incurred by big-ticket auction winners quickly add up to millions of dollars.

If you're a buyer, the best way to protect yourself is to use the escrow service listed on eBay itself (www.escrow.com). Sellers should encourage buyers to do the same thing.

Stealing First Base

This scam only occurs if you are too slow in contacting your bidders after an auction ends. Here is what happens: The scammer watches auctions for expensive items ending in the next few minutes. When the auction ends with a successful bidder, he then e-mails the winner with a payment link. If the bidder doesn't happen to notice that the person sending the e-mail does not have the same user ID as the seller, she happily sends the money off via PayPal. A couple of hours later, when you contact the winning bidder, she indignantly informs you that she already paid for the item. There isn't too much you can do about this scam except report it to eBay. The problem is the buyer's—not yours. (However, if this happens to one of my buyers, I usually sympathize and let her out of the deal, if she agrees to end the auction by mutual agreement. This way she doesn't have to worry about owing me money or having an unpaid item strike against her.)

With all scams, your best defense is to be on the lookout for anything that appears too good to be true. It probably is. While you don't want to be paranoid about every e-mail you receive, it does pay to be a little cautious—especially when you're doing business outside the United States and Canada.

POWER MOVES

❑ If you haven't yet signed up for PayPal, open an account.

❑ Visit the Seller Protection page on eBay (via the site map or by clicking on *Help* at the top of any eBay page and typing *seller protection* into the search box). Familiarize yourself with the eBay and PayPal protection plans for both buyers and sellers.

❑ Type the phrase *online security* into the eBay Help search box. This will bring up a series of links relating to fraud protection on eBay. Become thoroughly familiar with them so you can guard against scams and frauds.

WEEK
3

BUILDING AND GROWING YOUR BUSINESS

You have your auctions up and running, and you've learned how to make them more efficient to gain optimal sales potential. Now it's time to take your business to the next level. In this section, we'll show you how to reduce costs, manage your inventory, and automate routine tasks so you can run more auctions and increase profits. We'll also focus on special tools and upselling techniques, and e-mail marketing to your existing customer base.

In addition, we will show you how to make Fixed Price sales by setting up an eBay store, and explore the nuances and limitless sales potential of consignment selling on eBay, a topic we introduced in chapter 3. As you'll recall, consignment selling means offering goods for sale on eBay for other people who don't know how—or don't have time—to sell on eBay themselves. I call this selling *OPM*—Other People's Merchandise. If you can master this strategy, you will have an endless supply of merchandise to sell with no investment or risk on your part.

Finally, we will examine a few techniques for using eBay as a vehicle to spread your market beyond eBay and into the rest of the Web.

CHAPTER 21

✦ COST CONTROL ✦

CONTROLLING YOUR COSTS is important in any business—selling on eBay is no different. There are two ways to increase your profits: Launch more successful auctions or cut your costs. So far we have dealt primarily with techniques to increase your sales. However, as your business grows, it is easy to lose sight of pesky little expenses that can eat into your earnings. eBay listing fees, for example, are small, but can add up quickly. The same goes for eBay photo hosting fees. Packing and shipping supplies are another major cost for eBay sellers. Let's examine some of your typical costs, and how you can get them under control and make more money on eBay.

FOR THE RECORD

The first step when you're trying to control your costs is to figure out what they are. While monitoring your costs, you can simultaneously track your sales and profits. If you are just starting out, create an Excel spreadsheet like the one in Table 21.1.

The first line indicates total sales for the month. Only factor in payments you have actually received (not payments from sales concluded that month that have not

Table 21.1 Sales and Costs Worksheet

INCOME	JAN	FEB	MARCH	APRIL	MAY	JUNE
Sales	$1,400	$2,155	$2,855	$3,366	$4,125	$5,241
Cost of Goods Sold (COGS)	616	948	1,256	1,481	1,815	2,306
Gross Margin (Sales minus COGS)	784	1,207	1,599	1,885	2,310	2,935
EXPENSES						
eBay Fees	92	142	188	222	272	346
PayPal Fees	33	51	67	79	97	123
Cost of Shipping & Packing Materials	28	43	57	67	83	105
Shipping (UPS, USPS, etc.)	62	95	126	148	182	231
Monthly ISP/DSL Fees, etc.	22	22	22	22	22	22
Office Supplies & Expenses	25	29	36	42	55	63
Miscellaneous	10	15	20	25	30	35
Total	272	397	516	606	740	925
PROFIT (Gross Margin minus Expenses)	$512	$810	$1,083	$1,279	$1,570	$2,010

yet arrived). So, for example, don't add payments to this month's sales from a deadbeat bidder who refuses to pay, or from an auction that closes on the last day of the month but for which you won't receive payment until the following month.

The next line, Cost of Goods Sold (COGS), represents the amount you paid for the merchandise you purchased that month, including any shipping costs. When you subtract your COGS from your total sales, you end up with your gross margin.

Next you want to list all expenses related to your eBay business. I have listed the most common expenses, but you may need to add a few more, such as computer payments, car mileage to pick up and deliver goods, and advertising. Be sure to include these items in your total expenses for the month.

Once you total your expenses, subtract them from your gross margin to arrive at your profit for the month. As long as your eBay business is fairly small, this system will work quite well. If your business starts to grow, however, consider investing in a program like QuickBooks, an automated accounting system that costs about $200. While there are several other accounting software programs on the market, QuickBooks is the one used by most bookkeeping and accounting firms. Here's one distinct advantage of using QuickBooks: If your business is successful, you will need to retain a Certified Public Account (CPA) or a tax service like H&R Block to help with your taxes. Most CPAs and tax services use QuickBooks; if you can deliver a QuickBooks file to them, they can prepare your taxes more efficiently—and usually for a lower fee. If you employ a part-time bookkeeper, as I do, you'll discover that this program will easily pay for itself in money saved over having this person manage your books manually.

UNDERSTANDING YOUR EBAY FEES

Looking at Table 21.1, you can see that your eBay and PayPal fees represent a significant proportion of your costs. There's not much you can do to reduce your PayPal fees; these fees are a fixed percentage of what you sell. However, there are some steps you can take to reduce your eBay fees. Understanding how eBay calculates its fees is essential to learning how to control them, so first you must have a good grasp of eBay's fee structure, and how the various costs relate to one another.

eBay has several categories of fees:

* Insertion fees, or the cost to post an item for sale
* Final value fees, or the cost of selling an item
* Fees for additional listing options

Now let's explore the specific fees for each category. Note that the fees listed in this chapter were accurate when this edition went to press. However, eBay does change (translation: raise) its fees occasionally. You can find the current eBay fees at http://pages.ebay.com/help/sell/fees.html.

Insertion Fees

The first fee you'll encounter when listing an item for sale is the insertion fee. Insertion fees are a percentage of the starting price of your item. The percentage decreases as the price of your item increases. The fee varies based on whether you're selling in the auction or the Fixed Price format. The insertion fee for auctions is lower in media categories (Books, Music, DVDs and Movies, and Video Games) for the first three tier levels, as shown in Table 21.2.

Table 21.2
eBay Auction Insertion, Reserve, and Buy It Now Fees

EBAY AUCTION INSERTION FEES

Item Starting Price	Media Items Fee	All Other Items Fee
$0.01–$0.99	$0.10	$0.15
$1.00–$9.99	$0.25	$0.35
$10.00–$24.99	$0.35	$0.55
$25.00–$49.99	$1.00	$1.00
$50.00–$199.00	$2.00	$2.00
$200.00–$499.99	$3.00	$3.00
$500.00 and up	$4.00	$4.00

RESERVE PRICE AUCTION FEES

Reserve Price	Insertion Fee
$0.01–$199.99	$2.00
$200.00 and up	1% of reserve price (max.: $50.00)

BUY IT NOW FEES

Buy It Now Price	Fee
$1.00–$9.99	$0.05
$10.00–$24.99	$0.10
$25.00–$49.99	$0.20
$50.00 or more	$0.25

The insertion fee for Fixed Price listings is a little simpler. If it's a media item, the fee is $0.15; if it's not a media item it is $0.35, regardless of the item price (although Fixed Price listings must have a minimum price of $1.00).

BIZ BUILDER

The insertion fees for eBay stores are, by comparison, much lower. We will cover eBay store fees in chapter 26.

BIZ BUILDER

eBay often puts its fees on sale. It pays to check the eBay Announcements Boards frequently to take advantage of any eBay fee promotions, as eBay often gives less than a day's notice when temporarily reducing its fees. Occasionally, eBay offers free listing days, where you can list an unlimited number of items for free.

Final Value Fees

Once your item sells, you will be charged a final value fee. As with the insertion cost, this fee is based on a sliding scale. eBay has different final value fees for auctions and Fixed Price listings. Table 21.3 shows the fees for auction listings.

Table 21.3 eBay Auction Final Value Fees

CLOSING PRICE	FINAL VALUE FEE
$0.01–$25.00	8.75% of the closing value
$25.01–$1,000.00	8.75% of the first $25.00, plus 3.5% of the balance
$1,000.01 or more	8.75% of the initial $25.00, plus 3.5% of the value from $25.01 to $1,000.00, plus 1.50% of the remaining closing value

Here's an example of how the final value fee works:

If an item sold for $1,450.00, you would pay 8.75 percent of the initial $25.00 ($2.19), plus 3.5 percent of the next $25.01–$1,000.00 ($34.12), plus 1.50 percent of the remaining balance ($6.75). Add up all three amounts ($2.19 + $34.12 + $6.75), and you have your total final value fee of $43.06.

BIZ BUILDER

Final value fees are much higher than insertion fees. Therefore, it is very important for you to keep track of any nonpaying bidders and file a claim in the eBay Resolution Center to get these fees refunded. Also, if a bidder doesn't pay, you are usually eligible for the Relist Credit (where if the item sells the second time, you get a credit back for one of the insertion fees you paid). Essentially, this is a "free relist" although you do pay a second insertion fee, and that only gets refunded if the item sells.

The final value fees for Fixed Price listings vary depending on your item's category. There are four category-specific final value fee tables as well as one for *All Other Categories*, so rather than show all of them, Table 21.4 shows the *All Other Categories* fees. Some of the category-specific final value fees are lower than shown; some are higher. You can see all of the Fixed Price final value fee tables at http://pages.ebay.com/help/sell/fees.html.

eBay only charges you a final value fee if your item sells. If an item fails to sell at an auction the first time, you are eligible for the Relist Credit if it sells the second time, but you only get one shot at this. If it fails to sell the second time, you do not get another chance at the Relist Credit. You still pay a final value fee if the item sells. There is no Relist Credit for Fixed Price listings because the insertion fee is so low.

Table 21.4 eBay Fixed Price Listing Final Value Fees (in *All Other Categories*)

SELLING PRICE	FINAL VALUE FEE
$0.01–$25.00	12% of the closing value
$25.01–$1,000.00	12% of the first $25.00, plus 6% of the balance
$1,000.01 or more	12% of the initial $25.00, plus 6% of the next $25.01–$1,000, plus 2% of the remaining closing value

Optional Feature Fees

As we noted earlier, eBay offers several optional listing upgrades designed to make your listing stand out and to attract the attention of potential bidders. Tables 21.5 and 21.6 show the fees for these upgrades. The first fee listed is for auctions and Fixed Price listings running for three, five, seven, or ten days. The second fee listed is for thirty-day Fixed Price listings only.

Table 21.5 Optional Listing Upgrade Fees

Gallery Plus	$0.35/$1.00	Border	$4.00/$8.00
Listing Designer	$0.10/$0.30	Highlight	$5.00/$10.00
Item Subtitle	$0.50/$1.50	Featured First	$24.95/$74.95
Bold	$2.00/$4.00	Scheduled Listing	$0.10/$0.10
Homepage Featured	$59.95/$179.95	10-Day Duration	$0.40/Free
Gift Services	$0.25/$0.75	List in Two Categories	Listing fees double

Table 21.6 Featured Plus Auction Fee

STARTING PRICE	FEE
$0.01–$24.99	$9.95
$25.00–$199.99	$14.95
$200.00 or more	$19.95

Table 21.7 Image Hosting Fees

First Image	Free
Additional Pictures	$0.15 each
Picture Pack (1–6 images)	$0.75
Picture Pack (7–12 images)	$1.00

Additionally, you will incur expenses if you use more than one image (see Table 21.7).

If you choose to use a Picture Pack, you will get a free supersize feature that is only available when using a Picture Pack.

REDUCING YOUR EBAY FEES

Now that you understand how eBay charges for its services, let's take a look at how you can reduce your fees.

Insertion Fees

Right off the bat, you can see that eBay's insertion fees increase at various price points. If your starting price is on the cusp of one of these breaks, always go with the lower value. For example, if you started an auction listing at $50.00, the insertion fee would be $2.00. However, start the same item at $49.99—just one penny less—and your insertion fee drops by half to $1.00—you save $1.00. eBay does limit the number of identical results from the same seller that buyers will see on the Search Results page, but it only excludes items that have identical bidding activity and starting price. So if you have an item with a current high bid of $15.98 and another identical item ending a few days later that is at $10.50, both will show up in the Search Results. Which do you think new buyers will be bidding on?

When you list a large number of items, the listing fee maxes out at $4.00. If you are listing only a few items for sale, you should once again place your starting bid at the lowest price point consistent with what you expect the item to sell for. Say you are selling popular, relatively low-end items that typically receive many bids such as low-cost charms or a popular toy. Consider starting your auctions at $0.99—the lowest possible listing fee. Keep in mind, however, that if you are selling a high-priced specialty item in a narrow niche such as collectible movie posters or underwater cameras, you cannot risk doing this. Therefore, you have two options: List at a higher starting price and pay the higher insertion fee, or launch a Reserve Price Auction and start the item at a much lower price. I prefer the second option. Although the reserve fee is higher ($2.00 for items up to $200.00, and 1 percent for items over $200.00), as long as your reserve amount is reasonable and a high percentage of your auctions reach the reserve, the averages will work in your favor.

Special Feature Fees

We discussed how to use eBay's special features in chapter 16. Each of these features can potentially increase the number of bidders and the final value of your item. However, you have to calculate the potential return on investment (ROI), based on the expected value of the item you are selling. If you sell something in the $20 range, paying $2 for the Bold feature might get you a 15 percent increase ($3) in the final value, so this would be a good investment. However, the Highlight feature, at $5, would not be a good value—even if it increased your final value by 20 percent ($4).

eBay offers statistics on how well certain of these features perform, but these figures are averages for *all* auctions. A feature that gets an average 10 percent ROI for all auctions might not perform as well for your particular item. Also, this data is rarely new (sometimes it's as much as six or more years old). The only way to know for sure is to run test auctions. Whenever I find a new product I want to sell on eBay, I run auctions both with and without special features to determine if the performance warrants the investment. This kind of ongoing product research is critical to success in most business ventures, and it's essential when you're building a business on eBay.

There are two other costs that bear mentioning: Picture Hosting and Scheduled Listing fees. eBay charges $0.10 to schedule an auction to launch at a later time and $0.15 per photo if you include more than one in your listing. If you use four photos in an auction, you will be paying $0.45, plus another $0.10 (for a total of $0.55) if you schedule the auction to begin at a later time. If you are launching one hundred auctions a month, this adds up to $55.00 a month. In chapter 23, we will discuss automated services that offer image hosting and scheduling solutions. Some cost a minimal amount (under $20.00 a month), and the one we will talk about in detail is actually free.

As we discussed in chapter 15, you may be able to save money by hosting images on your own Web site, and just providing links to the images in your auctions. Many eBay sellers do this, but, in my opinion, it is too time-consuming to create and post the links every time you launch an auction.

The other major cost factor for eBay sellers is inventory—the products you buy to resell on eBay. We will discuss controlling your inventory costs in the next chapter.

POWER MOVES

❏ Set up a simple spreadsheet in Microsoft Excel and list your expenses. Be sure to include things such as your ISP and cable or DSL fees, as well as charges for telephone, postage, and office supplies. Take a step back and analyze your costs. Which line items are costing you the most each month? What can you do to reduce your monthly expenses?

❏ In chapter 10, you bookmarked the eBay fee schedule at http://pages.ebay.com/help/sell/fees.html. Go to this page and print out the full schedule. Study the fee schedule until you are thoroughly familiar with how eBay charges fees. You don't have to memorize the fees, especially those for optional features, but you should have a good feel for what they are and when to use them.

❏ Now calculate the eBay fees for several items listed and sold at different prices. For example, calculate the fees for an item that listed at $9.99 and sold for $20.00. Now do the same thing for an item that started at $49.99 and sold for $75.00.

❏ Using this information, study the auctions you have launched thus far, and evaluate your pricing. Have you been paying higher fees than necessary? What sort of ROI have you been realizing for optional listing features you've used? List steps you can take to lower your eBay fees, and write them in the binder next to your computer.

CHAPTER 22

✦ INVENTORY MANAGEMENT ✦

INVENTORY CONSISTS OF all the products you purchase to sell on eBay. Unless you engage in drop-shipping (as detailed in chapter 7) or selling on consignment for others (see chapter 27), your inventory will represent your largest investment and potentially your biggest financial risk. You incur this risk by purchasing inventory that either does not sell, or cannot sell at a high enough price for you to make a profit. Business owners call this *nonperforming inventory*.

In chapter 4 we stressed how crucial it is to research a product before you purchase it, so you can determine if it will sell on eBay. Product research is your best defense against being stuck with nonperforming inventory—but even excellent research is not foolproof. You can still end up with products that sell well at first and then fall in price as others begin selling them. In this chapter we'll examine how to manage your inventory so that you reduce costs and increase your monthly profits.

DEALING WITH NONPERFORMING INVENTORY

Purchasing large amounts of inventory at one time has its risks and rewards. Although you can get better prices by purchasing in large quantities, you need to consider how long it will take you to move the inventory.

eBay bidders pay close attention to an item's supply. When bidders see many identical items listed, they are reluctant to place high bids. They know that if they miss an item in one auction, they can just bid on another one. If you put too many of the same or similar items on eBay within a short period, you will drive down prices by increasing the supply. When you do this, you end up competing with yourself.

Despite your best research, you might find yourself with a product that's just not selling at a price that's profitable. When this happens, the best thing you can do is sell it quickly for whatever you can get. When you are sitting on inventory that is not selling, you are tying up money that you could be spending on inventory that *will* sell.

Retail store owners understand the cost of nonperforming inventory and the value of inventory that makes them money. That is why every retail store has a sale table. If an item is not selling well, store owners mark the price down to move it out quickly and free up money and shelf space for inventory that will perform better. As an eBay seller, it is imperative that you do the same thing if you want to make a profit. When inventory isn't moving, you need to create a virtual sale table.

There are two strategies for getting rid of inventory quickly. One is simply to launch the items on eBay at a lower price. The problem with this approach is that listing a large number of similar items at one time could drive the price even lower than what you were hoping to get. A better way is to list the items in Wholesale Large Lots.

Almost every eBay category has a subcategory called Wholesale Lots. This is where people sell items in bulk. If, for example, you purchased a large lot of cell phone batteries from a supplier and were only able to sell a few of them before the price started dropping, you could take your remaining batteries and either break them up into small lots or sell them as one large lot. Small lots will usually realize a higher per-item price than large ones; there are many small eBay sellers who cannot afford to purchase a case of forty-eight batteries, but who would be willing to buy a dozen at a time.

Another option is to use a Fixed Price multiple-quantity listing. Fixed Price listings are much cheaper to list and can run for thirty days. Unlike eBay store inventory, Fixed Price listings come up in the main eBay searches so you get more visibility. If you list a quantity over ten (say, fifty) of an item in a Fixed Price multiple-quantity listing, the "quantity" that appears on the description page will just say *more than 10 available*. If it's lower than ten, eBay will show the specific number of items that are unsold. If you list at a low price, you should be able to catch the impulse buyers and move your inventory quickly.

TURN YOUR INVENTORY OVER OFTEN

Inventory turn refers to how often you replace your inventory in a given period. Keeping your inventory turning at a brisk pace is essential to making large amounts of money on eBay. Consider the following example:

You find a source for overstock designer blue jeans, and you can buy a pallet load of one hundred pairs for $7 a pair. When you check the prices on eBay, you see that similar jeans are selling for between $18 and $29 a pair. The normal response is to list the jeans at the higher price. So you start launching auctions for the jeans at $29 a pair and find that you can sell about ten pairs a week. You are making a gross margin of $22 a pair before eBay and PayPal fees. Because you are selling ten pairs a week, you are realizing $220 a week. At this rate, it will take you ten weeks to sell all the jeans.

Now, let's say you lower the price of the jeans to $22 a pair, and you begin selling twenty-five pairs a week, as opposed to ten. Your gross margin on each pair is now only $15 but you are realizing $375 a week because of increased volume. Plus, you will sell all the jeans in four weeks instead of ten. Your margin for the four-week period is $1,500. You can now turn around and invest that $1,500 in more inventory, which you can sell again in another four-week period at the same price.

Compare the two scenarios: In the first one, you make $2,200 over a ten-week period at the higher price of $29. However, in the second scenario, you make $3,000 over the same ten-week period by selling the jeans at the lower price and reinvesting the profits. This is an example of using a lower pricing strategy to increase your inventory turn rate.

CONTROLLING YOUR INVENTORY

You can't control the flow of your inventory if you don't understand it. That's why it's important to keep good records. When you are just starting out, set up a simple Excel spreadsheet where you list your inventory (see Table 22.1). Create separate columns to list the item, the quantity you purchased, the quantity on hand, the date you acquired it, the cost per item, and the average selling price. (Every time you sell an item you should update the quantity on hand.) Keep a record of each sale in a ledger, so that you can determine the total final selling price for the entire lot.

Table 22.1 **Sample Inventory Record**

ITEM DESCRIPTION	INITIAL QUANTITY	QUANTITY ON HAND	DATE ACQUIRED	COST PER ITEM	AVERAGE (UNIT) SELLING PRICE
Men's Nautica Blue Jeans	44	17	12/1/2008	$19 pr.	$36.21
DKNY Silk Tops	12	8	1/7/2009	$24 ea.	$42.55
Nike Jordan Sneakers	36	33	2/14/2009	$47 ea.	$68.77
Nautica Blue Bathrobes, Unisex	12	4	2/22/2009	$14.20 ea.	$22
Fila Men's Running Suit	12	4	3/1/2009	$39 ea.	$76.88
G. Vanderbilt Women's Jeans	40	22	3/15/2009	$19.22 ea	$29.56

If you are going to run test auctions for the same item at different price points, set up a separate line item for each test. This will allow you to compare the performance of the different price points over time.

There are two other ways to track and control your inventory. If you decide to make an investment in QuickBooks (see chapter 21), this program has a built-in inventory function that allows you to enter inventory cost and performance data. The QuickBooks inventory function is fairly basic, although it's fine for most small businesses. If you sell a large number of different products, consider the more sophisticated inventory management program KwikInventory, made for Windows by Worth Data (www.barcodehq.com). Worth Data's system retails for around $300. You may also want to invest in a bar code printer and reader. These systems go for about $600, but there are plenty of used systems available on eBay for under $300.

The other way to manage your inventory is with an online system. In the next chapter, we'll return to auction management systems, which we touched on in chapter 15. Most of these services, including the ones I recommend, allow you to track your inventory, connect images and descriptions to each item, and even launch eBay auctions directly from your online system.

When you are first starting out, you will most likely be selling very few products. Setting up an inventory control system might seem like overkill, but as your business grows, you will need to organize and track your products. Knowing how much inventory you have on hand, how much it costs, how long it is taking you to turn it over, and how much it is selling for are all integral to running a successful eBay business. If you set up a system now while your inventory level is low, it will be much easier to integrate higher quantities later, when you're obviously busier, than to try to set up a system when you are also managing hundreds of auctions.

POWER MOVES

❏ Set up a spreadsheet to list and control your inventory. Be sure to track the dates you acquire your inventory, so you can assess how long it is taking you to move the inventory out.

❏ On this spreadsheet, track your average selling price (ASP) per item, so that you can identify your most and least profitable products. Use this information to determine which products (and how many units of each) to reorder.

❏ Implement strategies for dealing with nonperforming inventory. Consider listing items in a Wholesale Lots category or lowering your price to clear out slow-moving items.

CHAPTER 23

✦ AUTOMATING YOUR AUCTIONS ✦

IF YOU COULD HIRE A FULL-TIME employee for less than $50 a month, someone who would work with you in your eBay business—twenty-four hours a day, seven days a week—do you think that would be a good investment?

Uploading photos, writing descriptions, communicating with buyers, printing shipping labels, and posting feedback are just a few of the steps that you perform every time you launch or complete an auction. When you first start selling on eBay, you will be launching your auctions with the tools that eBay provides in the Sell Your Item form and managing your information from your My eBay page. As you grow your business, you should consider adding services and software that can automate some or all of these functions.

Automated services fall into three categories:

✳ eBay solutions (online and offline choices)

✳ Third-party offline software

✳ Online auction management services

Evaluating every product on the market to automate your auctions is beyond the scope of this book. Instead, let's look at the pros and cons of each type of service, and then evaluate one service that is fast becoming the choice of many eBay sellers.

EBAY SOLUTIONS

eBay offers both auction management software and online systems. The three basic choices are Turbo Lister, Blackthorne, and Selling Manager. We now turn to these eBay solutions.

Turbo Lister

This is a free download that allows you to create listings offline and launch them onto eBay. Through Turbo Lister, you can list multiple items at once and save listings to reuse again and again. Convenient templates allow you to create listings easily with a WYSIWYG (What-You-See-Is-What-You-Get) design editor (just like the HTML editor in the Sell Your Item form). Turbo Lister can also schedule your listings to launch at a later time.

Blackthorne

Formerly known as Seller's Assistant, Blackthorne is a software program that comes in two versions—Basic and Pro. These are eBay's all-in-one desktop listing and sales management tools, designed to automate the process of launching auctions. Blackthorne's tools help medium-to-high-volume sellers launch auctions on eBay without requiring a constant Internet connection. Both versions offer several customizable features. The Pro version includes sophisticated inventory control tools and detailed financial reporting. eBay charges $9.99 a month for the Basic version and $24.99 a month for the Pro version. Unlike Turbo Lister, which is primarily a launching and scheduling tool, Blackthorne has record-keeping and financial reporting capabilities. Blackthorne also allows you to automate the process of sending e-mails to winning bidders. You get a free thirty-day trial for either version, and if you download the program before subscribing, you can spend as long as you like preparing the listings. Once you're ready to launch a bunch of them, just sign up and the thirty-day trial starts at that point.

Selling Manager

This is eBay's online (that is, Web-based as opposed to desktop-based) sales management tool. You access Selling Manager through your My eBay page, which makes this tool very convenient. Selling Manager also comes in a Pro version. Selling Manager is for low-to-medium-volume listers, while Selling Manager Pro is better suited for high-volume listers.

Selling Manager is used in conjunction with Turbo Lister. Selling Manager provides additional automation for management of your ongoing listings as well as the postsale tasks. eBay charges $4.99 for Selling Manager.

With Selling Manager Pro you can relist multiple items at once; see a one-page snapshot of your business; track buying, selling, and account activities; create e-mails with custom templates; and print shipping labels and invoices. Plus you get bulk relisting capabilities and sophisticated inventory management and financial reporting tools. eBay charges $15.99 a month for Selling Manager Pro.

The eBay Advantage?

With the various eBay solutions, all your auction management is integrated into your My eBay page. You can easily compare the features (and cost) of each of these options in the table at http://pages.ebay.com/selling_manager/comparison.html.

The major drawback of all three eBay systems is the lack of photo hosting. Remember that eBay gives you the first photo free and then charges $0.15 for each additional photo. Most sellers use three or four photos in their auctions, so you can anticipate spending up to $0.45 a listing on photography. If you list one hundred auctions a month, this adds up to $45.00—in addition to the monthly cost of whichever eBay listing management tool you choose. eBay Picture Services addresses this, but you are still paying $4.99 for 50 MB, $14.95 for 250 MB, or $24.99 for 1 GB of storage per month. Unless you have a Premium-level eBay store, there are better options out there for the same or lower cost.

Another disadvantage is the inability to launch auctions in other (non-eBay) venues, such as Overstock.com Auctions. As you will see in chapter 28, once you have mastered eBay, you can easily increase your sales and profits by expanding beyond eBay.

THIRD-PARTY SOFTWARE

There are several companies selling software products that automate many of the common eBay functions. The two most popular are Spoonfeeder (www.spoonfeeder.com), and AuctionGenie (http://tinyurl.com/8b5qu). Auction Genie is the only software program that works with both Macs and PCs.

Both systems include most of the features offered by eBay's Blackthorne. AuctionGenie includes free photo hosting as part of its monthly cost, which appears to make it a somewhat better value. All three are primarily Windows-based, although AuctionGenie also has a Mac OSX version. The main advantage of these third-party systems over eBay's offerings is their ability to support multichannel selling. So you can create listings on other sites (channels) as well, such as Amazon, Overstock.com Auctions, and Yahoo! Stores.

ONLINE AUCTION MANAGEMENT SERVICES

There are over a dozen companies offering Web-based automation solutions for eBay sellers. The leading companies, together with their Web addresses and costs, are listed in Table 23.1.

Table 23.1 Leading Online Auction Management Services

Vendio	www.vendio.com	$14.95/month + image fees and per-item listing fee
InkFrog	www.inkfrog.com	$9.95/month
ChannelAdvisor	www.channeladvisor.com	$44.95/month (minimum)
Auctiva	www.auctiva.com	Free

All these companies provide basic automation services, although some do it better than others. My personal favorite for new sellers is Auctiva. Auctiva provides all the basic automation features, it's been around since 1998 (so it has a good track record), and it's free. What better price? Here are some of the features of Auctiva:

* HTML templates to create your auctions.

* Create an item listing for inventory you plan to list later.

* Prewritten, automated invoices, payment reminders, and shipping and feedback notices.

* One-page listing form (all the information is on one page so if you want to go back and revise something you can do it very easily).

* Free image hosting (up to twenty-four pictures per listing) with a free supersize feature.

* Free auction scheduling.

* Free listing templates (over 1,500 to choose from).

* Free watermarking for your photographs (so other sellers can't steal them for their auctions).

* Free scrolling window in all your listings to cross-promote your other items.

If you use Listing Designer, inserting three photographs per listing, and Scheduled Listing, using Auctiva to list your auctions will save you $0.50 per auction and $0.70 per Fixed Price listing. If you use more pictures (say the six-picture pack), you save $0.95–$1.15 per listing. That adds up quickly. If you launch one hundred auctions a month, that's $95.00–$115.00 in upgrade and picture fees you're saving every month.

Personally, I favor the online systems over desktop-based programs: They save the most time and you don't have to worry about computer crashes and losing your data. Using such a system is like having a virtual employee—one who saves you time, helps you launch your auctions more efficiently, and keeps your costs under control.

POWER MOVES

❏ Visit eBay's Selling Resources pages and read the information about the eBay-based automation solutions Turbo Lister, Blackthorne, and Selling Manager.

❏ Visit Auctiva.com (or any of the other sites listed in this chapter) and take a tour.

❏ Once you have selected an automation solution to try, either purchase a subscription or sign up for a free trial. Begin setting up your inventory and learning the system.

CHAPTER 24

✦ THIRD-PARTY PROMOTIONAL TOOLS ✦

YOU HAVE A GREAT PRODUCT that you can buy at a great price. You have mastered the art of title writing, using keywords, taking great photos, and all the basic steps you need for success. In addition, you've reduced your eBay fees and streamlined the management of your inventory. So what else can you do to increase your sales and profits?

eBay is a very competitive sales venue, so anything you can do to either stand out from the crowd or convince the customer to do business with you instead of clicking away to another auction will put money in your pocket at the end of the month.

Techniques for promoting your auctions fall into two categories: (1) those designed to drive buyers to your auctions, increasing your hits; and (2) those intended to generate buyer trust and confidence, increasing your bids. In this chapter, we'll explore some of the tools available from third-party vendors that can help lure buyers to your auctions and generate more and higher bids.

INCREASING AUCTION VIEWS

The single best way to boost the number of hits your auctions receive is by writing compelling, keyword-rich titles. If your auctions are getting very few views, the first thing you need to do is review the material in chapter 14 and make sure you are writing the best titles you can. The other factor that drives hits are the eBay promotional features covered in chapter 16, such as Bold, Highlight, Subtitle, and so on.

Assuming that you've done the best job possible in these areas, what else can you do to increase hits?

Auctiva Scrolling Gallery

Even if you decide not to use Auctiva to launch your auctions and host your pictures, you can still use the Scrolling Gallery (see Figure 24.1) for free.

Just sign up for Auctiva and select *Scrolling Gallery* from your list of options. You'll set up an eBay token that allows Auctiva very limited access to your listings (just to link your auctions together using the Scrolling Gallery) and presto—all the auctions you list from now on will cross-promote your other auctions.

This is particularly useful when you're selling similar items (such as clothes in the same size, or a range of items and their accessories) because buyers will look to your

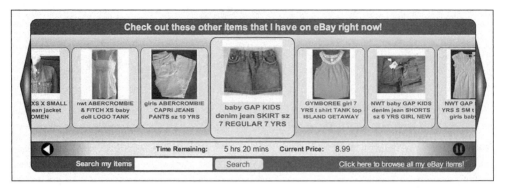

Figure 24.1   Auctiva Scrolling Gallery

other items to combine shipping. The disadvantage occurs if you have listed a lot of separate auctions for the same item. This can allow your buyer to see a different auction with a lower current bid, and shows him that there are many items available so he doesn't really need to bid/buy right now to get the item. So be aware of your listing strategy when you decide to use (or not use) Scrolling Gallery.

Web Site and E-mail Promotion

Another way to promote your auctions is with an *eBay* button that you can post on your Web site (if you have one) or attach to all your outgoing e-mails. If you go to the eBay site map under the heading Selling Activities, look for the link that says *Promote Your Listings with Link Buttons.* This will take you to a page where you can copy a snippet of HTML code that you can paste into a Web page or insert as your e-mail signature. The code will create a little button that says *Right Now on eBay* superimposed over an eBay logo. When shoppers click on this button, it takes them to a list of your auctions on eBay. There is no charge for this service; in fact, it can actually save you money if you have an eBay store. Whenever someone arrives at your store from an off-eBay location (such as from an e-mail link or from your Web site), eBay credits you 75 percent of the final value fee of anything the buyer purchases there. This is called the Store Referral Credit, and you do need to include some referral codes in the links to get it, but you can find all the details at http://pages.ebay.com/help/sell/referral-credit-faq.html.

Classified Ads

Here's another great way to promote your auctions that almost no one ever thinks of— classified advertising, both in newspapers and on the Web. This technique works best if you sell to a small niche market. For example, let's say you collect and sell old fountain pens. You can take out small classified ads in newspapers that read something like this:

> *Old Fountain Pens for Sale on eBay. Just type 1234567890123
> into the search box at www.ebay.com.*

The number could be the item number of a pen currently at auction or listed in your eBay store. This is the easiest way to lead someone directly to you, because the complete hyperlink to your auctions is too long and complex to put in a newspaper ad. If you have an eBay store, you could direct readers to http://stores.ebay.com/ *yourstorename*, which is also a good option because the URL isn't too long. If they type the address directly into the browser window, even though they aren't including the referral code, you are still eligible for the Store Referral Credit. This is because the URL is not an active link that could have been generated from eBay's own promotion.

If you are posting classified ads on the Web, you can use a simple HTML command to create a link to your list of auctions. Your online ad would read like this:

> *Old Fountain Pens for Sale on eBay. <a href=your link to auctions goes here>
> Click Here</a> to see my auctions.*

When you use the <a href=> code, the reader of an online classified sees this:

> *Old Fountain Pens for Sale on eBay.*
> <u>*Click Here*</u> *to see my auctions.*

When you use an HTML link, you can include the store referral codes; this way you can receive the Store Referral Credit when readers click on the link and are directed to your store inventory. You can find plenty of Web sites that offer free classified ads by just typing *free classified ad* into the Google, Yahoo!, or MSN search boxes.

BUILDING TRUST AND CONFIDENCE

Once you drive prospective bidders to your auction, you want them to bid. There are plenty of studies that show that anything you can do to inspire trust and confidence in customers will increase bids on eBay auctions, boost purchases through your eBay store, and increase purchases on a Web site. On eBay, your best strategy is to earn a high feedback rating and keep it at least 99 percent positive. But there are some interesting third-party tools to help you build buyer confidence as well.

SquareTrade

SquareTrade (www.squaretrade.com) offers warranty services for new and used items (see Figure 24.2). This can be a big deal, particularly in terms of used electronics. You do not pay for the warranty; the buyer does. However, you can promote the warranty through your auction, which does give you more credibility. Many buyers don't realize

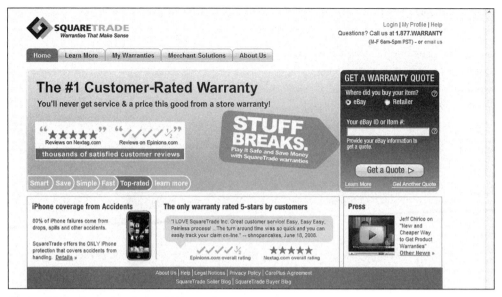

Figure 24.2   SquareTrade.com Warranties

that they can go to SquareTrade for warranties on most items bought on- or offline. Plus, most manufacturers don't offer warranties on used or refurbished items, or items sold by unauthorized dealers on eBay. However, SquareTrade warranties do cover all these situations. By offering it in your auctions, you're giving the buyer one more reason to buy from you. They don't necessarily know that they could buy from any seller and get the warranty direct from SquareTrade, so including this offer can make your item more attractive than others.

buySAFE

The bonding service buySAFE protects your buyers against fraud. If you sell low-value items (under $100), the service is probably not worth the cost (buySAFE charges a fee of 1 percent of the transaction value [final value] on each successful transaction). However, you might offer the Buyers Choice Plan, which allows the buyer to purchase a bond on the item if she chooses (there is no cost to the seller for offering this).

If you're selling big-ticket items, such as pricey antiques or collectibles, buySAFE certainly helps allay the fears of some prospective bidders who might otherwise hesitate to make a substantial bid on one of your pieces. Even if you have positive feedback in the thousands, someone considering buying an expensive antique has every reason to be cautious. When you sign up for and are accepted by buySAFE, the service automatically inserts a seal into your auctions informing bidders that they are protected against fraud, up to whatever limit buySAFE agrees to. If you are a fairly new seller, the fraud-protection limit will usually extend as high as $10,000. Once you gain more experience and your feedback rating climbs, buySAFE will often raise the limit to $25,000.

Figure 24.3 depicts the buySAFE Seal as it appears in an auction; Figure 24.4 shows the buySAFE page bidders arrive at after clicking on the seal.

Figure 24.3
buySAFE Seal

Another product from buySAFE is the Trading Assistant Bond for consignment sellers. One major concern of consignors is that they have to relinquish the item to the Trading Assistant when they sign the consignment agreement (before the item is even listed). That's okay for a $20 cookie jar, but what about a $1,500 diamond ring? Would you be comfortable leaving that with someone you don't know?

Many states are requiring Trading Assistants to be licensed and/or bonded. eBay specifically requires Registered eBay Drop-Off Locations (REDOLs) to be bonded, and buySAFE can provide that bond. It costs $250 a year for a $25,000 bond, which is not bad, considering it's a necessity for REDOLs and highly recommended for all Trading Assistants who specialize in higher-ticket items. The amount of extra business you will get because of the bond far outweighs the cost.

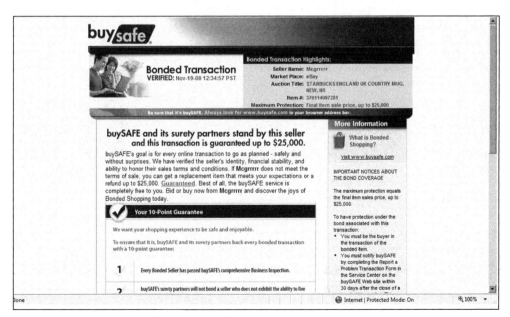

Figure 24.4   buySAFE Verification Page for Mcgrrrrr

SellersVoice

Silent auctions may be going the way of silent movies. Voice technology has been around for several years, but a relatively new company called SellersVoice has made adding audio clips to your auctions a breeze. SellersVoice has set up a special page for readers of this book at www.sellersvoice.com/skip to demonstrate how I use the technology in my auctions. Like other links cited in this book, this can be found at the book's Web site, www.skipmcgrath.com/3_weeks.

Using SellersVoice is easy. Once you sign up for an account (you can get a three-week trial for $1 at the link specified above), you call a toll-free number and record a message. I have found that a thirty- to forty-five-second message is ideal. After recording your message, you return to the SellersVoice Web site and copy a snippet of HTML code to your computer's clipboard. Now when you list an auction, simply paste the code right into your item description. This will place an audio toolbar into your auction text. See the example in Figure 24.5.

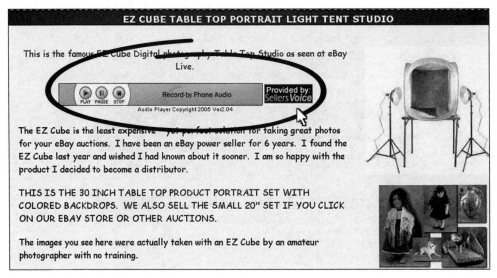

Figure 24.5   SellersVoice Toolbar in an Auction

I have performed several blind tests in which I launched identical auctions with and without a voice recording. The results varied, depending on the products I was selling, but in all cases I received more bids and gained higher final values when I used the voice feature. In one test, selling Starbucks collectible mugs, I averaged 19 percent more bids and achieved a 14 percent higher average final value.

The service seems a bit expensive at $29 a month. However, if you are currently realizing monthly profits of $2,000 or more, and you can increase that by even 10 percent, you'll see an extra $200 in sales per month. Subtract the $29 fee, and you have an additional monthly profit of $171. If you really build your business and take your sales up to the $10,000-a-month level, using audio could put an extra $1,000 or more into your profit column each month.

Don't worry if you don't have a professional-sounding voice or don't know what to say. The idea is to "humanize" your auction to increase bidder trust and confidence. The SellersVoice Web site has excellent tutorials and best practices to help you get started.

POWER MOVES

❏ As soon as you qualify, sign up for the SquareTrade program at www.squaretrade.com.

❏ Visit the other resources mentioned in this chapter, including:

> buySAFE (www.buysafe.com)

> SellersVoice (www.sellersvoice.com/skip)

❏ Become familiar with the buySAFE and SellersVoice offerings, and determine if any of these resources could benefit your business.

❏ Begin running online and newspaper classified ads for your auctions. Track the increase in sales to determine your ROI.

CHAPTER 25

✦ UPSELLING AND E-MAIL ✦ MARKETING TO YOUR CUSTOMERS

EBAY HAS VERY STRICT RULES regarding e-mail—especially when it comes to e-mail marketing to eBay members. In the early days of eBay, you could get any member's e-mail address right off the site. Now eBay has a system whereby you can only e-mail members through eBay's My Messages system. Furthermore, you can only see the recipient's e-mail address if he replies to you and doesn't check a box preventing his e-mail address from being revealed. This may sound a bit draconian, but it is actually for the best. From eBay's point of view, the company makes money when people buy and sell through eBay. From a buyer's point of view, eBay is now much safer, because, under the previous system, there used to be a lot more fraud and bid stealing.

················ BEST PRACTICES ················

RIGHT ITEM, WRONG SELLER

One popular scam worked like this: I see an auction end for a very expensive product, of which you are the winner. Because I can see your e-mail address, I immediately send you an e-mail claiming that I am the seller and providing a link you can click to pay me now. I am banking on the real seller failing to send out an authentic payment notice upon the auction's close, and that you are gullible enough to click on my link and pay me via credit card. Upon receipt of the payment, I promptly close the eBay account and disappear—until tomorrow, when I open a new account. eBay's current system prevents this once-popular form of fraud. It also attempts to keep spammers from getting your e-mail address and scamming you in other ways, or from trying to sell you who-knows-what.

Once a customer buys something from you on eBay, that customer is now "yours," in the sense that you have established a direct relationship with him. You can now freely communicate with him and make offers to him outside the eBay platform. This is perfectly within eBay's guidelines. (Actually, it's the law and there is nothing eBay can do about it.)

Does this mean you should now start deluging your customers with all sorts of offers? Not unless you want them to write back and ask to be taken off your mailing list. However, there are plenty of other ways to reach out to these customers. In this chapter, we'll explore profitable ways to go about building and marketing to your customer base. We'll also examine how to *upsell* (also known as *cross-selling*), by getting winning bidders to increase the quantity of their orders—or add related products to their original orders.

END-OF-AUCTION E-MAILS

The most common form of upselling is done in your end-of-auction e-mail. If you use an auction management system like Auctiva, you can create e-mails that go out to winning bidders and link to your eBay store or your Web site, if you have one. In the e-mail message, you can offer customers an incentive to buy more of the same product or another related item. Typical incentives include free shipping if customers buy a second item, or a discount on the second item purchased.

Here is a sample e-mail, designed to upsell, which you could send to a winning bidder:

> *Dear (Winning Bidder's User ID),*
>
> *Thank you for purchasing the Weber combined gas/charcoal barbecue grill, eBay item #123456789, through our auction. Your winning bid was $126.50 + $12.50 shipping and handling. The total is $139.00. I have provided a link below that you can click on to pay via PayPal.*
>
> *Almost everyone who buys one of these grills purchases a cover to keep the grill clean and dry when it sits outside during inclement weather. We offer a fitted cover for $24.00, plus $4.90 for shipping. However, if we ship it with your order, we will waive the additional shipping charge. If you want to take advantage of this offer, please click on the second link below that says Barbecue + cover.*
>
> *Payment link Barbecue*
>
> *Payment Link Barbecue + cover*
>
> *Please click here to visit our eBay store, where we sell a wide range of barbecue tools and accessories to go with your grill.*
>
> *Thank you once again for your business. We will ship your order immediately upon receiving payment and send you an e-mail with the tracking information.*

Best regards,
Skip McGrath, Mcgrrrrr

Note that the underlined words in the e-mail are clickable links to the payment gateway and to our eBay store.

The advantage of upselling from your Web site is that you raise your average selling price without incurring any additional eBay fees. If you upsell from your eBay store, you must still pay a final value fee. Here's the trick if you're linking to your eBay store: Make sure the link you provide in the e-mail includes the correct referral code for landing on your eBay store main page. This way, if customers buy anything from your store, you will get 75 percent of the final value fee credited back as the Store Referral Credit (see chapter 24).

E-MAILING CUSTOMERS ABOUT NEW PRODUCTS

Let's say you sold a quality product to someone at a decent price, posted glowing feedback about her, and provided her with a positive customer service experience all around. You now have the opportunity to market to that customer again.

There is nothing wrong with sending customers *occasional* e-mails when you have something special you think they would be interested in. For example, my wife and I sell Starbucks collectibles—Starbucks City mugs, Bearista Bears, and Starbucks coffee cards. Now, I don't want to send my customers an e-mail every time I'm auctioning a new Starbucks collectible, since I list several items every week. However, every once in a while I come across an unusual item—perhaps a mug with a spelling mistake on it, or a rare or hard-to-find Bearista Bear. In these cases, I send out an e-mail to my list of several hundred people who have purchased Starbucks merchandise from me in the past and alert them to the auction.

Invariably, I get one or two people who reply and ask not to be e-mailed again. Because my e-mails do not go for the hard sell, these requests are usually polite. For example, a customer might write something like this: "Hi, I bought a mug from you as a gift for someone and am not really a collector. So could you please take me off your mailing list? Thank you . . ."

Now let's look at a few other ways you can market to your customers.

BUILD AN OPT-IN MAILING LIST

A more effective approach than mass e-mailing is to ask your customers if they would like to be notified of future promotions, sales, and unusual or hard-to-find items. Every time you make a sale, after you post feedback and ship the item, send your customers an e-mail like this:

Dear (eBay User ID),

Thank you for purchasing the Aviator Bearista Bear through my auction. I hope your bear arrived in good condition and you are delighted with it. If you have any problems, please let me know immediately and I will do my best to make it right.

I have posted positive feedback for you and hope you will do the same for me.

Living in Seattle, the home of Starbucks, I often pick up hard-to-find Starbucks collectibles. Please reply to this e-mail if you would like to receive my monthly sales notice or an occasional e-mail if I come across a very special item.

Using this method, you will get fewer names to add to your list, but they will be highly qualified names. In addition, if you have an eBay store or a Web site, you can add a line to the e-mail with the store's and/or Web site's URL, and invite the customer to peruse your other offerings and purchase from you directly.

Obviously, this method of marketing only works if you have built a specialty niche. If you are selling used blue jeans one week and DVD players the next, there isn't much use in pursuing this type of marketing.

USING YOUR WEB SITE

Another form of upselling involves capturing your customers' e-mail addresses with an eye toward sending them future promotional offers available through your Web site. I do this using a service from PayPal that allows me to create a promotional code. For example, I can e-mail all my customers with a special code entitling them to 10 percent off any purchase from my Web site. When a customer visits the Web site and buys something, he is directed to the PayPal-enabled shopping cart. Once he enters his credit card or PayPal account information, a box comes up where he can enter the promotional code. PayPal then deducts the percentage I specified from the customer's order. You can also set the promotional code to disable the shipping calculation, thereby offering free shipping.

We've already talked about using Auctiva's Scrolling Gallery as a way to cross-sell your other items. Vendio offers a Scrolling Marquee, which is essentially the same thing as the Scrolling Gallery. If you use Auctiva or Vendio you can now put the Scrolling Gallery on your Web site to drive traffic back to your eBay auctions. You can see an example of this at the bottom of my homepage at www.skipmcgrath.com.

NEWSLETTER AND WEB SITE MARKETING

Another variation on the same theme is to start a subject-oriented newsletter. Many specialty sellers—especially those selling collectibles—create monthly or bimonthly newsletters and invite buyers to sign up for a free subscription. Here's how this works: First, you create a Web site to sell products in the same category as those you're listing on eBay. Then you publish your newsletter right on the site. The navigation bar on your homepage includes an internal link to your newsletter, and you might put a "teaser" box about the newsletter on the homepage to entice visitors to check it out. You then send out the newsletter's table of contents in an e-mail, with a link taking readers right to the applicable page on your site. This strategy is designed to drive prospective buyers to your Web site. Once they look around, you're counting on prompting them to purchase something.

Don't worry if you can't write well enough to produce a newsletter. You can always compile a digest of news and articles about your topic. For instance, let's say you sell mineral specimens to rock collectors. Conduct a Google search on several terms related to rock collecting and use the *News* tab of the Google search feature. Whenever you find a relevant article, include the title and the first sentence or two in your newsletter, with a link to the full article. It would look something like this:

> ### *Gem Show's Pool of Treasures Includes 96-year-old's Agate*
> *WHITTIER, CA—Clarence Pool has been an avid rock hunter for more than half a century. He became a dedicated Rockhound in his 20s, at the urging of another collector . . .* <u>Read More</u>

The underscored words <u>Read More</u> would be a hyperlink to the article itself. You can include a series of these on your newsletter page. Consider writing your own comments below each article. You should make sure that the link opens a new window, so your reader doesn't leave your Web site to go there.

You can also find free articles on hundreds of subjects at Web sites where authors post articles. You are free to post the article on your Web site as long as you credit the person who wrote it and include a link to the Web site it was posted on. Here are several Web sites from which you can copy or download articles:

* www.findarticles.com
* www.articlecity.com
* www.goarticles.com
* www.ezinearticles.com
* www.articleworld.net
* www.aracontent.com

Your goal is to build a content-rich Web site that makes your customers come back again and again.

CAPTURING E-MAIL ADDRESSES
FROM NONBIDDERS AND NONBUYERS

Did you know you can also capture e-mail addresses of people who just *look* at your auction, even if they don't bid or buy? The trick is to give something away for free. Yes, I said *free*. What you are going to give away is a free report. For example, suppose you are in the wedding business. You have a Web site that offers wedding gowns and supplies for sale, and you also sell some of your merchandise on eBay. At the bottom of every auction for a wedding-related item, you include a statement along the following lines: "As a FREE GIFT for looking at my auction, please click on my About Me page, where you can download my free e-book, *A Checklist for Planning the Perfect Wedding*."

The underlined words would be a clickable link to your eBay About Me page. While eBay does not allow you to link to other commercial Web sites from your auctions, it does allow you to do this from your About Me page as long as the page they click to does not offer anything for sale. So, once you set up your About Me page, include a link to the area of your Web site where customers can download the free report. Many people who look at your auctions without bidding on them will bite on your free offer. Once they arrive at your Web site, you provide the free report and hope that they bookmark the site or buy something. Or, even better, you can set up a subscription form for your newsletter and require a visitor to enter her first name, last name, and e-mail address before she can access the free report. Now you really have a prospect you can market to (until the wedding is over, that is). I use a service called Aweber at www.aweber.com to manage my newsletter lists.

THE EBAY E-MAIL MARKETING SYSTEM

In 2005, eBay figured out that many sellers were using the strategies outlined above and decided to try to compete for your business—and keep you and your customers on eBay—by offering a free e-mail marketing service.

If you look at Figure 25.1, there is a box on the right with a link that says *Add to Favorite Sellers*. When a member viewing your auction clicks on that link, he is taken to a page that looks like the one in Figure 25.2. At this point, he can sign up to receive e-mails from you. If you sell in several categories, there is a box where the buyer can select which category of products he is interested in.

Figure 25.1   Add to Favorite Sellers Option

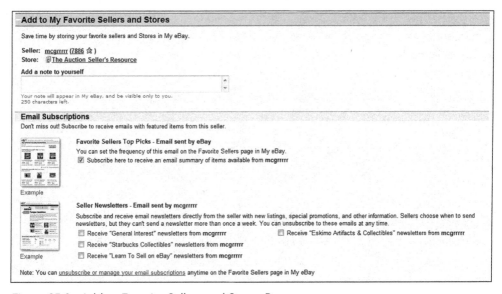

Figure 25.2   Add to Favorite Sellers and Stores Page

If you have an eBay store, once a buyer adds you to his Favorite Sellers list, you can e-mail him through the Manage My Store control panel. If you open an eBay store (see chapter 26), eBay allows you to build and market to your mailing lists in the following ways:

✳ Buyers can sign up to receive your e-mail newsletters when they add you to their Favorite Sellers list.

✳ Using a simple tool, you can create e-mails with links to your eBay store and your auctions, and then send them to your subscribers. You can control which subscribers receive your e-mails, based on their interests, purchase history, and so forth.

* You can create up to five mailing lists that target different interests or types of promotions. For example, you could have a DVDs mailing list (alerting buyers to new DVDs you have in stock) and a Sale Notifications mailing list (alerting buyers to special discounts you are offering). Buyers choose which of your mailing lists to sign up for when they add you to their Favorite Sellers list.

* You can measure the success of a targeted e-mail by viewing statistics, such as the number of bids and Buy It Now purchases it generated, and use this information to reach out more effectively to customers.

Depending on your eBay store subscription level (Basic, Premium, or Anchor; see chapter 26), eBay will allow you to send a certain number of free monthly e-mails to your subscribers. If you exceed your monthly allocation, you will be charged a per-recipient fee for additional e-mails. Monthly allocations and additional e-mail charges are outlined in Table 25.1.

Table 25.1
eBay Store E-mail Allocation Breakdowns by Store Type

SUBSCRIPTION LEVEL	MONTHLY FREE E-MAIL ALLOCATION	ADDITIONAL COST PER RECIPIENT (OVER ALLOCATION)
Basic Store	5,000 e-mails	$0.01 per e-mail
Premium Store	7,500 e-mails	$0.01 per e-mail
Anchor Store	10,000 e-mails	$0.01 per e-mail

For more on eBay store fees, see chapter 26.

E-mail marketing, both on and off eBay, allows you to generate more business. And more sales means more profits. If you can use your eBay auctions as a means of advertising for your eBay store, where listing and selling fees are lower—or, even better, for your Web site, where there are no listing or selling fees at all—then your profits will increase exponentially.

POWER MOVES

❏ Evaluate the products you currently sell. See if you can come up with combinations that would lend themselves to upselling; in addition, write up a list of products you could buy or create for the purpose of cross-selling. Once you have identified these items and determined their pricing, start featuring them in your e-mails to customers at the end of your auctions.

❏ Learn about eBay's e-mail marketing program. (To find out more about the program, click on the *Help* tab at the top of any eBay page and type *e-mail marketing* into the search box.)

❏ Visit www.Aweber.com and read about their programs for newsletter publishers. Consider how to create newsletters that would appeal to bidders and buyers of your specific product(s).

❏ Set up a system to capture and record e-mail addresses from your successful bidders.

CHAPTER 26

✦ OPENING AN EBAY STORE ✦

AN EBAY STORE IS BASICALLY a "mini" Web site on eBay, where you can sell products to eBay members at fixed prices. You can list your merchandise in an eBay store for either thirty days or as a permanent store listing (called Good 'Til Canceled, or GTC), which autorenews every thirty days until the inventory is sold or you take the listing down.

WHY SET UP AN EBAY STORE?

The key reason is to garner bigger profits. According to eBay's research, eBay store sellers realize, on average, a 25 percent increase in sales the first three months after opening their store. As a store seller, you'll also save on listing fees—just $0.02 a listing for each thirty-day period. Optional features are also much less expensive if you have an eBay store; for example, it costs only $0.01 for the Gallery feature in a store, as opposed to $0.35 to insert the Gallery feature in a regular auction listing.

BIZ BUILDER

eBay provides a dedicated search box within your eBay store, enabling buyers to search through your items and find exactly what they want.

You control the look and feel of your store. A professional-looking store gives you credibility as an online retailer—and makes shopping easier for your buyers. eBay offers a Business Resource Center where you can access tools to establish your store brand by downloading templates for business cards and more. This helps you build your brand on eBay and develop repeat business.

Since an eBay store is essentially a Web site, it has its own URL that you can use to drive buyers directly there, from both on and off eBay. You can even optimize your Web address so that it shows up in search engine results. (You can find complete instructions for doing this through the *Manage Your Store* link, once your eBay store is set up.)

An eBay store also allows you to cross-promote your products to prospective auction bidders. With an easy-to-use tool, you can control which items are cross-promoted; links to selected items appear at the bottom of your auctions. See Figure 26.1 for several examples.

Figure 26.1   eBay Store Cross-Promotions

TYPES OF STORES AND FEES

eBay charges less to sell through its Fixed Price store format than through auctions. There are three kinds of fees for eBay stores:

* Monthly subscription fees
* Listing and final value fees
* Special promotional fees

Let's look at each type, and what you get for your money.

Subscription Fees

eBay charges all sellers monthly subscription fees for their eBay stores. There are three subscription levels for eBay stores, each of which comes with additional features and benefits:

Basic: $15.95/month

Premium: $49.95/month

Anchor: $299.95/month

Basic Store

With a Basic Store subscription, you can showcase all your auction, Fixed Price, and Store Inventory listings in a custom storefront that you design. In addition, you can list an item in your store for as low as $0.03 per thirty days, and use the cross-promotion tool to cross-sell your inventory on all your Item, Bid Confirm, and Purchase Confirmation pages. The Basic subscription level also gives you a free subscription to

Selling Manager (usually $4.99 a month) and dedicated phone customer service between 6 a.m. and 6 p.m. Pacific Time.

Premium Store

With a Premium Store subscription, you get all the Basic Store benefits, plus additional exposure, including:

* Priority inclusion in the Shop eBay Stores section on Search and Browse pages.

* Featured placement on the eBay Stores homepage (http://stores.ebay.com).

* Prime positioning in the Stores Directory pages.

* Free subscription to Selling Manager Pro (usually $15.99 a month).

* Marketplace data and sophisticated traffic statistics, allowing you to see where your traffic is coming from.

* Dedicated phone customer service 24/7.

At $49.95 per month, a Premium Store may seem expensive, but when you deduct the $15.99 subscription fee to Selling Manager Pro (which you would probably need at this level anyway), the monthly store subscription fee drops to $33.96. All levels of eBay store allow you to choose up to three hundred categories and subcategories of merchandise to sell. This is helpful if you are selling different types of products and you want to direct customers to the right place in your store. For example, if you were selling men's, women's, and children's apparel, you could have a separate category for each one, and then subcategories within these main categories for size or type of item (just as eBay's auctions have). This would spare a woman visiting your store from having to page through dozens of men's and children's items. Similarly, if you were selling after-market car accessories, you could have separate categories for all the popular makes—such as Nissan, GM, Toyota, Chrysler, Honda, Ford, Mazda, and so on.

Anchor Store

The Anchor Store is quite expensive at first glance. However, if you are selling products with high keyword potential (that is, items that are frequently searched for), this option actually could be a good value. With an Anchor Store subscription, you get all the Basic and Premium Store benefits, plus:

* One million banner impressions per month for your store throughout eBay.com—including on the eBay homepage.

* Frequent placement of your logo on the eBay Stores homepage.

* Premium placement in the Shop eBay Stores section on the Search and Browse pages.

* 1 GB of image storage and a free subscription to eBay Picture Services.

When you open a store for the first time, eBay gives you the first thirty days of your store subscription for free. After the first thirty days, you're billed the normal monthly subscription fee. You can pay this fee through your primary eBay account by credit card, via PayPal, or by check.

Listing and Final Value Fees

When you list an item (either for auction or at a fixed price), the listing will automatically appear both in your eBay store (all subscription levels) and on eBay's Search and Browse pages at no extra charge. When a potential bidder clicks on *View Seller's Other Items*, he will see both your store listings and your auction listings.

By contrast, Store Inventory listings are Fixed Price listings that only appear in your eBay store and on store Search pages. They will not be included in the Search Results prompted by a search of all eBay listings. (If the number of auction and Fixed Price listings returned for a particular search is low, a selection of eBay store listings matching the same terms will appear at the bottom of the results. However, this doesn't occur for every search.)

The insertion fee for store items is based on the item price (as shown in Table 26.1). This fee covers any quantity of items with a single listing, whether you list one, one hundred, or one thousand of the same item. The insertion fee is charged every thirty days for Good 'Til Canceled listings. You cannot set the price for a Store Inventory item lower than $1. Therefore, the fees for Store Inventory (shown in the following tables) start with an item price of $1.

Table 26.1
eBay Store Insertion Fees

ITEM PRICE	INSERTION FEE
$1.00–$24.99	$0.03
$25.00–$199.99	$0.05
$200.00 +	$0.10

While eBay store listing fees are much lower than those for eBay auctions, the final value fees are higher. Table 26.2 is a schedule of final value fees for store listings as of this printing (go to http://pages.ebay.com/help/sell/storefees.html for the most recent fees).

Table 26.2 eBay Store Final Value Fees

CLOSING VALUE	FINAL VALUE FEE
$1.00–$25.00	12% of the closing value
$25.01–$100.00	12% of the initial $25 ($3.00), plus 8% of the remaining closing value balance
$100.01–$1,000.00	12% of the initial $25.00 ($3.00), plus 8% of the next $25.01–$100.00 ($6.00), plus 4% of the remaining closing value balance
$1,000.01 or more	12% of the initial $25.00 ($3.00), plus 8% of the next $25.01–$100.00 ($6.00), plus 4% of the next $100.01–$1,000.00 ($36.00), plus 2% of the remaining closing value balance

Finally, as with insertion fees, optional feature fees for Store Inventory listings are much lower than those associated with auction-style listings (see Table 26.3).

Table 26.3 Optional Feature Fees with an eBay Store

FEATURE	FEE PER 30 DAYS
Gallery Plus	$0.35
Item Subtitle	$0.02
Listing Designer	$0.10
Bold	$1.00
Highlight	$5.00
Border	$3.00
Picture Pack (up to 12 pictures)	$0.50
Scheduled Listing	$0.10

The Featured Plus fees are tiered (as shown in Table 26.4).

Table 26.4 eBay Store Featured Plus Fees

ITEM PRICE	FEATURED PLUS FEE
$1.00–$24.99	$9.95
$25.00–$199.99	$14.95
$200.00–$499.99	$19.95
$500.00 +	$24.95

SETTING UP SHOP

No matter which subscription level you opt for, setting up and branding your eBay store is fairly simple and only takes a few minutes. Best of all, you have complete control over the look and feel of your store. eBay allows you to:

* Customize your store's homepage.

* Select a color scheme for your header and left-hand navigation bar.

* Insert your own custom graphics into your header.

* Choose the default option of how you want your items displayed.

* Create up to twenty custom categories within your store.

* Provide additional information to your buyers, including descriptions about your store, yourself, and your store's policies.

Creating custom graphics for your store is important for branding purposes. If you don't have any experience in the field of online graphics, there are plenty of people on eBay who can do this for you. Simply type *eBay store graphics* into the eBay search engine, and you will find dozens of auction listings for people who offer this service. Most sellers charge between $50 and $150 for this service, but some may charge higher fees for more sophisticated graphics. There is a well-known company that provides professional store designs and marketing materials, called Frooition, at http://frooition.com.

Promoting Your eBay Store

The biggest PowerSellers on eBay generate the bulk of their sales from their eBay stores. The trick is to launch auctions that generate plenty of interest and traffic—and then convince everyone who looks at your auctions to visit your eBay store.

There are two ways that eBay lets bidders know you have a store: by placing a small store icon after your user ID and by including a link in all your auctions to *View Seller's Other Items*. Unfortunately, very few buyers actually click on these links. Your challenge is to change that—to encourage buyers to click through to your store.

As noted above, Premium and Anchor Stores allow you to set up separate categories in your store, like departments in a department store. The goal is to drive people viewing one of your auctions to a specific category in your store. Here's how it might work: Let's say you sell bird feeders and other bird-related products. You launch a few auctions for high-end bird feeders and promote them with some of eBay's special features, such as Featured Plus, Featured First, Homepage Featured, Bold, and Highlight, in hopes of generating a lot of traffic. Now in your auction, right under your product description, you include a paragraph that describes all the other bird-related items you sell. The paragraph would contain both an invitation and a clickable link to a specific category in your eBay store, like the one below:

> *<ext>If you love songbirds, please visit my eBay store,*
> *<a href=http://www.your_store_link_goes_here>BirdsForAll</a>, where*
> *you will find a large selection of bird feeders, bird baths, birdhouses,*
> *and books on birds and birding.</ext>*

The HTML code is the clickable link right to the appropriate category in your eBay store. The name *BirdsForAll* will appear in light blue and underlined, indicating to prospective buyers that they can just click on the link to visit your store. Bidders will read it as follows: "If you love songbirds, please visit my eBay store, BirdsForAll, where you will find a large selection . . ."

Another technique for turning auction browsers into store customers is to offer something for free. For instance, you could add the following sentence to the paragraph above with the clickable link: "As a free gift for visiting my store, you can download the e-book *How to Attract Songbirds to Your Yard*." In this case, you would simply create a short PDF file that anyone could download from your About Me page. (If you don't know how to attract songbirds to your yard, you can buy a book on the subject from the U.S. Government Printing Office and reproduce it. The GPO has books on thousands of subjects that you can freely reproduce because the copyright is in the public domain.)

Another way to attract visitors to your eBay store is to offer free shipping. I often do this by adding a statement to my auctions like this:

FREE SHIPPING FOR MY EBAY STORE CUSTOMERS

You do not have to wait for the auction to end to buy this Garmin GPS unit. It's available in my eBay store for immediate shipment. If you buy this item now from my eBay store, I will ship it for FREE anywhere in the U.S. If you are in Canada or overseas, I will give you a $5.00 credit toward the shipping cost. I also have several other Garmin models in my store in different price ranges. Click Here to buy now or to see all the items in my store.

While you'll have to pick up the cost of shipping, you'll be generating sales you would not have made otherwise. Many store sellers deliberately set the prices in their stores a bit higher to cover the cost of this giveaway. Once you get the bidders to check out your store, be sure to make it as easy as possible for them to buy. As we mentioned above, you need to direct the buyer to the correct category, because this saves him time and, hopefully, prompts him to buy other items of interest.

BIZ BUILDER

I make it a point to prominently feature the search box that allows buyers to search my store. Once a potential bidder is in your store, anything you can do to get her to the product she is looking for as quickly as possible will produce the best results. If you were selling apparel, for instance, you could invite buyers to search by size. If you sold different brands of cameras, you could place a message next to your search box inviting customers to search by brand, such as Nikon, Sony, or Kodak.

You can also promote your eBay store from outside eBay. eBay automatically submits your store's URL to several search engines, such as Google and Yahoo!. Be sure to use keywords in your store description and in each item title to increase your chances of getting hits from these search engines. To encourage you to bring in outside business, eBay offers a 75 percent discount on the final value fee of any item sold to someone you directed to your eBay store from outside of eBay. (This is known as the Store Referral Credit; see chapter 24.) But this discount is not automatic; you must include the correct referral codes in the links you submit to search engines or use in e-mail or Web site marketing (you can find the correct codes at http://pages.ebay.com/help/sell/referral-credit-steps.html). This can translate into huge savings. For example, if you sold an item for $75.00, the final value fee would be $7.00. If the sale came from outside of eBay, the fee would only be $1.75.

See chapters 24 and 25 for more ways to drive traffic to your store from outside of eBay.

POWER MOVES

❏ Visit the *eBay Stores* link from the eBay homepage. Click on several of the store listings and become familiar with how eBay stores are listed and how other sellers promote their stores.

❏ From your My eBay page, click on the *Manage My Store* link and sign up for a Basic Store subscription.

❏ Place some merchandise in your store, and start linking from your auctions to your store. Consider ways to entice bidders to your store, such as offering free shipping or a giveaway.

❏ Go to http://pages.ebay.com/storefronts/Subscriptions.html to compare the features of each subscription level.

CHAPTER 27

✦ EBAY CONSIGNMENT SELLING ✦

I LIKE TO CALL SELLING goods on consignment for others the "perfect eBay business." Oftentimes, the biggest problem eBay sellers face is finding products that they can resell at a profit. Luckily, there's an alternative. If you're having difficulty locating products of your own, you may be able to make money selling items for others.

For every successful eBay seller, there are others who can't figure out how to sell effectively or profitably on eBay. Also, believe it or not, there are still people who are not convinced that eBay really works, are afraid to try it, and/or are computer illiterate. There are also plenty of people who just don't have the time to learn the skills needed to sell successfully on eBay. That's where you come in.

In 2002, eBay launched the Trading Assistant program. A Trading Assistant is an eBay seller who sells products for eBay members who either don't know how to or don't want to sell their goods themselves. If you go to the eBay site map and look under the Selling Resources heading, you will see a link to the *Trading Assistant Program*. By 2008 there were 35,000 Trading Assistants helping others sell on eBay. While becoming an eBay Trading Assistant will take you more than three weeks, you can start selling on consignment at any time after you qualify for the program—and it's useful to understand how the Trading Assistant program works, so that, if you choose, you can incorporate this program into your long-term success plan.

THE TRADING ASSISTANT PROGRAM

When you join the Trading Assistant program, you tell the world that you are willing to sell for others. Trading Assistants charge fees or commissions for their services. Selling as a Trading Assistant allows you to leverage your selling expertise without having to find products yourself—clients provide the products and you are compensated for your efforts on mutually agreed-upon terms. Many sellers already do this as a way of making money on eBay; profit margins can be significant, especially for higher-priced items.

Do You Qualify?

To join the Trading Assistant Directory (see Figure 27.1), you must have sold at least ten items in the last three months, and maintain an average of ten sales per three months. You must have (and maintain) a feedback score of 100 or higher, and at least 98 percent

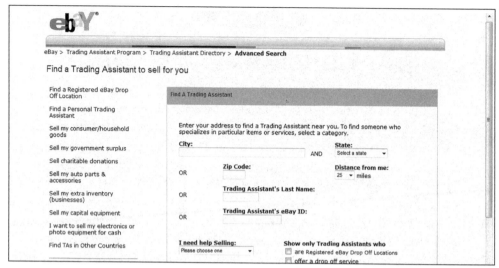

Figure 27.1 eBay Trading Assistant Directory

of your feedback must be positive. You also must be in good standing with eBay. Joining the directory is free.

eBay does not endorse the assistants listed in the directory. As eBay states in its description of the program: "Including yourself in our Trading Assistant Directory is a lot like running a classified ad for your services. Trading Assistants are not employees or independent contractors of eBay, nor do we endorse or approve them. Each Trading Assistant runs his or her own independent business, free from any involvement by eBay."

How It Works

Through the Trading Assistant program, eBay gives any eBay seller who qualifies an opportunity to start a consignment business. When an eBay member is looking for a Trading Assistant, she goes to the directory, where she can type in her location and search for an assistant in her area. Once the seller performs a search, she receives a list of Trading Assistants and their contact information. If your name comes up in the list, the seller (in this case the *consignor*, or the person who supplies your products) can either e-mail or call you to work out a deal directly.

eBay also provides Trading Assistants with promotional materials. There is a *Toolkit* link on the Trading Assistant page. From here you can download posters and flyers in Microsoft Word format that you can personalize, print out, and use in your marketing efforts. There are also business card templates and Trading Assistant images that you can use online.

Signing up to be an eBay Trading Assistant should be your first step in starting a consignment business.

THE TRADING ASSISTANT BUSINESS

There are thousands of eBay sellers running consignment businesses. These range from regular sellers who sell on consignment as a side business to full-time, large commercial businesses operating out of retail storefronts. eBay has extra regulations for retail storefronts (called Registered eBay Drop-Off Locations, or REDOLs) that are set up to provide consignors with a convenient place to drop off merchandise for consignment sellers to list on eBay. In addition to the standard Trading Assistant requirements, REDOLs must also carry a $1 million general liability insurance policy (on top of any other state requirements), have a $25,000 bond, be open at least five days a week with business hours posted, have outside signage, and adhere to a number of other standards as set out in the REDOL user agreement.

A woman in my hometown used to own a consignment shop right in the heart of the retail district. She sold good-quality antiques and collectibles on consignment and had a very nice business for several years. Three years ago she tried selling some of the goods in her shop on eBay. After some trial and error, she began doing very well. Earlier this year, she closed the shop; she now sells exclusively on eBay.

Like many consignment sellers, she finds people with goods to sell by placing ads in the local paper and on free community bulletin boards, approaching previous customers who know her, and by word of mouth.

Consignment selling on eBay is not a new idea. There was a huge boom of franchise consignment stores a few years back, but that model was largely unsuccessful for the actual sellers (because of the high franchise costs) and it fizzled out within about a year. eBay's REDOL requirements came into effect in 2008, and that reduced the number of storefront consignment sellers. But there are still thousands of Trading Assistants who are full-time consignment sellers whether or not they have a retail storefront.

How big can an eBay consignment business grow? That really depends on several factors, including how big you want your business to grow, what resources you have, and how much you can invest. I watched a large REDOL's auctions on eBay and I estimated they closed about $50,000 worth of auctions a week. The basic commission schedule for most consignment stores is 40 percent, so that works out to a gross margin of $20,000 a week. Now, you aren't going to take in this much without a sizable investment, several full-time employees, a hefty advertising budget, and so on. But I firmly believe that anyone who is skilled at selling on eBay can develop a small business that can realize a gross margin of $1,000 to $3,000 a week. This would require you to launch an average of twenty to fifty auctions a week. Many PowerSellers today routinely launch over a hundred auctions a week, so twenty to fifty auctions a week is certainly doable. In chapter 23, we discussed automating some of the common tasks that allow you to do this. One of the automation services we mentioned was InkFrog (www.inkfrog.com), which offers consignment tracking in addition to automation services. This feature allows sellers to keep track of sales and payments to consignors.

If you are going to sell at a high level, I strongly suggest that you get the Trading Assistant bond through buySAFE (as we discussed in chapter 24) because it will make consignors more willing to have you sell higher-priced items for them.

MARKETING YOUR EBAY CONSIGNMENT BUSINESS

Once you have honed your eBay selling skills, it's not hard to market your services. If you want to find consignors, you have to go looking for them. The eBay Trading Assistant Directory may bring you some business, but probably not enough to live on.

Finding consignors takes little time and money. Here's how I market my eBay consignment services:

* **CLASSIFIED ADS:** I run small newspaper classified ads that read something like this: "I will sell your treasures on eBay. Call Skip 360-555-1111" or "Raise cash by selling your unwanted merchandise on eBay. Professional eBay seller does all the work for you. Call Skip at 212-555-2222." Many newspapers offer deals on multiple placements of classified ads. Speak to your newspaper's classified ad rep about working out a volume discount.

* **NETWORKING:** I like to use what I call the "three-foot rule." (I think Europeans call this the "one-meter rule.") Everyone who comes within three feet (1m) of me learns what I do for a living. I always carry business cards or even a small flyer that explains what I do. Whenever I meet people, I tell them that I am a professional eBay seller and that if they have something they would like to sell, I would be glad to help them.

* **FREE BULLETIN BOARDS:** This works the same way as classified ads. Just create short ads on three-by-five cards and place them on community bulletin boards in senior centers, supermarkets, and laundromats. I always carry pushpins or thumbtacks so I'm ready whenever I come across one of these corkboards.

* **DIRECT MAIL TO ATTORNEYS:** Create a short letter that explains the services you offer and mail it to all the estate and bankruptcy attorneys in your county. When an attorney has to settle an estate or sell off the proceeds of a bankrupt individual or company, he often works with a local auctioneer. If you explain to an attorney that you can raise far more money for the estate or the creditors by exposing the merchandise in question to over 80 million prospective eBay buyers—rather than relying on a couple of hundred people who show up for a local auction—he will most likely be all ears.

* **CONTACT LOCAL RETAILERS:** Retail stores often have merchandise they want to get rid of. You can often get them more for it on eBay than they would get from a liquidation or surplus dealer.

There are many other ways to market your eBay consignment service, but these five techniques should net you enough business to keep you busy—and profitable—for quite a while.

POWER MOVES

❏ If you would like to try consignment selling, visit the eBay Trading Assistant page (on the site map, click on *Trading Assistant Program*, under Selling Resources) and read the requirements to see if you qualify.

❏ Create some small classified ads and three-by-five cards advertising your services as a consignment seller, and start placing the ads in local papers and the cards on community bulletin boards in supermarkets, laundromats, and the like.

❏ Once you have some experience as a consignment seller, if you decide to pursue this business more aggressively, visit my Web site, www.skipmcgrath.com, where you'll find my book on this subject, *How to Start and Run an eBay Consignment Business*.

CHAPTER 28

✦ BEYOND EBAY ✦

EBAY IS A GREAT PLACE to start an online business. It has a low barrier to entry and you can learn while you're making money. But there *is* life beyond eBay. My wife and I started selling on eBay in 1999. Today we still sell on eBay every day—but now we also sell on Overstock.com and maintain three different Web sites offering a variety of products.

While eBay is certainly the largest online auction site, there are a number of other successful sites, such as Bid4Assets, Overstock.com, Bonanzle, and E-Pier. In addition to auction sites, you can sell from your own Web site or create a Web store at www.PowerSellerBuilder.com (see page 242).

OTHER AUCTION SITES

Once you master eBay, you might want to explore selling your goods in other venues. If you sell very expensive items, one of the best auction sites is www.Bid4assets.com, which deals almost exclusively in high-priced goods. If you specialize in jewelry, check out Web-based auction sites that focus on those items, including www.bidz.com.

Overstock is a popular online shopping site that launched an auction format in early 2005. Since then it has grown substantially, and is now the second-largest auction site behind eBay in terms of gross merchandise sales. The Overstock auction site is separate from the Overstock.com site. You can find it at www.auctions.overstock.com.

In addition to auctions, there are all sorts of targeted selling sites. If you sell any type of handmade product, the most popular site is Etsy at www.etsy.com. Craigslist (www.craigslist.com) and Kijiji (www.kijiji.com) are well-known classified ad sites, which allow you to sell goods regionally.

YOUR OWN WEB SITE

In the past, setting up your own Web site was a daunting challenge. If you didn't know how to write HTML code and upload pages, you would have to hire a Web designer to do it for you. This could cost anywhere from $500 to several thousand dollars, and once the site was designed and launched, you needed help to maintain it. Over the past few years, an array of new Web services have come on the market, allowing anyone with minimal computer skills to design and maintain an e-commerce Web site. If you have the skills to launch an eBay auction, then you can build a Web site.

These companies use a system of predesigned templates and shopping carts. All you have to do is point and click to select colors and designs and to upload photos, and then just type text into an HTML editor that looks like a Microsoft Word document to create the headlines and text for your Web site.

Here is a list of some of the more well-regarded Web site–creation companies:

* www.powersellerbuilder.com
* www.hostway.com
* www.register.com
* www.homestead.com

Using the first site on the list, PowerSellerBuilder.com, I was able to design and upload an e-commerce Web site in less than four hours. (You can check out two Web sites I designed with PowerSellerBuilder.com at www.ezauctiontools.com and www.firepit-grills.com.) PowerSellerBuilder.com has over five hundred color and design combinations, and offers e-mail accounts, newsletter and autoresponder functions, FAQ pages, photo albums, message boards, and a shopping cart that allows you to use PayPal so you don't need to apply for a merchant credit card account.

PowerSellerBuilder.com also offers several tools to help promote your Web site, such as free Web site submission to major search engines like Yahoo! and Google; the ability to add titles, keywords, and metatags to your Web pages to make it easier for search engines to find you; free submission to Google's online shopping engine, Froogle; and discounts for Yahoo!'s Overture keyword advertising program.

As of this writing, PowerSellerBuilder.com charges $29.98 a month. This is more expensive than simple Web site builders, but it also includes a shopping cart and telephone and e-mail support. There are many advantages to having a Web site. As we've discussed, you can capture customers on eBay and drive them to your Web site, where you can sell products to them without paying additional eBay fees. As you build a customer base, you can market to them from your Web site as well. A Web site can also help build your credibility and brand your business.

I use eBay to drive traffic to my Web sites, and I use my Web sites to drive traffic to my eBay auctions and stores. Once you get the hang of managing Web sites and auctions, you will see how easy it is to make your business venues complement and support each other.

ONWARD AND UPWARD

I hope by now you are well into your third week of activity and closing auctions successfully. The most important advice I can give you at this point is this: Don't give up!

Things will go wrong—they always do. As with any new venture, you will certainly make mistakes and they can frustrate and demoralize you. Whenever you make a mistake, go back to the basics and analyze what went awry and what you can do differently the next time. Take risks and experiment—but remember to stay within eBay's guidelines when you do. When you take risks, such as selling a new product, be sure to take small risks instead of one large one. Don't commit to buying a large amount of inventory until you have thoroughly tested the market.

Finally, remember that eBay is a community. eBay members love to help each other. If you are having problems, go on the eBay message boards and ask for help. You'll be amazed at how many people will reach out to assist you with terrific advice.

Besides being profitable, selling on eBay is supposed to be fun. If you always try to view your business in this context, you will enjoy yourself, your mistakes will be less frustrating, and you will probably make more money in the end.

Good luck on eBay!

✦ APPENDICES ✦

✦ AUCTION CHECKLIST ✦

HERE IS A SHORT CHECKLIST you should consult before launching your auctions:

- ❑ Have I checked my listing for any spelling or grammatical errors?
- ❑ Is my type readable? Is it too large or too small?
- ❑ Did I use short paragraphs with breaks between them?
- ❑ Are my photos clear and not too big to cause slow loading?
- ❑ Have I checked all my fees and options?
- ❑ Did I use the correct auction duration (number of days)?
- ❑ Does my auction end at a good time and on a good day (such as Sunday at 7 p.m. EST)?
- ❑ Did I include clear shipping information, costs, return policy, and other terms?
- ❑ Is my item description accurate, clear, and complete?
- ❑ Did I include information as to the product's size, weight, and so forth?
- ❑ Did I mention any flaws?
- ❑ Did I include a return policy?
- ❑ Did I clearly spell out the payment terms?
- ❑ Does my title communicate what I am selling?
- ❑ Does my title contain lots of keywords for item searches?
- ❑ Did I invite bidders to e-mail me with questions?
- ❑ Did I include active links to my eBay store and my About Me page?
- ❑ Is my About Me page up-to-date?
- ❑ Did I include a Buy It Now price?

APPENDIX B

✦ POPULAR SOURCES OF ✦ WHOLESALE MERCHANDISE

HERE IS AN ANNOTATED LIST of popular sources for merchandise at wholesale prices. eBay PowerSellers often buy from these wholesalers. Most of these companies require you to have a state resale license (or sales tax ID number). You can also find this list and click through to the sites directly at www.skipmcgrath.com/3_weeks. (Don't forget the underscore!).

LIQUIDITY SERVICES (www.Liquidation.com) is one of the largest closeout and surplus dealers on the Web. Its customers include major department stores, such as Macy's, Target, and BJ's Wholesale, as well as small businesses looking to move out surplus merchandise from their stores.

Using an auction format similar to eBay's (with comparable fees), Liquidation.com has hundreds of bulk auctions to bid on at any given time. In addition to providing access to a variety of lot sizes—pallet loads, box lots, and trailer loads—the site also sells a variety of surplus merchandise, including overstocks, closeouts, shelf pulls, and refurbished products. Best of all, this company has good customer service.

The merchandise available at Liquidation.com is available for a wide range of prices: A typical pallet can cost anywhere from $200 to $2,000. Recently, I saw a pallet of video game sets—Game Boys, Xbox 360s, and PlayStation 3s among them—that were selling for an average of $40.00 each. Another pallet had a thousand pairs of new, name-brand blue jeans—Polo, Lee, Boss, and the like—selling for less than $1.70 each.

Merchandise at Liquidation.com changes every day and you can sign up for e-mail alerts to make sure you don't miss any specials that would be of interest to you.

GOVERNMENT LIQUIDATION.COM (www.govliquidation.com), is the official Web-based auction site for the Department of Defense and is also owned by Liquidity Services. Through this site, the DOD clears out its military surplus goods, unneeded office equipment, computers, appliances, tools, and just about anything else you can imagine. In 2005, the U.S. Air Force sold more than ten thousand surplus Palm M515 units. I bought a lot of twenty-five for just $70 each—about one-quarter of the retail cost.

Warning #1: Before bidding on an item at Liquidation.com, be sure to check the shipping cost. Because dealers who list with this site are located all over the country, the cost of shipping a pallet load of goods can get very expensive; so try to buy from suppliers who are nearby. For example, if you live on the East Coast, you should expect that a pallet from California would be subject to high shipping prices. Before placing a bid, either get a shipping estimate or be sure to bid from sellers who are fewer than one thousand miles (1,609km) from your location.

Warning #2: Be wary of buying returns. If you are unsure about the quality of merchandise you're considering bidding on, e-mail the seller to ask if the goods you're interested in contain *product returns* or *warranty returns*. Product returns are merchandise that customers returned to the store for some reason. The reasons for return could be anything: Maybe the item was the wrong color or size, or maybe the customer found it defective. Warranty returns are items that were brought back to the manufacturer for warranty repair. Some manufacturers will simply ship a new item to the customer and sell the returned item as is, rather than pay the cost of repair. In general, I would not buy warranty returns unless you can repair the product yourself or plan to sell it for its parts.

VIA TRADING (www.viatrading.com) is another large closeout dealer that buys and sells surplus, overstocks, and returns from major department store chains. In my own dealings with Via Trading, I've found that company representatives are very honest in describing their merchandise; that is, you won't be surprised about the quality of the goods you order. However, there is one caveat: Via Trading only deals by the pallet load. And though many of its pallets sell for as little as $250, whenever you're considering pallet loads of merchandise, always be sure to check the shipping charges first.

BUYLINK (www.buylink.com) is a collective of several hundred small distributors and manufacturer's reps. You have to register, enter your sales tax ID number, and wait about two business days for a confirmation e-mail before you can get a rundown of prices. But once you are registered you can place orders for a variety of gift products, home and garden accessories, and new collectibles.

GREATREP (www.greatrep.com) is a Web site that lists several hundred specialty gift wholesalers and many small manufacturers. Not all of them will deal with eBay sellers, but most of them will. The advantage of Greatrep is that you can find niche products that other sellers don't have. Once you register on the site, you will receive an e-mail with links to access the manufacturers' listings. Some of the manufacturers do not have Web sites, but phone numbers are listed so you can just call them.

AMERICAN TOP LEATHER (www.americantopleather.com) is a manufacturer of leather goods specializing in apparel and accessories. This is *not* your source for those cheap, $17 leather jackets you'll see selling on eBay. American Top Leather produces merchandise in several qualities, ranging from average to excellent. The company has a great line of motorcycle jackets and outstanding saddlebags that sell extremely well on eBay at a very nice markup.

LUXURY MAGAZZINO (www.luxurymagazzino.com) is the best-known supplier of designer goods among eBay PowerSellers. Luxury Magazzino bought the www.luxurybrandsllc.com domain and customer list after Luxury Brands went bust, which is why, if you attempt to visit Luxury Brands, you'll be redirected to the Luxury Magazzino Web site. However, Luxury Magazzino is not the same company under another name. The site sells all the famous designer labels—and, best of all, you can purchase them in small quantities. I recently bought a lot of six Prada Tussoto handbags for about $450 total, and they all sold for between $150 and $175 each.

Not all Luxury Magazzino products sell well on eBay, however. Once again, before committing to a large purchase, research the items on eBay to make sure they are selling well. Hint: Always search Completed Listings so you can find out what something actually sold for instead of merely what the current high bid is.

MADISON AVENUE CLOSEOUTS (www.madisonavenuecloseouts.com) is a great source of good-quality clothing for men, women, and children. The company also carries men's big & tall and women's plus sizes, which are great sellers on eBay.

The pricing is excellent, and you'll frequently find great specials. In my experience, the product descriptions are very honest in terms of quality and makeup of the goods. However, you do have to request that information via e-mail, as it's not readily available on the Web site.

T-SHIRT WHOLESALE (t-shirtwholesaler.com) sells a lot more than T-shirts. This is a great source for name-brand men's and women's tops of all kinds.

THE SILVER SOURCE (www.silversource.com) is one of the largest and most reliable sources of silver jewelry on the Web. The Silver Source has been supplying flea market dealers and jewelry stores for more than twenty years and the company expanded to eBay sellers in 1998. The Silver Source literally has thousands of styles of almost every type of jewelry—rings, pendants, necklaces, toe rings, and more. Sterling silver rings start at less than $2 each. The minimum order is $100.

TEEDA (www.teeda.com), another jewelry company, specializes in cubic zirconium, marcasite, and sterling silver jewelry at excellent wholesale prices.

MBK WHOLESALE (www.mbkwholesale.com) is a large general wholesaler that carries a wide range of gifts, collectibles, and As Seen On TV (ASOTV) items. MBK is a regular source for many large PowerSellers.

DRAGON DISTRIBUTING (www.dragondistributing.com) is a leading wholesale distributor specializing in the distribution of automotive and consumer electronics to independent dealers. Dragon carries all the hot brands of car-audio amps, speakers, cables, and accessories. You will need a sales tax ID number and a commercial checking account to do business with Dragon.

Dragon is headquartered in Asia, but the company has warehouses in the United States. Before you buy, make sure to determine where the goods will be shipped from and get a shipping estimate. If they are coming from overseas, you will need a customs broker to clear the shipment and pay any duties involved. A & A Contract Customs Brokers (www.aacb.com) is very experienced at working with eBay sellers and can handle all your importing needs.

TELEBRANDS WHOLESALE (www.telebrandswholesale.com) is probably the leading supplier of ASOTV goods for eBay sellers. There are several companies in this industry, but, in my opinion, TeleBrands is the best. The company sells most products in one-case lots and the prices are typically 50–60 percent below the advertised-on-TV price. The other big ASOTV supplier is **SALCO**, which runs a drop-shipping operation for eBay sellers at http://ezdropshipper.com.

BOONE'S ANTIQUES (www.boonesantiques.com) is a wholesaler of antiques—yes, you can buy antiques wholesale. Boone's Antiques supplies antiques dealers and decorators all over the country. The Boone's main store is in Wilson, North Carolina. (Actually, *store* is an understatement, considering it is four acres [1.6ha] in size.)

✦ THIRD-PARTY RESOURCES ✦ FOR EBAY SELLERS

EBAY HAS SPAWNED an entire industry of companies that supply products and services exclusively for eBay sellers. Some of the most popular companies are listed below; you can also find links for them on my Web site for this book: www.skipmcgrath.com/3_weeks.

AUCTION MANAGEMENT SERVICES

Auction management services allow you to automate the auction process, which gives you the time to list more items for sale, and consequently, make greater profits. Valuable features provided by most auction management services include the following:

Predesigned templates	Image hosting and placement
HTML editors	Image editing
Bulk listing tools	Tools to print shipping labels
Automated payment notification	Automated checkout
Auction scheduling	Recurring launching
Sales reporting	Access to other venues
Inventory reporting and control	Hosted online stores

The main advantage of online auction management systems is that they work 24/7, even when you're not online. Also, if your computer crashes, your data is still safely stored on the Web. However, the main disadvantage of an online service is the cost: Auction management services charge by the month, by the transaction, or both. You should carefully compare costs before selecting a service. Some of the best-known auction management services on the Web are listed below:

Auctiva	www.auctiva.com
AuctionHawk	www.auctionhawk.com
Channel Advisor	www.channeladvisor.com
InkFrog	www.inkfrog.com
Vendio	www.vendio.com

Readers of *Three Weeks to eBay Profits* can take advantage of special free-trial offers from these online management services by accessing them through the Web site for this book: www.skipmcgrath.com/3_weeks.

AUCTION MANAGEMENT SOFTWARE

The auction management systems described above are all Web-based, but you also have the option of purchasing auction software for use on your computer. These software programs offer many of the features of an online service, with only a few exceptions. Software will only allow you to handle automated checkout, automated payment notification, and image hosting when you're connected to the Internet. This means you must manage and revise your auctions offline and then connect to the Web when you're ready to make updates, upload images, send payment notices, and so on. The main advantage of software is the cost—once you've purchased the program, you own it (as opposed to online services, which charge by frequency of use). However, as with any software, you're relying on your home computer: If you don't sufficiently back up your sales records and your computer crashes you risk losing your data. Here are the most popular software products and their corresponding Web sites:

AuctionSubmit	www.auctionsubmit.com
Foo Dog	www.foodogsoftware.com
e-Lister	www.blackmagik.com/elister.html

PRODUCT RESEARCH SERVICES

HammerTap (www.hammertap.com)

HammerTap is an invaluable research tool for eBay sellers. By sorting through the multitudes of auctions, the program identifies top-selling items up for bid in your particular niche of the eBay market. HammerTap allows you to drill down and narrow your search to find the most successful brand or product feature within a category of merchandise—information that will help you effectively evaluate your products' sales potential.

HammerTap can also uncover auction trends that yield higher sell-through rates in your own auctions. Use the data available on HammerTap to discover which day of the week is best to end your auction listing, assess whether or not to use a reserve, choose starting prices that attract more bids, and much more. In addition, HammerTap has an *Auction* tab on its Search Results page that enables you to investigate successful auctions via a variety of factors, including their popularity, starting price, total sales, number of bids, seller's reputation, reserve sell-through rate, or category. It's a great way to learn exactly what determines an auction's success.

If you use the link www.hammertap.com/skip, you'll find a special HammerTap discount deal just for readers of this book.

Terapeak Research Service (http://www.terapeak.com)

Terapeak is one of the newer research services for eBay sellers. It offers all the features of HammerTap plus a keyword analysis tool.

Terapeak provides the following information about a product:

* Average sales price

* Total sales for your item

* Total listings

* Success rate

* Total bids received

* Demand for the item

* Prices realized on eBay

* Best time of day to sell

* Top-ranked sellers and total bids they have received

* Total sales market share

* Sell-through rate

Terapeak also allows you to download the data to Excel for further offline analysis.

Find Hot Niches (http://www.findhotniches.com)

Find Hot Niches is a monthly service that researches the hot keywords used in more than one hundred product niches. This is a great way to discover new niches and pinpoint the best keywords for any niches you select.

AUCTION NEWS AND INFORMATION

AuctionBytes (www.auctionbytes.com)

AuctionBytes, run by David and Ina Steiner, is the authoritative, independent news source for eBay and the online auction community. The Steiners publish a daily newsletter and a weekly wrapup featuring longer stories, advice, and articles written by online auction experts. The site also contains several free resources and links to hundreds of Internet services.

AUCTION PROMOTION TOOLS

SellersVoice (www.sellersvoice.com/skip)

SellersVoice is an online service that allows you to easily add audio to your eBay auctions. According to research conducted by SellersVoice, adding audio can increase the number of bids received by as much as 30 percent and final values by as much as 19 percent. For testimonials, links to my auctions featuring audio, and a free trial from SellersVoice, visit www.sellersvoice.com/skip, or go to the Web site for this book, www.skipmcgrath.com/3_weeks, where you will find links to all the specials and offers mentioned here.

Google AdWords (https://adwords.google.com)

Google AdWords is a pay-per-click service that you can use to drive business to your eBay store. The ads appear as small boxes on the right side of every Google Search Results page that relates to your search term. For example, let's say you're selling digital camera supplies and someone googles the term *tripod*; if you have purchased the keyword *tripod* through AdWords, a sponsored advertisement for your store will appear next to the natural search results. When the consumer clicks on your ad, she will be taken directly to your store.

Not including the one-time activation fee, AdWords users have two payment options. If you select *cost-per-click-pricing*, AdWords will charge you when someone clicks on your Google ad; if you opt for *cost-per-impression advertising*, you'll be charged when your ad is viewed on the Google Search Results page. Advertisers' fees are determined by their bids on specific keywords that, when searched by Google users, will call up their paid advertisement. The higher your keyword bid, the more prominent the placement of your ad on the Google Search Results page.

Yahoo! Search Marketing (www.content.overture.com)

This is another pay-per-click advertising service that puts a link to your eBay store just ahead of the natural Yahoo! Search Results. The ad is formatted so that it looks more like an actual Yahoo! listing, although it's preceded by the heading Sponsored Results directly above it.

Miva (www.miva.com)

Miva is a much smaller pay-per-click service. It doesn't deliver as many hits as Google or Yahoo!, but the cost per click in much less. Therefore a lot of sellers use Miva to test their keywords. Once they determine which keywords work best, they roll their campaigns out on Google or Yahoo!.

buySAFE (http://buysafe.com)

buySAFE is a bonding company that provides your buyers with protection against fraudulent transactions on eBay and the Internet. This is very useful if you sell high-priced merchandise, as it gives your customers confidence in you. buySAFE has a store where shoppers can look for merchandise that is insured by buySAFE. This service is free to buySAFE customers. buySAFE also provides the $25,000 Trading Assistant bond required for REDOLs.

✦ SAFETY TIPS FOR ✦ BUYERS AND SELLERS

COMPARED TO THE REST of the Internet, eBay is actually one of the safest venues for online buying and selling. Fraud is quite rare and affects only a tiny fraction of the millions of dollars of business done on eBay every day. Nevertheless, with 84 million potential buyers, eBay does attract its share of online criminals—dishonest people bent on stealing your money any way they can. Below are some strategies you can use to ensure a safe buying and selling experience.

BUYING ON EBAY

The most common type of fraud on eBay occurs when someone sells an expensive item that he doesn't possess and/or has no intention of delivering. For example, let's say you have been looking at one of those new Hitachi plasma TVs that sell for over $4,000. You see one from a seller for under $3,000 and you bid on it. You send the money and the TV never arrives. A week later you e-mail the seller and get no reply. When you check the seller's account on eBay, it has been terminated. Your money is gone and so is the seller.

While this scenario may sound frightening, this type of fraud is easily prevented if you follow these simple steps:

1. Check the Seller's Feedback

In chapter 11, we discussed the concept of feedback. eBay's feedback reports on other members can tell you a lot about the sellers with whom you are considering doing business. Look at an eBay member's user ID; a number in parentheses immediately follows it. That number is that member's unique feedback score.

If you look at Figure D.1, you can see this user's feedback score is 7,886 and his feedback is 99.9 percent positive. You can click on *How Is Feedback Percentage Calculated?* to see the full breakdown of the seller's feedback (including the total number of feedback comments received and the number of positive, neutral, and negative comments received). On the Feedback Profile, you are shown the last twelve months of transactions in the Recent Feedback Ratings box. Only the last twelve months of feedback count in the feedback rating (the percentage of comments received that are positive). In the Recent Feedback Ratings box you can see the last month, six months, and twelve months of feedback received for this user.

Figure D.1: A Sample eBay Feedback Report

If you see a negative in the 1 month column, you should scroll down to see what the issue was. Often you'll see that it was a new buyer who didn't understand feedback yet, but if there are a number of negatives here, this is a red flag—particularly for high-priced items.

If you are buying a T-shirt or a coffee mug for $20, the chance of out-and-out fraud is pretty slim. Most fraud-minded sellers tend to focus on items with high values, such as diamond rings or plasma TVs. So I wouldn't hesitate to buy a low-cost item from a seller who may have a low feedback score as long as his Feedback Profile is primarily positive. If you look again at Figure D.1, you can see that eBay displays the actual comments that buyers left. If someone has recently received negative feedback, I sometimes scroll down the page to read the actual comment.

2. Don't Buy Expensive Items from New Sellers

If you look at the top of Figure D.1, beneath the seller's user ID, you can see how long she has been registered on eBay. Most fraudulent transactions are by sellers who have been registered for less than thirty days. I would be very hesitant to bid on or buy an expensive item from a brand-new seller. If you are considering bidding on an item, you can also click on the link that says *ID History*. This page will show you if the seller has changed her user ID since she registered.

3. Never Send Cash, a Money Order, or a Certified Check

eBay requires paperless payments, which means all forms of payment must be electronic. The options are PayPal, ProPay (if the seller is a PowerSeller and offers it), or credit/debit card, using the seller's merchant credit card processor. For expensive items, I highly recommend using PayPal. PayPal's buyer fraud protection does not have a dollar limit, so if you buy a $3,000 TV and it turns out that the seller took your money and skipped town you are covered for the full value (including shipping). The other advantage is that the seller never sees your credit card number. If the seller only offers credit card processing through his own merchant account, you have to give the seller the full number, address, and three-digit security code. This is much riskier than using PayPal, where the seller never sees this information.

4. Always Ask Sellers for a Tracking Number or Delivery Confirmation

UPS and other shipping services track all packages to their destinations. Similarly, the U.S. Postal Service offers Delivery Confirmation. Tracking prevents a seller from claiming he sent a package when he actually didn't. If you pay via PayPal and have to file a claim for an item you never received, the seller must prove delivery confirmation (for items under $250) and have full tracking for items over $250. If the seller cannot provide this, PayPal will find in the buyer's favor.

5. Read the Auction Description Carefully

One recent scam involved some sneaky members selling the empty box that the popular Microsoft Xbox game system comes in. The auction description described the Xbox system in great detail with lots of photos. Unfortunately, buried in the text was the following statement: "You are bidding on the box only." Buyers reading this line assumed that, by *box*, the seller was referring to the Xbox—when, in fact, the seller was only offering the empty box in which the product was originally packaged. Another variation of this scam is selling a link to a site where you can get the item for free, or for a specific price.

6. Make Sure You Are Buying Authentic Products

Unfortunately, there are a lot of knockoffs and outright counterfeit items for sale on eBay. eBay aggressively polices this through its Verified Rights Owner (VeRO) Program, but it can't catch everyone. If you are bidding on a brand-name item, such as a Rolex watch or a Prada handbag, this is another situation where you should check the seller's feedback and ID history very carefully. Again, you are covered by PayPal if it does turn out to be a knockoff (assuming, that is, that you paid via PayPal).

7. Look for buySAFE-Bonded Sellers

As we discussed in chapter 24, buySAFE is a bonding service underwritten by the Liberty Mutual Insurance Company that insures buyers against fraud. Whenever you see the buySAFE seal in an auction, you know two things: The seller has been thoroughly vetted by buySAFE, and, if that seller defrauds you, buySAFE will reimburse you for your loss up to the amount of the seller's bond. If you click on the buySAFE seal in the seller's auction, you can see the amount of the bond, which can be anywhere from $5,000 to $25,000. (If you are selling expensive merchandise, you may want to consider using buySAFE so potential bidders feel more comfortable buying from you.)

8. Report Suspicious Auctions to eBay

If you come across an auction that looks suspicious—such as a seller from Taiwan who has only been on eBay for a few weeks, and who is selling an expensive piece of jewelry and demanding cash as payment—take action. In this situation, you should not only refrain from bidding on the item, you should click on the link at the bottom of the auction that says *Report This Item*. Upon receiving the report, officials at eBay's Trust & Safety will examine the listing and cancel it if they think it contains a high risk of fraud.

9. Safeguard Your Registration Information and Password

Phishing is jargon for sending out spoof e-mails designed to lure recipients into entering their eBay passwords and credit card information into fraudulent Web pages that look just like the PayPal or eBay sites. To avoid falling victim to these online predators, remember a couple of simple pointers: Neither eBay nor PayPal will ever send you an e-mail asking you to click on a link to update your account information. Legitimate e-mails will always be addressed to you by name and will direct you to the eBay or PayPal homepage to log in as you normally would.

One popular scam is to send a fake My Messages notification. The user clicks on the *Respond* button to reply to the e-mail through eBay, and is instead taken to a spoof site. Once the user logs in, the scammer has his login information and access to his eBay account. A variation of this is a fake e-mail alerting the user to a "Final Notice for Payment" for an auction he did not bid on. It's all fake; the e-mail contains a link that leads the user to a phony PayPal site where the scammer can access your PayPal login information.

You can easily avoid falling for these scams by installing the eBay toolbar and activating the Account Guard feature. When this is active, if you try to enter your eBay or PayPal password into any site that is not an official site of these companies, a warning box will appear before you click *Submit*.

10. Beware of the Evil Twin

A more recent method of stealing your personal information is the Evil Twin. This scam takes advantage of wireless connections in airports and coffee shops. The Evil Twin is essentially a wireless version of a phishing scam—you think you're connecting to a genuine hot spot, but are actually connecting to some guy with a laptop and a wireless network card sitting perhaps a few feet away. Because he is closer to you than the base station, you might actually log on to his network instead.

Once you are logged on, the thief can capture a record of your keystrokes. Therefore, you have to be careful about entering personal information, such as passwords and credit card information, when you are on one of these networks.

SELLING ON EBAY

Like buyers, sellers can also fall prey to scams such as phishing and the Evil Twin. However, other scams specifically target eBay sellers. Here are some important tips for anyone considering selling on eBay:

1. Be on the Lookout for Counterfeit Certified Checks and Money Orders

Never accept certified checks or money orders. The reason eBay went to paperless payments was because counterfeit checks and money orders accounted for highest instances of fraud on the site. Even if a buyer insists on one of these methods, it's better to cancel his bid than to take the risk. If a buyer threatens you with negative feedback if you won't accept one of these payment methods, report him to eBay. eBay takes threats like this very seriously and the buyer will likely be suspended.

2. Always Ship Using a Service That Provides Tracking

Just as some sellers will *claim* they shipped your unreceived merchandise, there are some buyers who will claim they never received their item and demand a refund or a replacement. That's why I usually ship with a service such as UPS or FedEx that provides dated tracking for all packages. If the item I am shipping is expensive, I check the box on the shipping form to require a signature upon delivery. Whenever I ship via USPS, I always opt for Delivery Confirmation, which is the USPS's service that confirms receipt. If you insure the package with the U.S. Postal Service, then it is signed for at each step of the way. You don't get a signature from the customer, but the postal carrier who delivers it signs a form certifying the delivery. You can add Signature Confirmation to a USPS parcel, too, and I recommend that you do that if your item is over $250.

3. Carefully Select the Locations to Which You Will Sell

I have been selling internationally for several years now, but there are some countries I simply will not sell to because fraud is so rampant there. Chief among those are Russia, Thailand, and Nigeria. When you launch an auction on eBay, if you select International Shipping, you can select the countries or parts of the world where you will do business. Until you gain some experience, I would limit your sales to the United States and Canada. Later you may want to add European nations and Australia.

4. Use a Post Office Box or Postal Service as Your Registered Address on eBay

Once you conduct a transaction with someone, she can find your address within the eBay system. I once had someone who purchased an item from me show up at my front door wanting to pick it up. In general, it's not a good idea to have your address available anywhere on the Internet if you can help it. Companies such as Mail Boxes Etc. and The UPS Store offer mail receiving services.

5. Take Detailed Photographs of and Insure Expensive Items

There are some unscrupulous buyers who receive something and then decide they didn't really want it. So they may break it or put a scratch on it, and then demand a refund. If the item is insured and the buyer breaks it, you can simply file an insurance claim and the insurance company will take over from there. The company will almost always investigate the claim, especially if the item was expensive. If the buyer put a scratch on the item or otherwise damaged it, you will have a dated photograph to prove it was fine when you shipped it.

✦ GLOSSARY AND GUIDE ✦
TO COMMON ABBREVIATIONS

active user: An eBay member who has bought, bid on, or sold merchandise at least once in the last twelve months.

ADDY: An abbreviated term for *e-mail address*.

AdWords: Google's term for *pay-per-click advertising*.

AG: An abbreviation for the term *about good*, used to describe the condition of an item.

a.k.a.: An abbreviation for *also known as*. (Also sometimes written as *a/k/a or aka*.)

A/O: An abbreviation for *all original,* an auction term used to describe the condition of an item. *A/O* is often used in the auction title to save space.

ASAP: An abbreviation for *as soon as possible*.

as is: A term identifying auction items that are sold without warranties as to the condition of the property. Items sold without warranties may be damaged or have missing parts. See also *caveat emptor*.

ASOTV: An abbreviation for *As Seen On TV*.

ATM: An abbreviation for *at the moment* (not to be confused with *automated teller machine*).

auction: The standard selling format on eBay. A seller offers one or more items at a set starting price; buyers then visit the listing page and bid on the item during an established period of time. When the auction ends, the high bidder (or bidders) buys the item from the seller for the amount of the winning bid.

average selling price (ASP): The average price at which an item sells, or the average price of all items sold by a particular eBay seller in a given period. When calculating ASP, only count items that have actually been paid for; do not count sales to winning bidders who have not yet paid.

BC: An abbreviation for *back cover*.

bid increment: The amount by which you must increase your bid over the current high bid in order to bid on an item at auction. The bid increment is established by the current bid price.

bid rigging: The unlawful practice whereby two or more bidders conspire to influence an item's value either by not bidding at its auction or by placing fake bids. See also *collusion* and *shilling*.

BIN rate: The percentage of items sold with BIN (Buy It Now) or any Fixed Price format.

blocked bidders: A seller's list of specific eBay members who are prohibited from participating in that seller's auctions.

BTW: An abbreviation for *by the way*.

Buy It Now (BIN): The BIN option allows a seller to set a purchase price that, when selected by a bidder, ends an auction immediately and sells the item on the spot.

B&W: An abbreviation for *black-and-white*, generally used in reference to photos.

calculated shipping: A seller's option that posts a shipping calculator in an auction description. When a buyer enters her zip code, the calculator estimates applicable shipping costs.

caveat emptor: A Latin term for "Let the buyer beware"; also a legal maxim stating that the buyer incurs all the risk in a transaction.

COA: An abbreviation for *certificate of authenticity*; a legal guarantee that an item is genuine (usually certified by an expert).

collusion: A practice in which two or more eBay bidders conspire to influence an item's value either by placing fake bids (to inflate the price of the item) or by refusing to bid at all (to deflate the price of an item). See also *bid rigging* and *shilling*.

consignment selling: An arrangement in which one person sells merchandise on eBay on behalf of the item's owner, and in turn receives a commission for his efforts should the item sell. See *Trading Assistant*.

CONUS: An acronym for the continental United States (not including Alaska and Hawaii).

conversion rate (CR): The percentage of auctions closed successfully (i.e., with items sold) out of the total auctions listed by a seller.

DBA: An abbreviation for *doing business as*. This is the legal term for using a business name instead of your real name. For example, you incorporate as *John Jones, Inc.*, but the name you do business as is *The Sell More Company*.

deadbeat bidder (DBB): A winning bidder who fails to complete a transaction.

dingbat bidder: A bidder who doesn't yet understand how eBay works; known to send e-mails with such basic questions as "What does *new with tags* mean?"

DNR: An abbreviation for *one dollar no reserve*; a listing that starts at $1 with no reserve.

DOA: An abbreviation for *dead on arrival*; a term used when the item you just purchased doesn't function properly upon receipt.

drop-shipping: A business model in which a seller hires a wholesale vendor to ship products directly to the seller's customers. With drop-shipping, the seller lists the item on eBay at a price that is higher than the drop-shipper's wholesale price. Once a sale is made, the seller collects the payment and shipping fee from the buyer, and then sends a payment to the drop-shipper, who in turn ships the item directly to the seller's customer. (Also often written as one word: dropshipping.)

DSL: An abbreviation for *digital subscriber line*; a high-speed Internet connection through a dedicated phone line.

eBay store: An individualized "mini" Web site on eBay where sellers can market their products to eBay members at fixed prices. Sellers list their merchandise in an eBay store for either thirty days or Good 'Til Canceled, which autorenews every thirty days until you manually cancel the listing.

emoticon: A specific group of characters used to form facial expressions in e-mails. For example, :-) is a smiley face.

escrow: A buyer's deposit or fund entrusted to a third party that will hold the payment for an item, or items, until the seller makes delivery of merchandise to the buyer.

FAQ: An abbreviation for *frequently asked questions;* a list of common questions and their answers made readily accessible for new and inquiring users.

FBA: Fulfillment by Amazon. This is a service whereby a seller purchases a large lot of wholesale merchandise and has it shipped to Amazon in bulk. Amazon then becomes your drop-shipper. When you make a sale on eBay, you send the buyer's address to Amazon and Amazon packs and ships the individual item to the buyer.

FedEx: An abbreviation for the shipper Federal Express.

feedback (FB): Short comments posted by parties in an eBay transaction regarding their satisfaction with the transaction. A feedback comment becomes a *permanent* part of a member's reputation and is open for public viewing by the eBay community.

file transfer protocol (FTP): A method of exchanging files over the Internet.

final value (FV): An item's final selling price, not including shipping costs.

final value fee (FVF): The eBay seller's fee upon making a successful sale.

Fixed Price listing: An item for sale at a Buy It Now price. There is no bidding with a Fixed Price listing; buyers purchase items immediately at the set price.

flame: A series of angry e-mails or posts to a message board, often written in all capital letters.

free on board (FOB) (also known as *freight on board*): A term indicating that goods will be placed onto shipping transport without a loading fee. The FOB location is the point at which the buyer takes ownership of goods while they are in transit; consequently, this is when the buyer becomes responsible for shipping charges. For example, if I quote a price for a pallet of goods as *FOB Trenton, NJ*, the buyer's total price includes the cost of freight from Trenton to the delivery location.

gently used: A term indicating that an item was previously owned, but shows little wear.

gross merchandise sales (GMS): The total dollar value of your sales over a specified period of time.

HP: An abbreviation for *homepage*—not to be confused with Hewlett-Packard.

HTML: An abbreviation for *hypertext markup language*. This is the code that computer programmers use to create what you see when you view a Web page.

HTML Editor: An eBay application that appears in the Sell Your Item form; it allows you to enter text in plain English much as you would into a word processing document. The HTML editor then converts the text into HTML code. This feature allows you to create attractive listings and to create or modify your About Me page without taking the trouble to learn HTML.

hyperlink: A clickable photo or line of text on a Web page that takes you to another page on the Internet (also known simply as a *link*).

IE: An abbreviation for Internet Explorer (not to be confused with the abbreviation *i.e.*, meaning "that is").

IMHO: An abbreviation for the phrase *in my humble opinion*.

IMO: An abbreviation for the phrase *in my opinion*.

Internet service provider (ISP): A business or organization that offers users access to the Internet and related services. Well-known ISPs include EarthLink, AOL, MSN, Yahoo!, and some telephone companies. Sometimes called Internet access providers.

ISBN (International Standard Book Number): This is a number assigned to books and music CDs. eBay uses this number to automatically insert photos and descriptions into your listings using the Pre-Filled Item feature in the Sell Your Item form.

jpeg: An acronym for *Joint Photographic Experts Group* (often abbreviated as *jpg*); the required file format for pictures on eBay; pronounced JAY-peg.

link: See *hyperlink*.

LOL: *Laughing out loud* (sometimes seen as ROFL, for *rolling on the floor laughing*); this abbreviation is used frequently in e-mails to and from buyers and in posts on the eBay message boards.

lot or **lots:** Similar items sold in bulk quantities. Lots are normally sold at discount or wholesale prices.

LTD: An abbreviation for *limited edition*.

MIB: An abbreviation for *mint in box*; see *mint*.

MIMB: An abbreviation for *mint in mint box*; see *mint*.

MIMP: An abbreviation for *mint in mint package*; see *mint*.

mint: An item that has never been opened or used and is in perfect condition.

MIP: An abbreviation for *mint in package*; see *mint*.

MNB: An abbreviation for *mint no box*; see *mint*.

MOC: An abbreviation for *mint on card*; see *mint*.

My eBay: An eBay page that displays your ongoing auctions, their status, and your auction history.

NARU: An abbreviation for *not a registered user* (i.e., a suspended eBay user or a user who has closed his or her eBay account).

NBW: An abbreviation for *never been worn*.

NC: An abbreviation for *no cover* (i.e., a book missing its dust jacket or, in the case of a paperback, its cover).

newbie: A term for someone who is new to eBay.

NM: An abbreviation for *near mint*; a very subjective term. See *mint*.

NPB: An abbreviation for *nonpaying bidder*. See also *deadbeat bidder*.

NR: An abbreviation for *no reserve*; used frequently in auction titles to indicate that there is no reserve price for the item being auctioned.

NRFB: An abbreviation for *never removed from box*.

NWT: An abbreviation for *new with tags*.

OEM: An abbreviation for *original equipment manufacturer*.

OOP: An abbreviation for *out of print*.

PayPal: The payment service owned by eBay, and one of only two payment options allowed on eBay.

PayPal Verified buyer: A buyer whose address and account information have been confirmed through PayPal.

phishing: A fraudulent practice whereby an unscrupulous person (or group of people) attempts to gather personal (usually financial) information about an unsuspecting eBay user. In a typical scenario, you receive a counterfeit e-mail that appears to come from eBay, PayPal, or your bank, and contains a link leading you to a fake Web site, which is designed to look like a well-known, branded site but has a slightly different URL. This tactic is used to trick online shoppers into disclosing their credit card numbers, bank account information, social security numbers, passwords, and other personal information, which can lead to identity theft. All genuine e-mails from eBay will appear in the My Messages folder on your My eBay page.

PM: An abbreviation for *Priority Mail.*

PPC: An abbreviation for *pay per click.*

Primail: An abbreviated term for *Priority Mail.*

private auction: An auction in which the item title and price do not appear on the feedback profiles of either the buyer or the seller.

proxy bidding: eBay's bidding system. A bidder enters the maximum amount he is willing to spend on an item. The auction begins at a low starting price and, as it continues, eBay automatically increases the high bid in set increments until the proxy bidder emerges as the winner or his maximum price is exceeded.

relisting: The process of listing an unsold item again.

reserve not met: An auction term that means no bid is high enough to match the seller's minimum acceptable price; see *Reserve Price Auction.*

reserve price: The minimum price a seller is willing to accept for an auction item.

Reserve Price Auction (RPA): An auction in which the seller sets a minimum acceptable price. Sellers sometimes disclose the reserve price to prospective bidders.

Resolution Center: The eBay service that allows members to report and track all transaction problems. For instance, sellers can report auction winners who have neglected to pay for their items, and buyers can report sellers who have failed to ship items that have been paid for.

retaliatory feedback: When a nonpaying bidder posts negative feedback because you complained about him to eBay.

RMA: An abbreviation for *Return Merchandise Authorization*; a seller's authorization of a product return. Many sellers require buyers to e-mail them first and get an RMA before returning an item for a refund.

RSVP: An abbreviation for the French term *répondez s'il vous plaît* (meaning, please reply).

Second Chance Offer (SCO): An option that allows sellers to offer identical items to losing bidders after an auction ends—either because the winning bidder was unable to complete the transaction or because the seller has more than one of a particular item for sale.

Seller Resources: An area of the eBay site map featuring valuable resources for sellers—from advice on effective selling strategies, ways to promote your merchandise, and shipping options, to eBay news and updates, and tips on category trends and market research.

shilling: A practice in which a seller conspires with another eBay member to place phony bids to artificially inflate the price of an item. See also *bid rigging* and *collusion*.

SIG: An abbreviation for *signature*.

site map: A Web page that presents a visual and organizational guide to all features on a Web site. The eBay site map offers links to all resources and tools available on eBay.

SKU: An abbreviation for *stock keeping unit*; a numerical identifier used to distinguish individual items in an inventory. Most auction management systems, including eBay's Turbo Lister, have a field for SKU.

snail mail: A slang term for regular mail delivered via the U.S. Postal Service.

sniping: The practice of bidding in an auction at the last possible moment so that others don't have the opportunity to place a higher bid. Several companies actually make automated software that will snipe for you if you are not on the computer during the final minutes of an auction.

spam: Unwanted e-mail designed to sell something; on eBay, spammers send unsolicited e-mail to bidders in auctions with which they have no involvement. eBay will suspend your account for doing this.

spoof Web site: See *phishing*.

TM: An abbreviation for *trademark*.

Trading Assistant (TA): An experienced eBay seller who meets eBay requirements and will sell another person's items on eBay for a fee or commission. See also *consignment selling.*

unwanted bid: A bid that does not meet the seller's terms, stated in the auction. For example, a seller states in her auction that the item will only be shipped to U.S. locations; however, the bidder is located overseas. In this situation, the eBay seller may cancel the bid without any adverse repercussions.

UPS: An abbreviation for *United Parcel Service.*

upselling or **cross-selling:** The tactic of offering a winning bidder an additional quantity of his item or a related product (such as a set of earphones to someone who buys an MP3 player) upon purchase. You can make the offer via e-mail when you send the winning bidder payment instructions.

URL: An abbreviation for *Uniform Resource Locator;* the address that identifies a Web site on the Internet. The URL comprises the protocol (e.g., http://), followed by the domain name (e.g., www.skipmcgrath.com) and the specific file reference (e.g., /ebaynews/).

USPS: An abbreviation for *United States Postal Service.*

VeRO: An acronym for eBay's *Verified Rights Owner* program, which enforces copyright and trademark laws within the eBay marketplace. If you sell counterfeit goods on eBay, the rights owner can file a VeRO complaint and have your auctions shut down.

VG: An abbreviation for *very good.*

VHTF: An abbreviation for *very hard to find.*

wholesale: The practice of purchasing a quantity of goods at a discount, for the purpose of reselling at a (hopefully) higher retail price.

winning bidder notification (WBN): Notification sent to the winning bidder at the end of an auction. The e-mail may be sent by eBay, PayPal, a seller, or a seller's auction management system. The WBN typically tells the buyer the final value of the item he has won and the shipping cost, and either includes instructions or provides a link to a payment page.

WYSIWYG: An abbreviation for *What You See Is What You Get*; a program that displays what your final HTML page will look like while you're creating it. eBay and other auction management services provide WYSIWYG HTML editors to help sellers create their auction listings.

Yahoo! Shops (or Yahoo! Stores): A shopping portal operated by Yahoo!.

✦ INDEX ✦

tracking shipments, 152, 162, 261, 263

UPS for, 152, 154, 162, 163, 263

U.S. Postal Service (USPS) for, 151–152, 161–162

Wizard, 90, 154

your business address and, 264

Silver Source, 251–252

Site map, 21–22

Skype, 88

Software, for automating auctions. *See* Automating auctions

Software, selling, 28–29

Spoofing or phishing, 16, 181–182, 262–263

Spoonfeeder, 203

Sports memorabilia, 29

SquareTrade warranties, 210

Standard auctions, 73–74

Starting and ending auctions, 101–102

Stealing first base, 182–183, 215

Subtitle, 83, 144–145, 192, 229

Success, defining, 2

Success plan, 113–117

  business plan, 116–117

  defining metrics, 115

  evaluating earning potential, 113–114

  final thoughts, 243

  Power Moves, 117

  setting goals, 114–116

Surplus merchandise. *See* Closeout merchandise

Symbols key, 165–166

T

Tax. *See* Sales tax

Teeda, 252

Telebrands Wholesale, 252

Ten-Day Duration, 148

Terapeak, 39, 43–46, 255

Thank-you notes, 107

Thomas Register, 56–57

Thumbnail picture, 84, 146

Timing of auctions, 101–102

Title of listing, 82–83, 125–128, 134

Toolbar, 24

Trade shows, 62–63

Trading Assistant program

  business of, 237–238

  buySAFE bond for, 211

  classified ads for, 238

  contacting retailers about, 239

  described, 36

  discussion boards, 25

  how it works, 236–237

  income potential, 36

  marketing, 238–239

  networking for, 238

  notifying estate/bankruptcy attorneys about, 239

  potential of, 238